PRAISE FOR

Work+Life

"*Work+Life* gets points for comprehensiveness. . . . The approaches Yost suggests—making a formal proposal, studying negotiating techniques, and reviewing your situation regularly—are clearly likelier to succeed than grumbling and wishing things were different. And she cites cases that suggest win-win solutions can be found even in places where they seem improbable. . . . A working mother with an MBA from Columbia University who has been a mid-level bank executive and . . . a work/life strategy consultant . . . [Yost is] in the unique position of having looked at these issues from three sides: boss, worker, and intermediary."   —*The Washington Post*

"Work is no longer necessarily a nine-to-five proposition. . . . In this volume, the author argues that, in order to maintain a life outside work, one must think creatively and establish personal boundaries—what she calls the work+life fit. In this information-packed volume, she explains how to do it. Illustrating each point with stories of real people who found a good work and life fit, Yost takes readers through the process of seeing the possibilities for creating a non-standard work schedule, asking for what they want, getting to yes with the professional powers-that-be, and practical, logistical tips for making a program that works for them. It's a goal-oriented book. With Americans working harder and longer today than they did twenty years ago, many readers may appreciate this scheduling guide, which is as much pro-business as it is pro–personal life."

—*Publishers Weekly*

"*Work+Life* offers practical instructions for finding work/life balance, putting together a proposal and convincing your manager that it would be in the organization's best interest to allow you flexibility in working hours and location."   —*The Philadelphia Inquirer*

"A practical step-by-step volume that lays the groundwork for change, anticipates problems, then takes readers through implementation."

—*Minneapolis Star Tribune*

"Convinced there was a better way, Yost opened her own consulting business with the revolutionary premise that the best solutions come from the employees, not the employer. 'People think that they either have to stay with things exactly the way they are or quit,' she says, 'but there are countless options between those two extremes.' As for selling the boss on one of them, Yost says you'd be surprised. 'Nine out of ten times, even in the most restrictive work environments, managers will work it out,' she says, 'They don't want to lose good people. It's their worst nightmare.'"

—*The Newark Star-Ledger*

Work+Life

Finding
the Fit That's Right
for You

Cali Williams Yost

RIVERHEAD BOOKS
New York

THE BERKLEY PUBLISHING GROUP
Published by the Penguin Group
Penguin Group (USA) Inc.
375 Hudson Street, New York, New York 10014, USA
Penguin Group (Canada), 10 Alcorn Avenue, Toronto, Ontario M4V 3B2, Canada
(a division of Pearson Penguin Canada Inc.)
Penguin Books Ltd., 80 Strand, London WC2R 0RL, England
Penguin Group Ireland, 25 St. Stephen's Green, Dublin 2, Ireland (a division of Penguin
Books Ltd.)
Penguin Group (Australia), 250 Camberwell Road, Camberwell, Victoria 3124, Australia
(a division of Pearson Australia Group Pty. Ltd.)
Penguin Books India Pvt. Ltd., 11 Community Centre, Panchsheel Park, New Delhi – 110 017,
India
Penguin Group (NZ) cnr Airborne and Rosedale Roads, Albany, Auckland 1310, New Zealand
(a division of Pearson New Zealand Ltd.)
Penguin Books (South Africa) (Pty.) Ltd., 24 Sturdee Avenue, Rosebank, Johannesburg 2196,
South Africa

Penguin Books Ltd., Registered Offices: 80 Strand, London WC2R 0RL, England

PRINTING HISTORY
Riverhead hardcover edition / April 2004
Riverhead trade paperback edition / January 2005
Riverhead trade paperback ISBN: 1-59448-065-6

The Library of Congress has catalogued the Riverhead hardcover edition as follows:

Yost, Cali Williams.
    Work + life : finding the fit that's right for you / Cali Williams Yost.
        p.   cm.
    ISBN 1-57322-268-2
    1. Vocational interests.   2. Vocational guidance.   I. Title: Work and life.   II. Title.
HF5381.5.Y64   2004   2003062900
650.1—dc22

Printed in the United States of America

10   9   8   7   6   5   4

To Andy, Emma, and Maddie—you are everything

To Doris and Les—for being the first to believe

*To Cate—for teaching me to live life fully and completely
because it can end too fast and too soon*

Acknowledgments

This book is the culmination of a journey that began more than 10 years ago when I decided to follow my heart, take the risk, and start down a radically different professional path without any idea of where it would lead. Along the way, I met and was supported by incredible people. Without them, this book simply would not be.

Words are difficult to find to describe my gratitude and my love for my editor and longtime friend, Wendy Carlton. When we met 20 years ago at college, I never dreamed that we would one day work together professionally. Wendy, I could go on for pages about how much your encouragement and effort on behalf of this book have meant to me, but that could be its own handbook on friendship. From when I first mentioned to you that I wanted to leave banking and go into this heretofore unheard of work/life field, to when I hesitantly approached you years later saying, "I have this idea for a book, what do you think?"—you've encouraged and cheered me along. For the past five years, you've shepherded me step-by-step through the world of publishing. You've advocated for me and my book in ways that, at times, have left me speechless with gratitude. Your skill as an editor has been a privilege to observe. And it will always be one of my life's greatest joys to have shared this experience with you. I love you, Wen. Thank you.

To Susan Petersen Kennedy, again, words are difficult to find to describe this remarkable woman. After years of simply knowing you as "Wendy's great boss," you spent three hours with me at lunch patiently and supportively listening to my very tentative vision about a book to help business people find more balance in their lives. It would take years for me to hone that vision into *Work+Life*, and I'm still so grateful for your time and your insights not only on that day but on the days since, especially now that I understand that you are very much more than simply "Wendy's great boss." You're a visionary, and I am so glad this book came to life at Riverhead. Thank you.

To everyone else whose enthusiasm for and commitment to this book has been so affirming, especially Marilyn Ducksworth who "got it" on every level from our very first meeting and helped me to articulate my message even more clearly; Bonnie Soodek, for seeing the possibilities; and my agent, Sally Wofford Girand, for taking a chance on an unknown author with a message she was living personally. And, to everyone at Riverhead who contributed their time and tremendous talent to collectively make this book what it became. Thank you.

When following your dreams, the difference between success and failure often comes down to one person taking a chance on you. For me, that person is Dana E. Friedman. As the cofounder and copresident of Families and Work Institute, you took a chance on a former banker with little to offer but a passionate enthusiasm for work/life issues. When you left FWI for Bright Horizons Family Solutions, I followed. My admiration for you and your work as one of the work/life pioneers is immeasurable. It's because of you, and those other visionaries, that we even have the term *work/life* in our cultural and corporate vocabulary. Wanting to do my best for you and to prove that your faith in me was warranted, I pushed myself to learn everything I possibly could from you, from other experts, from the research, and from our projects. The result is this book. Literally, without you, there would be no book. Thank you.

Also, thank you to the brilliant and committed colleagues whom I had the privilege to work with and to learn from while at FWI and BHFS. From FWI, this includes Ellen Galinsky, cofounder and president of Families and Work Institute, and Debbie Schwartz, who patiently taught me many of the research tools that helped me learn so much over the years. Others who taught and inspired me with their own expertise and passion are: Arlene Johnson, Deborah Holmes, Terry Bond, James Levine, Robin Hardman, Ed Pitt, and Nina Sazar O'Donnell. At BHFS, I could not have asked for a better teammate than Nancy Kane, or more wonderful colleagues than Stephanie Skidmore and Beth Pressler.

And, finally, the incredible cheering section of my family and friends. Perseverance is critical to success, but it certainly does help to surround yourself with people who at times may believe in you and in your dream more than you do.

To my husband, Andy. In addition to Wendy and Dana, I can think of no other person who bears as much direct responsibility for this book's coming into being. From day one, you've given me your support on so many levels. Whether we were struggling to put each other through school, having two beautiful children, or supporting the writing of this book, not once did you say anything but, "You can do it. It's a message people need to hear." How many people can ever hope to have that kind of encouragement from their spouses? You've sacrificed a lot for this, and I'm very blessed. And to my amazing babies, Emma and Maddie. You are my greatest gifts.

To my parents, Peg Williams, and Doug and Jane Williams. Mom, thanks for giving me your questioning mind, your love for words, and your helping soul. Dad, thanks for raising me without any limitations and for your enthusiasm and belief in this project. Jane, thank you for your consistent and loving presence in my life, and for your unending encouragement. Even though your collective opinion that I am "brilliant and talented" might be a bit overstated, biased, and somewhat subjective, it certainly did keep me going more times than you will know. Every child deserves that, and I'm so lucky to have the three of you to give it to me. I love you all. Thank you to siblings, Lauren, Cindy, David, and Janey, and their families for all of their love.

As every working mother knows, it's your baby-sitters that really make it all possible. For me, those are Marcelina DosSantos and Shannon Killeen. Over the past six years, you've loved my girls like they were your own. The knowledge that they are happy has allowed me to focus on this project without distraction. Thank you!

To my friends. This is another area of life in which I have been truly blessed. There is a core group of patient, positive, funny, and sometimes endlessly supportive souls who on more than one occasion had to say, "You go, girl!" For this I will forever be grateful. This group includes: Stephanie Flower, Barbara Hughes, Margaret Dempsey, Fran Moum, Ainsley Hilfiker, Jane Gamboli, Kathy Werner, Mary Lea Crawley, Camille Rudge, Geralyn Lalevee, Nancy Reiner, Hope Sherman, and Esslie Hughes.

Thank you to the parish of Grace Church Madison. While I've always felt very supported by the universe with this project, the clergy—Lauren Ackland and Marshall Shelly—as well as the parish of Grace, especially George Hayman and Mary Barrett, have done more than they will ever know to help me sustain and connect with that feeling of support. Thank you all.

Also, I would like to thank others who over the years have offered their personal and professional support at critical junctures, and to whom I am most grateful. They include: Joanne Spigner, Marggi Vangelli, Alice Johnson, Laura Johnson, Judsen Culbreath, Mary Azzolini, Sherrill Curtis, Grace McQuade, Airelle Eckstat, and the Junior League of Morristown. And especially my college English professor Pauline Fletcher, who went out of her way one day after class to tell me, "You know you are a gifted writer." While I may have filed that away for years, I drew upon it often when writing this book. It's an example of how our encouraging words can someday help change another's life.

Finally, to the thousands of men and women I've met over the years who have shared their work+life realities with me. Thank you for contributing to an effort that will hopefully help people find a better way to combine work and life.

Contents

Step 1   The Work+Life Fit Fundamentals

Step 2   The Work+Life Fit Roadblocks

Step 3   The Work+Life Fit Roadmap

Foreword

Dana E. Friedman, Ed.D.

For the past twenty years, a group of tenacious people—employees, human resource managers, researchers, policy analysts, management gurus, feminists, and dads—have been trying to morph companies into caring, people-friendly cultures. They have researched employees' needs, organized task forces, and amassed return-on-investment data, all to make the case to an intransigent culture that employees' needs, interests, and responsibilities outside work matter to what they do when they are at work. Traditionally, employees were expected to leave their personal problems at home. The difficulty in today's demographically altered world, is that there is no one at home.

Many of us in the forefront of this "work/life movement" thought that we had reason on our side. We saw the growing portion of the workforce comprised of working mothers. We saw the aging of the country and the increased elder-care responsibilities of the workforce. We saw the new work ethic of Gen Xers who wanted to "get a life." It seemed logical that if a company ignored the personal concerns of its workforce, it would be ignoring the predominant concerns of an increasingly large portion of its labor pool. It meant that recruitment efforts, benefit plans, productivity incentives, and work schedules were likely to be out of sync with employees' needs and rendered ineffective. It seemed obvious that the oil that kept the workforce running smoothly in the industrial era was not going to keep the squeaks out of the human machinery in the post-industrial age.

This common sense reasoning wasn't compelling enough. But the advocates for change got lucky because of other challenges facing the business community. The recession of 1990 spurred a tremendous amount of activity in corporate work/life offerings. As the organization expert Harry Levinson once said, "Organizations change only when they are in pain." The economic downturn and a labor mismatch that resulted in thousands of layoffs as well as a shortage of skilled workers provided two "painful" reasons to respond. First, companies needed to attract well-educated, technologically competent workers, and they felt that work/life policies gave them a competitive edge. Second, during downsizing, companies became concerned about low morale, particularly for a group of employees who must now do more with less, not knowing if they might be next on the unemployment line. Work/life policies became "survivor benefits" for those who survived downsizing.

Indeed many companies did respond to the family and personal needs of their employees. They have been given honors and awards by *Working Mother* and *Fortune* magazines. They have been the subject of lead stories in both the *Ladies' Home Journal* and *The Wall Street Journal*. Their CEOs have been the keynote speakers at conferences sponsored by the White House, Business Roundtable, and the National Mothers' Centers. They have created the world's most fabulous on-site child care centers, user-friendly work arrangements, onsite concierge services, and generous retirement benefits. They have evaluated their programs and policies to determine the impact on absenteeism, turnover, and morale and published their research widely to help other companies see the benefits of a work/life agenda.

This is all good news, and quite amazing when you think just how much some companies have changed in the past twenty years. But it is important to look behind the glitzy benefits and examine the corporate culture. As a consultant to many of the most progressive firms, I have been constantly shocked by the disconnect between what was in the employee handbook and what it was "really like" to work there. Some companies that are well known for their work/life policies do not have universal buy-in from all first-line supervisors for these policies. A company may have a wonderful referral service that can help an employee look for child care or elder care, but if her manager won't let her make a personal call during work to talk to the referral counselor, then the program isn't of much help. More important, that employee's perception of the company is not one of family-friendliness—thanks to that manager.

Some of the best firms out there haven't figured out that they've been concentrating on the wrong part of the problem. They have focused on developing policies and programs that will prevent employees' personal lives from interfering with work. What they should be focused on instead is preventing the stresses and strains of work from interfering with employees' personal lives. When employees face work inefficiencies, long hours, and a jerk for a boss, they take their frustrations home. When work problems affect life at home, employees bring more issues back to the workplace. Thus, the real culprit in high turnover and low morale is the way work is organized and how employees are managed, evaluated, and rewarded. The person who most influences these aspects of work is the manager.

While the business elite in the Fortune 500 have adopted some work/life policies and programs, what about the small and mid-sized firms that employ over 90 percent of all workers? There appears to be very little recognition there that work/life issues are paramount in the minds of employees. What smaller firms do have, however, is an informal culture that typically allows a lot more flexibility. You may be dealing directly with the president of the firm, for there are very few layers of management. It's harder in a small firm for a manager to say, "Gee, I'd really like to let you change your schedule, but, you know, they won't let do it me 'upstairs.'" In a small firm, there is probably someone right down the hall who overheard you talking about it. But the work/life supports that exist in a small firm are most likely incidental, not intentional. The majority of firms today are not pro-active or strategic in their efforts to respond to the changing needs of the workforce.

This book is critical because of these realities. Whether you work in a large company with a household name or a small firm on Main Street, in the end, it is going to be up to you to negotiate with your manager about how you can do your best work and still have a personal life. Your confidence in your value to the organization, and your faith in the solution you propose will help enormously. This book will help you figure out just where you need to put the fulcrum in your personal balancing act and how to make your case to management. And if your request for help is rejected, you will also find ideas for how to adapt and when to give it up.

With the pace of life making demands on us in a way that it didn't in the past, and companies asking employees to do more and more and more, employees are the only ones who can draw the line. I think of part-time workers who are on the phone with the office on the days they are supposed to be off, dealing with their customers when they thought they'd be dealing with their kids. Part-timers don't complain about this. They are so grateful to have permission to take some time off, they take whatever their company dishes out. I call these people the "grateful dead."

With the dramatic changes that have taken place over the past few decades, it is clear that individuals have done most of the accommodating. They've changed their relationships with spouses and kids and revised their expectations. Now it is time for institutions to change. But they are taking their sweet time about it. So you need to figure out on your own how best to adapt to the new realities of work in America. And as this book points out, it is probably not helpful to ask, "What's wrong with this picture?" but rather, "What's right with it?" You need to be as proactive and strategic as companies must be when trying to find the right fit between your life at home and your life at work, and this book will give you all the tools you need to do just that. The book that smart, savvy employees everywhere need to help them take the initiative is finally here—*Work+Life* is it.

Work+Life

Introduction:
How Do You Find
a Better Way to Fit Work
into Your Life?

You are put on earth, with a unique set of skills and talents, to fulfill a purpose in both your work *and* personal life. That purpose evolves as you go through different stages of life. Your goals will change, depending on whether you are single or married, parenting, retiring, or caring for an aging relative. They will vary similarly if you go from assistant to manager or from corporate employee to small business owner. Whatever your individual work/life scenario, the trick is to find a "fit" that gives you the time and energy for both your work and life: work+life.

The mission of this book is to give you the tools you need to find that work+life fit, as well as the stories to inspire your efforts. If it changes the way you think about work and the role it can play in your life, then I've done my job. Rather than seeing work as a "given," consider it a flexible and malleable part of life that allows you to use your gifts and strengths to make a living, but not necessarily to the detriment of your personal life. In other words, your *life* determines

1

how much time and energy you devote to work, instead of work dictating what's leftover for your life.

Now, I'm not implying that choosing a primary focus on work is wrong. But what happens when you are caring for a child or an aging parent, volunteering, pursuing an avocation, going back to school, or trying to work during retirement? You need more time, energy, and flexibility to manage these personal responsibilities and interests. In fact, without it, you feel drained and stressed. You suffer, and your work suffers.

"Well," you may say, "that's just the way it is. Work is work." After years of working in business, first as a banker and manager, then as a work/life strategy consultant to Fortune 500 companies, and now as a work+life coach, I can assure you it doesn't have to be. You *can* find a better way. I've worked with too many men and women, in too many industries, with too many different types of work/life realities, to believe anything less is possible for you.

Twenty years ago, the parameters around your work and your personal life were clear. Regardless of the type of company you worked for, the hours were generally nine to five, Monday through Friday, no questions asked. You knew the rules and operated within them, or you were free to work elsewhere, or not at all.

Now, globalization, reengineering, and technology have opened up new market opportunities and increased productivity, but they've also created a 24/7 workweek and reduced job security. And slowly those external, company-mandated boundaries between your life and work disappeared; yet nothing replaced them.

Suddenly, everyone was looking around for the old corporate norm that said, "Okay, enough for today. You can go home." But it wasn't there. So everyone started working harder, longer, and faster. The result has been work/life conflict for mothers and fathers, for those caring for aging parents, and for anyone else who has interests and responsibilities outside of work. While their personal sources of conflict differ, they all share the desire for a new way to allocate time and energy between work and life.

Because the old 9-to-5 corporate culture will never return, you need to change the way you think about, approach, and interact with work. Instead of looking to someone else to set the parameters around work, you need to create the new boundaries yourself. Believe it or not, you have the ability to influence the role that work plays in your life. Work doesn't have to dictate what the rest of your life looks like. Will it take effort on your part? Yes. Will it require patience and perseverance? Yes. Is it worth it? Absolutely, if it leads you to a more complete and fulfilling existence.

But if you are like most people, you have no idea where to begin. You need a framework to help you identify and think through the steps necessary to develop and achieve a successful work+life fit. This is exactly what the Three Steps in this book provide. And they can help *anyone* at *any* stage of life to achieve *any* type of work+life fit, including:

▶ The father who wants to work from home every Wednesday in order to coach his daughter's soccer team;

▶ The retiree who wants to work up to 30 hours a week at various times without benefits, because he or she wants the flexibility to pursue other interests but isn't quite ready to call it a day at work;

▶ The mother who used to work 50 hours a week but now job-shares three days a week and participates in a two-hour weekly staff meeting via speakerphone on one of the days at home;

▶ The adult son or daughter of an aging parent who works four 10-hour days in order to have the fifth day off to take that parent to the doctor and the grocery store;

▶ The single, childless person with a passion for photography who works from 7:00 A.M. to 4:00 P.M. on Tuesdays and Thursdays and answers e-mail and voice mail in the evenings in order to take a photography class;

▶ The volunteer who works nine, 9-hour days in a row and takes every other Friday off to coordinate activities in a soup kitchen, but is available by cell phone if needed;

▶ A former stay-at-home mother who transitioned back into the workforce and now works Thursday, Friday, and Saturday as an event planner; and

▶ Anyone who wants to work from 8 A.M. to 6 P.M. on Monday and Friday, but from 1 P.M. to 7 P.M. Tuesday, Wednesday, and Thursday simply to have a little more time for his or her personal life.

Each of the Three Steps builds upon the other, leading you to your goal. Step 1 introduces you to the Eight Work+Life Fit Fundamentals that challenge limiting thinking and embrace new realities that allow you to see all the possibilities for your life and work.

Armed with your new beliefs, you move on to Step 2 and learn to recognize and bypass the four most common Work+Life Fit Roadblocks. This is a critical step because these roadblocks can derail you at any point; therefore, it's important to know what to look out for before you begin.

You'll then be ready in Step 3 to make your work+life vision a reality by following the Work+Life Fit Roadmap. The roadmap is an easy-to-follow, step-by-step process that leads you from creating a vision of your new work+life fit, through comparing that vision with all of the relevant realities in your work and personal life. Doing so improves your chance of success as you implement your final work+life fit arrangement.

By understanding how the Three Steps to a Better Work+Life Fit evolved, you can see how and why they depart from traditional, corporate-initiated efforts to resolve work/life conflict. Efforts that, unfortunately, have had limited success, considering the millions of employees who continue to experience this productivity-draining conflict.

It began in 1991. I was an ambitious assistant vice president working for a large bank in New York City. A colleague had just announced that she was going to have a baby. I was happy for her, but even happier for myself when I learned that her high-profile portfolio would be reassigned to me (a real coup since Janet was more senior and experienced than I was). Seizing this opportunity, I arranged introductory meetings with my new customers, one of whom was the CEO of another financial institution.

As I walked into this CEO's office, he extended his hand and spoke the following words: "It's very nice to meet you, Cali. I look forward to working with you now that Janet will no longer be my account officer, but you realize this makes no business sense."

He went on to explain how *his* company encourages women returning from maternity leave to telecommute for a few months in order to ease the transition back to work. "Trust me," he said, "I'm not doing this because I'm a nice guy. I'm doing it because in banking, your money is as green as mine is. The only thing that really makes us different to the customer is their relationship with their account officer. Customers would rather work with someone they've known and trusted for a long time—like Janet—even if she's only in the office three days a week. Truthfully, it's just as easy for me to work with a new person from one of your competitors as it is to work with a new account officer from your bank. Plus, the account officers we've supported are so loyal afterward, they never leave!" He was speaking an irrefutable, yet unacknowledged truth: Helping your employees address both their work and personal responsibilities makes good business sense.

Up to that point, I'd been feeling pretty pleased with myself, but suddenly I realized something very basic was wrong with my situation.

They'd reassigned Janet's accounts to me even before she had her baby, even before anyone knew whether or not she would return from maternity leave. In other words, after years of successfully cultivating and maintaining a core group of profitable accounts, Janet would be expected to start from ground zero when she came back. Needless to say, she chose not to return, and, as a result, everyone lost. The bank lost a seasoned, well-respected account officer with strong customer relationships. The customers lost an account manager whom they knew and trusted. Janet lost a career to which she had devoted more than 15 years. And this all meant that the bank's shareholders lost.

While none of my new customers left the bank, the reality was I didn't know their needs or their histories as well as Janet did. As a result, I'm sure I overlooked certain new business opportunities that she would have identified. The associated lost opportunity costs meant lost profits. Given the clear business argument for retaining Janet and her expertise, I kept wondering why the bank hadn't offered her some type of flexibility, such as working part-time or from home. As my client the CEO had said, it made no business sense.

During this same period, I also became responsible for managing a group of individuals all of whom were older than I was. As my own employees faced various work/life challenges, I gave more and more thought to what the CEO had said.

For example, John, one of my account officers, became a father for the first time. It was the end of the year, and he had a limited amount of vacation left to be with his wife and newborn. At the time, there was no such thing as paternity leave. So John returned to work after a week, but you could tell his mind was elsewhere. He fell behind on his new customer call requirements; his loan proposals went unwritten; and he spent much of the day on the phone with his wife (understandably). After a couple of weeks, he snapped out of it. But wouldn't it have been better for the bank to give John an extra week off to be with his wife and new baby? Would he have come back ready to work instead of resentful? I probably would have gotten a whole week of productivity rather than a warm body filling the chair.

The problem was that neither John nor I knew what to do. There wasn't a process to help him or me, as his manager, think through solutions that made sense for both him and our business. As a result, both John and the business unnecessarily suffered.

While this all occurred little more than 10 years ago, it was a lifetime in terms of corporate awareness of work/life issues. Not only my employees, but also the employees of my corporate customers, were experiencing the negative effects of work/life conflict. And even though I was a banker, I couldn't stop wondering why these issues weren't a more urgent strategic priority. There had to be a better way. Shortly thereafter, I realized that I wasn't the only person who felt this way and that there was an emerging field of academics, consultants, and businesspeople dedicated to studying, developing, and implementing work/life policies and practices in corporations. Soon I found myself keeping in my desk a folder six inches thick and bulging with every work/life-related article I could find. It was clear that I had found a new passion. And I believed that resolving employee work/life conflict was a matter of helping companies implement the right work/life policies. I was wrong.

.   .   .

The transition from banker to work/life consultant wasn't easy. It required changing my own work+life fit twice in two years. First, I went from full-time employee to full-time MBA student, because I believed that I would be an effective messenger only if companies and individuals thought that I understood the realities of business. So, I left my well-paying banking position, borrowed money, and lived on my husband's salary while going to school full-time.

When I graduated, I then went from student to full-time senior research associate and consultant with Families and Work Institute (FWI), one of the country's premier work/life research and consulting organizations. At FWI, I worked side-by-side with work/life pioneers exploring cutting-edge ways to address these issues. I consulted to Fortune 500 companies, while organizing and participating in national work/life conferences and managing national studies of work/life topics. Now, I thought I would really be able to make a difference.

In our consulting work, corporations hired us to identify and strategically address the work/life issues that their employees faced. We conducted and analyzed employee focus groups, manager interviews, and surveys in order to develop customized recommendations for each company's needs. But project after project, client after client, I noticed the same frustrating disconnect between what employees told us they needed and their use of the work/life supports that, in many cases, the company already had in place. This gap between the need for and the use of work/life supports was consistent across companies and industries. Where was the message lost? Maybe good corporate policies weren't enough.

In the continuing quest to reduce this gap between employee need and use, we focused our consulting work more specifically on what seemed to be the primary culprits: unsupportive managers, unsupportive workplace cultures, and inefficiency in the way work gets done. To this end, we helped companies train unsupportive managers and alter powerful, unwritten rules in a work culture like "face time." We also helped them revolutionize inefficient and unnecessary work practices, with an eye to recouping time lost for personal responsibilities.

And, indeed, the gap seemed to shrink a bit. But it still remained wide. Having work/life policies on the books, training managers, improving work efficiency, and changing the corporate culture weren't enough. There had to be something more. But what?

My simultaneous involvement in two very different projects finally provided the clarity that I sought. The first project was professional and the second, personal.

In 1997, I moved from FWI to Bright Horizons Family Solutions. Shortly after joining BHFS, a longstanding client with a strong commitment to work/life issues approached us to figure out, once and for all, why more employees weren't taking advantage of the flexible work arrangements they offered. This was particularly troubling since a majority of employees consistently said flexibility was what they most needed. So we talked to over 100 employees and managers throughout the company who had been involved in successful flexibility. We asked them to tell us why and how it either did or did not work from both the employee and manager perspectives.

After analyzing data from interviews, a survey, and numerous focus groups, it seemed that offering the same set of standard flexible work arrangements to all employees didn't work because:

▶ There *is* no one standard flexible work arrangement that works in all cases for everyone. Most successful arrangements are a creative blend of adjusting time spent on the job and/or location where the job is done; a blend that works in the context of an employee's particular job.

▶ Everyone's job is unique. Five employees in the same department can have different jobs. Successful flexibility depends upon a careful analysis of the individual elements of a particular employee's job and tailoring a type of flexibility that supports those elements.

▶ The individual work style of the employee must be compatible with the type of flexibility in their arrangement. For example, telecommuting might be difficult for someone who works better around other people.

Managers offered another important insight that helped explain why the historically corporate-driven approach didn't work:

▶ Managers believe that employees need to develop, propose, negotiate, and manage their *own* flexibility. They generally support flexibility as a way for their employees to take care of their work and personal lives as long as it doesn't mean more work for them. As one manager put it, "I'm okay with it (the arrangement) as long as it's not another rock in my backpack."

It was clear that the problem lay with the company-initiated, top-down, one-size-fits-all approach to addressing work/life issues. *Successful flexibility wasn't company-initiated and managed; it was employee-initiated and managed.*

Successful arrangements weren't uniform and applicable to a broad cross-section of the company; they were creative and accommodated the unique tasks and responsibilities of a person's job, as well as his or her work style. The source of the gap had become clearer, as had the solution: encourage employees to create, negotiate, and manage a work+life fit compatible with the tasks and responsibilities of their job and their work style.

But if employees were supposed to do all of this, where were they supposed to begin? Where was the comprehensive tool to help them analyze the relevant work realities to create a work+life fit? It didn't exist. And this still didn't explain why, if two people work for the same company and have the same type of job, one would find a better work+life fit and the other wouldn't. Success had to be determined by something more than work realities.

My simultaneous involvement in a second, more personal project showed me that creating and implementing a successful work+life fit required considering both work *and* personal realities. I became pregnant with my first child, which forced me to reconsider my own work+life fit.

As most people do, my husband and I believed the baby was a gift that would enhance our lives but would essentially change very little. I was an MBA working in a field that I loved, doing work in which I passionately believed. Besides, I worked for a supportive boss—one of the pioneers of the work/life field no less—and I had access to a slot in one of our company's AAA-rated child-care centers. I felt as if I would be immune from the heartbreaking struggles I heard about from employees and managers in focus groups and interviews. Oh, how wrong I was.

As the time of our daughter's birth approached, I sat down and analyzed all of my work realities—my job, my work style, and the needs of our business—in order to come up with a mutually beneficial work+life fit. I decided to propose working part-time, three days a week, with little or no travel for at least nine months. Yeah, things were looking good.

But then, I stopped to consider the realities of my personal life and everything changed. These personal realities included my husband, our child-care situation, our personal finances, and most important, how I *really* wanted work to fit into my life.

We felt very fortunate to have access to a top-notch child-care center, especially since we didn't want, or have room for, a live-in nanny. However, my husband's commute to New York City meant that he left at 7 A.M., and arrived home after 7:30 P.M. And he had little flexibility in his schedule. Therefore, I would be fully responsible for coordinating all child-care drop-offs and pickups, which made the prospect of business trips seem daunting. If you are a consultant who works with multisite, multinational corporations, travel is essentially a given. Okay, maybe things weren't so perfect.

Now to our finances—ugh! At first, the concept of not having my salary seemed unimaginable, especially after struggling for so many years as a graduate student. How could we make it? I'm a bit embarrassed to admit this, but for the first time in our lives, we developed a budget. We kept track of our expenses, refinanced our mortgage and car loan, and to our great surprise, the impossible began to seem possible. I could actually consider working part-time and, with some sacrifices, I wouldn't have to earn any money for a while.

But, in the end, the deciding factor was my vision of how I wanted work to fit into my life. When I was completely honest with myself, I knew that my focus was changing. I was beginning to see that if I wanted to help people resolve their work/life conflicts, it wasn't going to be by developing corporate strategy. At the time, only a portion of large companies embraced the business case for implementing a comprehensive work/life strategy. And even then, corporate work/life initiatives were only half of the answer. Employees still needed to do their part, but they had no tools. What about the majority of employees who worked for companies, both large and small, that for whatever reason weren't dedicating *any* resources to work/life? Where would they even begin? I wanted to create that missing tool that allowed individuals to initiate the process of finding a better work+life fit for themselves. And I wanted more time with my new baby.

Chances are, had I proceeded with my original vision, based solely on my work realities, it would have failed. It would have happened the first time no one was available to pick up my daughter from child care or when I found myself frustrated in drafting another corporate work/life strategy recommendation and knowing it wasn't really the answer.

Clearly, a process for creating and implementing a work+life fit needed to consider both work *and* personal realities. Another piece of the puzzle had fallen into place, but how do you explain the individuals with work and personal realities that supported their visions who still weren't able to make it happen? In examining these scenarios, I discovered that there were two critical, yet overlooked, steps a person had to take before they started the process of creating and implementing a work+life fit.

Again, I reviewed the stories of employees with whom I'd worked over the years. And I saw that implementing a successful work+life fit is as much about having the right attitude as it is about carefully analyzing your work and personal realities.

When I meet someone with a successful work+life fit, the same thing often strikes me: how completely ordinary he or she is. It's easy to assume that the reason people succeed where others have failed is that they are somehow extraordinary. When in fact their jobs aren't particularly unusual, they don't have particularly unique talents, and though always good performers, they aren't usually off-the-charts exceptional. The difference lies in their attitude toward the whole process and their belief in being able to make it happen.

They are more positive, more internally motivated, more empowered. In contrast to someone with the same job who felt trapped by limiting misconceptions about work and life and who wanted someone else to give them the answer, they seemed to share a "can do" approach to seeking a solution. They demonstrated that success depends, at least in part, on the willingness to:

- ▶ Take the initiative
- ▶ See the infinite number of work+life fit possibilities
- ▶ Propose your work+life fit to your manager in spite of fearing the answer might be "no"
- ▶ Know that you add value to the company
- ▶ Create a business case to support your formal proposal
- ▶ Understand that anyone can seek a better work+life fit for any reason, as long as it not only meets your needs but the needs of the business

▸ Know that as your work and personal life evolve, your work+life fit will change
▸ Be patient and persevere

There was still one catch. Over the years, I'd observed that even some of the most positive people with well-thought-out arrangements would often give up before, or even after they achieved their goal—as if they'd hit a roadblock that came out of nowhere and couldn't get around it. The four most frequently cited reasons for their abandonment can be characterized as:

▸ **The success roadblock:** when your new work+life fit is incompatible with your definition of success, which includes money, advancement, prestige, and caregiving;
▸ **The fear roadblock:** when fear, real or imagined, keeps you from achieving a better work+life fit;
▸ **The resistance roadblock:** when you experience resistance to your new work+life fit from within yourself and from others; and
▸ **The in-the-box-thinking roadblock:** when you don't consider all of the different types and combinations of flexibility when creating a work+life fit.

Because these roadblocks can appear at any point in the process, it was clear that the second of the three steps had to involve recognizing and bypassing the roadblocks before you are derailed. The Three Steps to a Better Work+Life Fit were complete:

▸ Step 1: Embrace the Eight Work+Life Fit Fundamentals that help you to see the possibilities for a better work+life fit;
▸ Step 2: Recognize and bypass the Four Work+Life Fit Roadblocks; and
▸ Step 3: Follow the Work+Life Fit Roadmap to envision, negotiate, and implement a work+life fit that includes both your work and personal realities.

As I said in the beginning, when you hear the story of how the Three Steps evolved you can see how different they are from traditional, corporate-driven attempts to help employees resolve their work/life conflicts. But don't think for a minute that companies are off the hook. On the contrary, their continuing efforts in the area of work/life play a critical role in the process working at its optimal level.

In fact, the goal is to create a partnership with your company, with the company undertaking the critical task of creating an environment that supports the discussion between you and your manager. A company does this by training and rewarding managers, and publicly acknowledging the employee and the manager when a work+life fit succeeds. Companies must also challenge aspects of their corporate cultures and inefficient work processes that undermine a positive work+life fit.

But while the company is an important partner, it is not the focus of this book. *The focus of this book is on you, and giving you the tools to envision, propose, negotiate, and implement the work+life fit you want.* The goal is to help you come to the table as an equal partner with a well-thought-out formal proposal that considers your needs as well as the needs of the business and that you can successfully implement.

The book contains inspiring stories of people with whom I have worked over the years. While the stories generally are composites of many different individuals in order to preserve privacy, I hope they will serve as role models of this new way of thinking about work and how it fits into your life. As you read about their successes and struggles, focus less on *what* they did (because the work+life fit you want may be different) and more on *how* they did it. Let their courage to ask, as well as their creativity in forming a work+life fit suited to their unique realities inspire you. Let it encourage you to seek and to tailor your own solution.

There are plenty of excellent work/life-related books, but they target either a specific demographic (e.g., mothers or fathers) or a specific work/life issue (e.g., child care or caring for an aging parent). This book, however, assumes that while the specifics of the conflict may differ, men and women face many of the same work/life challenges. Regardless of the underlying source of your conflict, whether it's child, elder, lifestyle, or retirement-related, the process for creating a solution is the same for everyone. In fact, you can apply the Three Steps to resolve *any* work/life conflict at *any* stage of your life.

Is this another self-help book geared to helping you live your "authentic life"? Yes and no. Yes, the goal is to help you determine what you want out of life and what makes you truly happy. The difference, however, is that this book helps you achieve your goal by addressing the sometimes seemingly intractable reality of work. In other words, after you discover your passion for writing poetry or realize you must make more time to care for your aging parents, you still face the reality of a 60-hour workweek. The steps outlined here will help you adjust your work reality and reallocate time and energy to these other important parts of your life.

"Okay," you say, "this is all fine during economic growth when jobs are a dime a dozen, but it's different in a recession when you are just lucky to have a job." Even in a recession, I believe there are business cases to be made for pursuing your vision. Companies still need to retain talented people who know how to get the work done. If there is less work, you might suggest reducing your hours. You get more time and energy for personal responsibilities and the company, in turn, reduces salary expenses while retaining your experience and knowledge. And again your experience and knowledge will be needed when the inevitable recovery begins. That's just one of many potential justifications that this book will discuss for a new arrangement in a difficult economic climate.

In an economic recovery, once again, jobs will become more plentiful. Take advantage, and choose consciously the role that you want work to play in your life rather than allowing the wave of long hours and excessive workloads to overtake you as it may have in the past. In both scenarios, stop, think strategically, and find a better work+life fit. Building your supporting business case, in all economic environments, is an important part of Step 3.

As someone who is pro-business, I believe that if companies are going to compete in the future in all economic environments, they will have no choice but to support their employees' efforts to achieve the best work+life fit possible. This is especially true as demographic changes are projected to cause labor shortages within the next few years.[1] It's estimated that within ten years, the American workforce will have a 6 million-worker deficit between the number of new graduates and the number needed to replace retirees.[2] The smartest companies know that the only true source of their competitive advantage is their unique employees. Allowing employees to have who they are, both personally and professionally, respected in the workplace will not only unlock their greatest personal potential, but the greatest potential of the company.

But I also believe that if we want companies to do more, then more employees need to start doing their part by initiating well thought-out arrangements. Only then will companies be forced to create even more supportive cultures. It's a "chicken *and* the egg" situation. For years, many have argued that companies must take the initiative first and make employees feel comfortable asking for support. I disagree. From all of my experience, I now believe that companies need to do more *and* that more employees must ask. Use the Three Steps to a Better Work+Life Fit to help you confidently and successfully propose, negotiate, and implement a work+life fit that not only benefits you but that ultimately benefits your company as well.

You can choose how work fits into your life. You can find work+life satisfaction. It has worked for others and it can work for you. In the end, both you and your employer will benefit. Enjoy the journey!

What Is
Work+Life Fit?

What is work+life fit? Like the term work/life balance, work+life fit describes how work interacts with the rest of your life. But it doesn't imply that your ultimate goal is to find a "balance" by *dividing* your time and energy equally between two separate spheres. Instead, work+life fit more accurately reflects reality and the need to "fit" work flexibly and creatively into your life as a whole. In other words, given the realities in your work and personal life, work may at this time be the predominate focus of your life, while at other times it may only fit partially, or maybe even not at all.

Think of your life as a pie representing the fixed amount of time and energy you can expend daily—not only the number of hours, but also the emotional and physical energy.

How you allocate this fixed amount of time and energy depends in large part on the stage of life you're in. In some stages of life, you may allocate a majority of your time and energy to

100%
of Your Fixed
Time *and* Energy

work, leaving only a tiny sliver for your personal life. (Note: Through-out the book, please define work any way you would like—both paid and unpaid.) At other times, you may need to allocate more time and energy to your personal responsibilities.

Over the past twenty years, however, work/life conflict has in-creased for many because both work and personal life are demand-ing more of that fixed time and energy, yet you have nothing more to give.

The Three Steps to a Better Work+Life Fit can help you reallocate your fixed time and energy between your work and personal life in a way that meets yor needs and the needs of your company.

Having a deeper understanding of the source of a problem can help you to address it more effectively. So let's take a look at the trends that are causing so many people like you to seek relief.

A majority of the research I will share with you comes from both the 1997 and 2002 editions of *The National Study of the Changing Workforce* (*NSCW*) published by Families and Work Institute (FWI), my former employer. This study is particularly important for a couple of reasons. First, while at FWI, I worked personally with the re-searchers who conducted this study. As a result, I know that their re-search methods are some of the most rigorous and beyond reproach. Therefore, you can feel very confident using this data in whatever way you choose throughout the process. Second, the number of people surveyed as part of this study is so large that the findings can be generalized to the population as a whole. In other words, the find-ings from the *NSCW* data reflect the reality of the entire U.S. work-force and not just a small subsection of the population. Hopefully, you will see yourself somewhere in the research.

The "Personal Life" Piece of Your Time and Energy Pie

Eighty-five percent of the American workforce currently lives with some form of "family."[1] However, the remaining 15% also has friends and family for whom they feel responsible. This means 100% of all current and potential employees have personal relationships and interests outside of work to which they want to devote some amount of their attention in a given day.

In other words, it's *not* just employees with children who want a better work+life fit; it's *anyone* who has a life outside of work that they value. One of my clients who is a buyer for a retail chain described it this way, "I may be single and childless, but I have relationships with my friends and hobbies that are important and require my attention, not to mention my parents who aren't getting any younger." People with small children or ailing parents may have a more urgent and less negotiable need for a better work+life fit, but it doesn't make their need any more valid than that of someone without child- or elder-care responsibilities.

That said, we're going to focus on child care and caring for an aging parent to illustrate how the demands upon your time and energy lead to work/life conflict. This is simply because it's easier to quantify the number of employees specifically caring for a child or an elder than, say, those cutting back on their schedule in a partial retirement or returning to school part-time.

Almost half of all employees care for a child under 18 years old. Twenty-five percent have cared for an elder over the past five years, and almost one in ten had to find the time and energy to care for both a child under 18 and an elder. This group is often referred to as the "sandwich generation."[2]

The reality of employees having children and aging parents has not changed. What *has* changed is the family structure within which these responsibilities are dealt with. Twenty years ago, less than half of the married men with children under 18 years old had wives who worked.[3] Thus, a majority of married men could devote all of their time and energy to work unfettered, because a majority of their wives devoted 100% of themselves to dealing with personal demands. Modern-day corporate America was built around this reality.

Today the picture is much different. Three-quarters of all married employees—both men and women—have an employed spouse. Not to mention the fact that almost 67% of working dads are married to working moms, which is a big increase from 49% twenty years earlier. In other words, dual-career couples with children under 18 have gone from being the minority to being the majority. And this doesn't even include the 20% of employees with children under 18 who are single parents, most of whom are women.[4]

Today the majority of women with children are working and, therefore, can't devote all of their time and energy to personal demands. As a result, men are forced, out of both desire and necessity, to divert some of their time and energy from work to family. An engineer who is married with children explained his situation, "My wife has a job that she not only loves, but that helps us to make ends meet. We split the drop-off and pick-up duties of child care and sometimes when she travels I'm on full-time duty. I wonder if my boss understands that I am still committed even though I get in at 9 A.M. and have to be out the door no later than 5 P.M. if I am going to make it to the caregiver's on time?"

Even more than child care, caring for an aging parent is an equal opportunity responsibility. On average, both men and women spend the same amount of time per week—11 hours approximately—caring for an aging relative, and they are equally as likely to take time off from work or to reduce their hours to provide that care.[5] As a senior executive of a Fortune 500 company once said in a focus group, "My wife isn't going to take care of my mother now that she finally has a career of her own. She raised the kids, and in her mind it's my turn."

As a result of these changing roles, increasingly men and women are devoting similar amounts of time *and* energy to personal responsibilities, not just caring for children and aging parents, but also housework, yard work, errands, community involvement, sleeping, eating, and exercising.

While it's easy to track the actual hours you devote to your personal demands, it's more difficult to measure the average amount of *energy* you expend on them—it's a more subjective and individual experience that only you can quantify. While it may be less concrete, energy is no less important. Because I believe it's the piece of the puzzle most people overlook when trying to solve their work/life conflicts. On paper, it looks like you have enough time to get everything done, so why are you still overwhelmed? Because you haven't considered how much energy you are expending doing it. Depending upon myriad unique variables—age, personality, health, etc.—each of us has a different fixed amount of energy to expend. What's easy for one person can be difficult for another, thus requiring more energy.

In exercises #1 and #2 at the end of this chapter, you will have a chance to start estimating how much time *and* energy you feel you devote to various personal responsibilities and tasks. For example, taking your mother to the doctor may take an hour, but you estimate that worrying about her health consumes 15% of your energy every day. Helping your child with homework every night may take two hours, but it takes a lot more energy to complete trigonometry homework with a ninth-grader than spelling words with a second-grader.

To illustrate how demands on your time and energy contribute to work/life conflict, let's say that hypothetically you estimate that you expend, on average, 60% of your time *and* energy on your personal responsibilities and interests every day.

This would hypothetically leave 40% leftover for work. So where's the problem? The problem is that work now requires more of your time and energy than it did 20 years ago.

The "Work" Piece of Your
Time and Energy Pie

You are working more hours per week and expending more energy during this longer workweek than you either did or would have 20 years ago. This may not surprise you, but, again, what may is the magnitude of the change.

From 1977 to 1997, the average person's workweek increased from 43.6 hours to 47.1 hours.[7] Twenty percent of all employees worked paid or unpaid overtime at least once a week with little or no notice, and/or traveled overnight for business—both activities added even more hours to an already longer week.[8]

And the increase over the past 20 years is not just in the time devoted to work, but also in the amount of *energy* expended during those hours:

- ▶ 88% of employees say they have to work very hard, versus 70% in 1977;
- ▶ 68% of employees say they have to work very fast, versus 55% in 1977; and
- ▶ 60% do not have enough time to finish everything that needs to get done, versus 40% in 1977.[9]

In other words, even though you are working harder and faster and longer, you aren't getting your work done, which means workloads have increased.

Fitting the Pie Pieces Together—
The Source of Work/Life Conflict

So, we all still have the same amount of time and energy we've always had. Responsibilities related to caring for a child or an aging parent also remain relatively unchanged. But today, if you are like a majority of mothers, you work and can no longer devote all of yourself to these personal demands. Therefore, if you are a working dad, you are picking up some of the slack. As a result, you have less undistracted time and energy to devote to work. Compounding the conflict is the fact that you aren't only working longer hours, but you're expending more energy during those hours. And you still aren't able to finish your work. Just thinking about it makes me tired!

In our hypothetical illustration, we assumed that your personal responsibilities required approximately 60% of your time and energy per day. However, since work now demands not only more of your time but also more of your energy, we'll say work—which includes time commuting—requires 65% of your time and energy on average every day.

Wait. That's a total of 125%, or 25% more time and energy than you're humanly able to offer. That is unless you want to burn out or become unproductive, stressed, or physically ill, which are all results of unresolved work/life conflict. Clearly, something has to give.

Most people are diverting time and energy away from their personal lives and responsibilities and giving it to work. As a result, more than one-quarter to a third of all employees say that they "very often or often" in the past three months:

- Felt used up at the end of the workday (36%);[10]
- Brought work home once a week or more (31%);[11]
- Didn't have time for family and other important people (27%);[12]
- Didn't have the energy to do things with their families or other important people (28%);[13] and
- Weren't in a good mood at home because of their jobs (26%).[14]

In other words, on average 30% of the entire U.S. workforce says they frequently take time and energy from their personal life and give

23

it to work. Like you, they find that work is not fitting into their lives the way they would prefer. Surely, they would rather feel energized and present at home rather than drained and in a bad mood. Imagine the toll that takes on relationships with family and friends, not to mention the ability to enjoy any activity outside of work. Sound familiar?

Jessica, a banker, describes the difficult trade-off by saying, "I guess it's just easier to say 'no' to your family and friends than to your boss or clients. You just tell yourself, 'they'll understand and still be there.'" She paused and then added, "But will they really still be there?"

That's a pretty gloomy picture, but what if the same thing is happening in reverse? Maybe an equal number of employees are consciously reserving energy for their personal lives at the expense of work. Unfortunately, this is not the case. Only about 5% of all employees say that their family or personal lives:[15]

- ► Often kept them from getting work done on time;
- ► Often drained them of the energy they needed to do their job; and
- ► Often kept them from concentrating on the job.

Let me reiterate that there is nothing wrong with choosing to devote a majority of your time and energy to work as long as it gives you satisfaction. Indeed, I've met many work-primary people who seem content. In fact, at certain times of my life, focusing primarily on work has been my reality.

However, the majority of people are not satisfied with their work+life fit. On the contrary, they are stressed, nervous, and overwhelmed. In fact, more than half of all employees sometimes or more often felt nervous or stressed in the last three months.[16] More than a third were so overwhelmed that they often or sometimes had difficulty dealing with everyday life.[17] That level of stress and dissatisfaction emerges when you give time and energy to work by robbing from the personal relationships, experiences, and activities that keep you physically healthy and give your life meaning.

For example, perhaps in order to find extra time and energy for work, you sleep fewer hours at night even though you're tired. You exercise less and get dinner at the drive-thru "just one more night" instead of preparing a healthy meal. Maybe you're finding it easier to let the sitter feed the kids and put them to bed before you get home. Or perhaps you've decided not to coach your son's soccer team next fall. And there doesn't seem to be enough time to take an evening walk with your partner anymore. Not to mention that you've stopped taking calls from your aging parents because you don't want to hear, "When will I see you?" one more time. It's been months since you've gone to church or synagogue, and you haven't signed up to lead story circle at your daughter's school. Forget your book club, fishing, knitting, or planning your best friend's birthday party—who has the time or the energy? Apparently, you don't.

You can keep this up for a while, but eventually you too will join the ranks of the stressed and dissatisfied. And the stress not only makes you unhappy; it can make you sick. Maybe you are like Ellen, a bank administrator who explained to me how "From the time I wake up until the time I collapse into bed, it's just one big headache." More than a third of all workers often or sometimes suffer from minor stress-related health problems such as headaches, insomnia, or stomach pains.[18] Maybe you need a better work+life fit simply because you are literally sick and tired.

Whatever the reason, hopefully by now you understand that you aren't making a change because "you can't hack it." No. It's because very real and overwhelming pressures in your work and personal life conspire to demand the impossible of not just you, but many people.

But, if you're like most people, you insist on comparing yourself to those who are currently able or willing to devote more or most of their time and energy to work. You forget that life is cyclical and that a work+life fit that's appropriate today might not be right tomorrow. You may even think that you're the only one experiencing work/life conflict and suffer in silence. When I facilitate focus groups and workshops, participants often say, "It's helped me so much to know I'm not the only one with these problems. I thought there was something wrong with me." There is nothing wrong with you. Maybe you just didn't realize that you could choose to do things differently.

What Would Help You to Achieve a Better Work+Life Fit? Time and Flexibility

Clearly, you have very valid reasons for needing to do things differently. But exactly what do you want? According to the research, you want time and flexibility; time away from work, and the flexibility to find that time. In other words, you want a work+life fit that reduces the size of the time and energy pie piece devoted to work. And, again, on this point you are by no means alone:

- ► Almost two-thirds of *all* employees, both men and women in all stages of their careers, would like to work less. This is 64% of all employees who want to work fewer hours. In fact, both men and women would reduce the number of hours they work per week by an average of 11 hours.[19] Those 11 hours probably represent the portion of their "time and energy" that they would like to reallocate away from work and give to their personal lives.
- ► 70% of working fathers and mothers say they don't have enough time with their children.[20]
- ► A study of 6,000 employees ages 18 to 65 years old found that a majority (51%) want nontraditional work that allows them to either work from home or part-time or the flexibility to drop in and out of the workforce.[21]

Why Should Your Employer Help You Achieve a Better Work+Life Fit?

In Step 3, you will develop a business case to support your individual proposal. But for now, let's look at how your employer benefits, in general, from supporting your search for a better work+life fit. It's important to know how unresolved employee work/life conflict affects the corporate bottom line. Specifically, what is the strategic business imperative?

I'll play devil's advocate. I'm the CEO of a company and I just finished reading the first part of this chapter. I might be thinking, "My employees are giving the company even more of their time and energy, which means more productivity for our shareholders. So what if that time and energy is coming from their personal lives. That's not my problem. I pay them to work. Right?" Wrong. Thankfully, more and more companies have figured out that this approach is just plain bad for business, whether it's a period of economic growth or recession.

It's important that more companies are offering work/life supports, though the level of employee use still doesn't match their need. And even in a weaker economy, I'm hearing more stories from clients about managers who support their efforts to improve their work+life fit, as long as those arrangements take the needs of the business into consideration and don't mean more work for the manager ("not another rock in my backpack").

This increased supportiveness does not represent a collective change of heart within corporate America. Corporations and their managers are not just trying to be nice. Rather, the trend toward greater supportiveness represents a proven, profit-oriented, strategic decision; helping employees achieve a better work+life fit directly affects the financial performance of the organization. Again, regardless of the prevailing economic climate, companies will always need to attract and retain the best, most productive human resources if they are going to compete and succeed. A study conducted in 2001 by MetLife found that 78% of the 481 benefit professionals surveyed felt that retention of employees is their first priority. And more than half said that attracting employees was still a critical goal.[22] Very few of the best and brightest employees are going to be able to devote 100% of themselves to work. Adding urgency for companies are labor shortages that are projected to begin as early as 2006 and, by some estimates, to escalate to a shortfall of as much as 36 million employees by 2031.[23]

The business case—whether you are a company, a manager, or an individual trying to justify a work/life initiative—focuses on four general outcomes:

▶ Increasing productivity
▶ Increasing employee commitment
▶ Recruiting and retaining the best employees
▶ Benefitting the company financially

A number of recent studies support the existence of these positive corporate outcomes, including:

Increasing Productivity

▶ In 2001, Frederich Reichheld, partner emeritus of Bain & Co. and author of *The Loyalty Effect,* conducted a study of 100 employers. He found that a 5% swing in retention rates resulted in earnings swings of up to 25% to 100%—up if retention is higher and down if retention is lower. Fostering loyalty boosts productivity, customer retention, and referrals, attracts talented staff, and is even *more* important in a down market.[24]

▶ In 2001, Brigham Young University published a study of IBM employees entitled "Finding an Extra Day a Week: The Positive Influence of Perceived Job Flexibility on Work and Family Life Balance." They found that of employees who worked 40 to 50 hours per week and were *not* allowed to alter their starting or ending times, work a compressed workweek, or work from home, 46% had trouble balancing work and life. *But* of those with the same hours *and* flexibility, only 28% said that they had trouble. According to the researchers, "In a heavy workload environment (like IBM), perceived flexibility in the timing of work enables the employee to work an extra day a week before work/life balance becomes difficult."[25]

► In 2000, Boston College published a study entitled "Measuring the Impact of Workplace Flexibility" in which they interviewed 59 users and nonusers of flexible work arrangements at Amway, Bristol Myers Squibb, Honeywell, Kraft, Lucent, and Motorola. Eighty-seven percent of those surveyed said that flexible work arrangements had a positive impact on productivity and work quality, and 80% said the arrangements improved retention. Managers were also enthusiastic with 70% saying flexibility had improved the employee's productivity, 65% saying it improved quality of work, and 76% saying it improved retention. *And* three-quarters of those managers saw no change in their own workload because of an employee's flexibility.[26]

Increasing Employee Commitment

► In 1997, the Economic Policy Institute surveyed 1,500 production workers at 19 plants to study the impact of work/family practices. They found that workers had a more positive perception of their family life, which increased their organizational commitment, reduced stress on the job, and reduced the amount stress spilled over into their personal life.[27]

► Dupont conducted an employee survey in 2001 that found that those using work/life programs are more committed, more likely to go the "extra mile." And 3 out of 4 employees said that they plan to stay with the company 15 years or more. Of all of the work/life programs, flexibility was the most valued with nearly half of the respondents taking advantage of flexible schedules.[28]

Recruiting and Retaining the Best Employees

▶ A 2003 study by *The New York Times* Job Market of 500 hiring managers found that nearly three-quarters of job seekers said that work/life balance was at the top of the list of factors that are important to them. Two-thirds said they look to see if a company is making it a point to hire and cultivate diverse employees, and half want to know the company's ranking on Fortune's 100 Best Companies to Work For list.[29]

▶ The 1997 "Working Trends" study of 1,000 workers conducted by the John J. Heldrich Center for Workforce Development at Rutgers University and the Center for Survey Research and Analysis at the University of Connecticut found that balancing work and family is more important than any other employment factor, and one in four workers surveyed said their employers don't offer any work/life benefits. Eight-seven percent said that flexible schedules would help them, and more than half would telecommute but only 17% of employers offered it.[30]

▶ A study conducted in 2000 by PriceWaterhouse Coopers and Universum (a German company) of 2,510 graduating students from 36 universities from five continents and 11 countries found that balancing work and personal life is now the most important goal of these students, with 57% saying that it is their most important career goal. *And* they don't believe it will compete with their long-term career development.[31]

Benefiting the Company Financially

▶ The Watson Wyatt 2001 Human Capital Index studied 750 North American and European companies with 1,000 employees or more that supported flexible work arrangements as one of a number of human resource practices. It found that these companies had a 3.5% higher market value than companies without flexibility.[32]

▶ A study conducted in 2000 by Vanderbilt University and Hewitt Associates compared companies on Fortune's 100 Best Companies list to those companies *not* on the list and found that those on the list had higher-than-average annual stock returns, better operating performance, and higher return on average assets.[33]

▶ In 2002, Watson Wyatt found that offering flexible work arrangements increased shareholder returns by 3.5% because of a "surge in productivity" by workers using time more efficiently and increased employee retention.[34]

These studies are just a sampling of the mountain of research from the past decade that, in a nutshell, makes the following business case:

By reducing employee work/life conflict through the creation of a supportive work environment (for example, supportive corporate culture and flexible work arrangements), you directly increase job satisfaction, loyalty, and retention, and you decrease burnout. This, in turn, directly improves employee productivity and customer satisfaction, which results in the ultimate objective—increased revenues and profits. Reducing employee work/life conflict just makes good business sense.

Even without all of the research and case studies to back it up, you already knew intuitively that achieving a better work+life fit would make you more satisfied with your job, more loyal to your company, less likely to quit, and a heck of a lot less burned out. You would be willing and able to work more efficiently, which would make your company more profitable. Sounds like a compelling business case to me.

So what is work+life fit? It's simply acknowledging that you only have a certain amount of time and energy to give all aspects of your life every day. And given the increasing demands work now places on everyone, not just parents or those caring for an aging parent, you need to analyze your work and personal realities and create an arrangement that helps you find a better way to fit work into your life as a whole. Or, going back to the pie analogy, you need to reduce the size of that pie piece devoted to work, and do so in a way that benefits not only you, but also your employer.

Now that you know what work+life fit is, let's complete the steps to make yours better!

GETTING STARTED

Creating Your "Work+Life Fit" Workbook

Throughout the book, there are exercises to complete at the end of each chapter, with each one building upon the other to ultimately bring you to your new work+life fit. Therefore, it's helpful to have one central place where you can keep track of all of your work. Here are some fun and creative suggestions that may make the process more organized and efficient:

- ► First, create your Work+Life Fit Workbook by using any combination of binders, notebooks, or folders. Just make sure you have enough space to write down your answers to the exercises, to keep track of questions you may want to refer back to, to store articles related to your work that you may come across, etc.
- ► Personalize your Work+Life Fit Workbook in some wonderful creative way that makes it all your own. You may also want to get a couple of special pens to work with.

► As the first three pages in your Workbook, make a copy of the:
- Eight Work+Life Fit Fundamentals (pages 12–13),
- Four Work+Life Fit Roadblocks (page 100), and
- Work+Life Fit Roadmap (page 182).

Having these three pages in the front of the workbook allows you to easily refer to all Three Steps to a Better Work+Life Fit at a glance, which will help you to stay on track throughout the entire process.

How Do You Currently Allocate Your Time and Energy Between Your Work and Your Personal Life?

The goal of these exercises is to *start* visualizing the source of your work/life conflict by working with the concept of time and energy and how it plays out in your life as you begin the Three Steps. It will help you to start thinking about which areas you may want to address as you work through the rest of the chapters.

EXERCISE #1

- Draw three circles of equal size on a piece of paper, lined up side-by-side. Each circle represents the total amount of time and energy you have to give per day.
- Label circle #1 "Personal Life Pie Piece." Draw a line indicating the total percentage of time *and* energy you devote to your personal life, then shade that section in. In the hypothetical example, we drew a line allocating 60% of the pie to personal responsibilities. What do you estimate your allocation would be? Remember it's more than just the concrete number of hours; it's the amount of energy that you expend within those hours.
- Label circle #2 "Work Pie Piece." Draw a line indicating how much of your total time and energy you devote to work, then shade that sec-

tion in. In the hypothetical example, we allocated 65%. What would your allocation be in real life?

- Label circle #3 "Current Work+Life Fit." Imagine that you lay your personal life circle #1 over your work circle #2. See where they overlap. Shade in the portion where the overlap occurs in circle #3. In the hypothetical example, we were expending 25% more time and energy on average than the fixed amount we had to give. How much do your two pie pieces overlap? Seeing in black and white how much more you give on a daily basis to your work and life than you are physically able to give as one person can be a real motivator for completing the rest of the process. The goal is to eliminate that overlap!

EXERCISE #2

This exercise takes the work you just did a step further and helps you to determine the actual allocation of time and energy within different areas of your work and personal life.[35] Look at the following list (please change the categories below to reflect the aspects of your life that are most important to you). Assign percentages according to how much time and energy you devote to the following areas in your life (like the previous exercise, the total may exceed 100% of your fixed time and energy if you are overextending yourself):

Work
Family/Relationships
Leisure
Community
Religion

EXERCISE #3

How would you reallocate your time and energy so that the total that you expend *doesn't* exceed the 100% that you have to give? Assign percentages to the amount of time and energy you would like to devote to each of the following areas in your life, but the total this time *can't* exceed 100%:

Work
Family/Relationships
Leisure
Community
Religion

EXERCISE #4

Compare the allocations from Exercises #2 and #3. For example:

	Actual Allocation	*Desired Allocation*
Work	60%	40%
Family/Relationships	50%	50%
Leisure	5%	9%
Community	0%	0%
Religion	0%	1%
Total	115%	100%

By comparing your actual and desired allocation of time and energy, you can begin to see the areas that you need to target. In the example above, this person estimates that he overexpends by 15% his total time and energy every day. When considering how he would reallocate to eliminate his conflict, he would choose to take time and energy away from work and find more leisure time. While he still has much to learn before he can finalize his new work+life fit, this gives him a place to start as he begins the Three Steps.

Step 1

The Work+Life Fit Fundamentals

THE EIGHT FUNDAMENTALS in Step 1 will challenge the way you think about work and life. They will help you see, and therefore be able to pursue, the possibilities for a better work+life fit. Because, as we've said, it's attitude that often separates those who are able to make it happen from those who seem to give up.

Why is it important to embrace these fundamentals? By design, each step builds upon the other. Before you can make any change in the way work fits into your life you need to believe that it's possible, which, for many, is a drastic shift especially when all you may see are misconceptions and limitations. In fact, much of my time with clients is spent simply shifting their thinking from the limitation of "yes, but" to the positive reality of "why not!"

That's not to say that overcoming the roadblocks in Step 2 and creating and implementing a new work+life fit in Step 3 aren't important steps. But they won't work without first challenging the self-defeating "well, that's just the way work is" beliefs that can keep you stuck in work/life conflict.

Taking the Initiative

Misconception: *I must wait for someone else—my manager, or human resources, or prospective employer—to solve my work/life conflict.*

Reality: *I can take the initiative and do the work to create and propose a better work+life fit.*

When it comes to influencing the way work fits into their lives, most people feel powerless. They are paralyzed by the belief that someone else needs to hand them a solution. Chances are, you're no different. If you already have a job, you look to your manager or human resources to solve your conflict. And if they don't, you simmer in resentful misery or you leave. "I would love to have stayed with my job after (insert work/life event of your choice), but they never offered me a different arrangement, so I had to leave." If I had a dollar for every time I heard that statement over the years, I'd be a wealthy woman.

Or if you're looking for a job, you assume the description of a potential opportunity is nonnegotiable and wait for the person hiring to offer an alternative. If he or she doesn't, you either decline the opportunity or accept it "as is," knowing full well that you're walking straight into work/life conflict.

In fact, this sense of powerlessness is so common that when I run workshops it doesn't take very long before at least one person becomes visibly disturbed as they quickly face two realities.

First, they realize that I won't be handing them a solution tailored to their unique work/life conflict. And second, while I will give them a framework within which to create a solution themselves, they are going to have to do the work. You see, for many it seems easier and much less scary if someone else finds the answer to their work/life conflict, even if it will most likely fail because:

▶ No one knows the realities in your work and personal life better than you do; therefore, how could anyone else possibly develop your solution?

▶ Managers have way too much on their plates already to be saddled with solving your work/life conflict. They typically support your new work+life fit as long as it doesn't mean more work for them; and

▶ Finally, while there are exceptions in a number of forward-thinking organizations, human resource departments, unfortunately, in most instances aren't able to address work/life issues in a strategic, customized way. This is particularly true in small and mid-sized companies without the resources to devote solely to work/life initiatives.

Like it or not, only you know how work needs to fit into your life given your work and personal realities. Only you can negotiate the appropriate work+life fit with your manager or prospective employer and manage it day in and day out. And only you can enjoy the sense of empowerment and fulfillment that comes from resolving your own conflict.

Let's look first at your manager's perspective. Like most of the managers I've met, chances are your manager already has enough to deal with without having to sit down to figure out exactly what you need. Plus, how is she supposed to understand all of the relevant personal realities—your work+life vision, your finances, your partner's schedule—which affect your work+life fit? She can't.

You need to have some compassion for the position most managers are in today. Not only are they responsible for managing a large number of direct reports, but they often handle direct client or product responsibility as well. I know this was the case for me when I worked in banking. In addition to supervising the work of a unit of account officers and support staff, I was responsible for managing my own portfolio of accounts. Needless to say, this didn't leave a lot of extra time to tailor individual work+life fit solutions for each one of my employees.

You may be saying, "Okay, if my manager can't give me the answer, I'll go to human resources. They'll tell me what to do." Unfortunately, as I noted earlier, human resources in most companies is probably even less likely to tailor a work+life fit that meets both your needs and the needs of the business. Why? First, think about the basic role of HR in any organization. It is to create and administer the fewest number of policies that apply to the largest number of employees. In other words, their job is uniformity and standardization where at all possible.

But uniformity and standardization are antithetical to creativity, which is critical when developing a new work+life fit. In addition, many, but not all, human resource departments see work/life initiatives solely in terms of policies and programs, rather than as a strategic management tool to be used to enhance productivity and profits. Although human resource executives say that they are responsible for recruiting, retaining, and increasing productivity of employees, only 1% believes that work/life initiatives are an important tactic for accomplishing those goals.[1] They see it as an accommodative policy and not a strategic management tool. Therefore, it's not surprising that they often can't articulate the business case strongly enough to get management to buy in.

This doesn't mean that HR isn't important in helping you to take the initiative to create and implement your own work+life fit. HR may not be able to give you the answer, but it can help create a supportive environment within which you can confidently approach your manager to discuss your work/life issues. HR can also offer manager training and incentives that encourage managers to work toward a solution with you, as well as provide child care, elder care, and other programs that support the implementation of your work+life fit. And you should absolutely use HR for those purposes.

Let's look at one more reason why you might be holding out hope that someone will take you by the hand and offer a solution. Employee loyalty. On one level, employee loyalty is very admirable and important. But on another level it's misguided, especially as it relates to work+life fit. What do I mean by misguided? I'm talking about a misplaced sense of loyalty that causes you to expend time and energy at work that you would prefer to devote to your personal life, because you trust that "they'll take care of me." Economic history, both past and present, illustrates time and again that your company won't.

In recent years, we've witnessed that when economic forces dictate, companies will expand and contract their workforce without giving much thought to employee loyalty. And in this high-tech age of globalization, this pattern of expansion and contraction is likely to continue. Therefore, out of necessity, *employer* loyalty is, and will most likely continue to be, conditional, and there will be a continuing move away from job security.

Therefore, *employees* should be loyal and committed to their companies, but conditionally as well—the condition being you will work for them as long as you are given support and respect to negotiate and achieve your desired work+life fit. Because the reality is that "jobs are less secure, more demanding, more time-consuming, and more hectic, which leads to less employee satisfaction with their (work+life fit)."[4]

This is a wake-up call to realize that personal relationships and supports are really the only constant in today's ever-changing globalized world. And making them strong does require an investment of time and energy outside of work. Unfortunately, most working people fail to make the choices that ensure they have the time and energy they need.

In focus groups, people use very personal language to describe how they feel about their company, such as "We're like family" or "I love my company." In fact, more than 73% of employees say they are either very or extremely loyal to their employers. This is in spite of the fact that:[5]

▶ One-third of these same employees feel they are likely to lose their jobs in the next couple of years; and
▶ Almost two-thirds feel they have little chance for advancement.

In other words, although employees do understand that their employer's loyalty is conditional, they still offer *un*conditional loyalty in return. And only 15% of employees say they are likely to make a genuine effort to find another job in the next year.[6]

Let's reframe these percentages in terms of a personal relationship. You are dating someone. Not only do you feel that there is a 30% chance this person will leave you in the next two years, but that there is a 60% chance they will never marry you. Regardless, a majority of the time you feel very or extremely loyal to this person, and you only consider looking for a new relationship 15% of the time.

Does this sound like a healthy, mutually beneficial partnership? If you wouldn't put up with this type of unbalanced relationship in your personal life, why would you in your work life? Perhaps you do "love" your work environment and consider your colleagues to be "family." There's nothing wrong with that; however, if you choose not to pursue a better work+life fit out of this sense of love and loyalty for your employer, your affection may be a bit misplaced.

Hopefully, you're beginning to see why it's incumbent upon you to take the lead on your own behalf. Use your dedication and commitment to your company as incentive and leverage to achieve the work+life fit that you want, not as an excuse to muddle along despite unresolved conflict.

ALLISON'S STORY

Allison, a mid-level marketing manager at a large Fortune 500 manufacturing company, is overwhelmed. After having her daughter Janet

a year ago, she returned to her job full-time and continued to participate in a community volunteer organization to which she devotes
about 20 hours a month. Because she loves her job and her volunteer
work, she has tried to give them the same amount of time and energy
that she did before Janet was born. But she loves Janet too. And she's
finding that there simply isn't enough time and energy to give her at
the end of the day. Too often she kisses Janet at bedtime and realizes
she hasn't spent one minute on the floor just playing with her. And
she can't remember when she last had a complete conversation with
her husband.

There are days when she sits at her desk and realizes she's been
staring at the same proposal for an hour. And instead of looking
forward to her volunteer work reading to the kids at the battered
women's shelter, she resents it and finds herself rushing to finish the
books. Then there are the days she just cries; cries driving to work, in
the bathroom stall, making dinner.

She thinks to herself, "Can't anyone see I need a break? Why doesn't
my manager tell me to leave early? He keeps saying how glad he is to
have me back, but can't he see I'm losing it? I went to HR and they
handed me a brochure listing all of the work/life programs and policies
the company offered, but I've never seen anyone else in my group use
any of these things. I don't even know what questions to ask. Maybe I
have no choice but to leave. And why doesn't the committee chair of
my volunteer project get the hint when I say wouldn't it be nice if we
read to the kids once a month instead of twice? But is that what really
I want—to leave my job, only volunteer once a month? I don't know.
All I know is that I don't want what I have now, that's for sure."

Imagine her excitement when she learns that her volunteer organization is sponsoring one of my Work+Life Fit Workshops. Allison
arrives late and frazzled. She apologizes profusely and starts to introduce herself, barely getting out, "My name is Allison . . ." before
dissolving into tears. She asks me to continue while she composes
herself and listens attentively while tears continue to stream down
her face. But soon I begin to notice that instead of feeling empowered

by learning about the Three Steps to a Better Work+Life Fit, she is visibly frustrated. Finally, she confesses, "I thought you were going to give us solutions, not just tell us the steps we have to take."

Hearing her disappointment, I explained that neither I nor anyone else could solve her very unique, very personal work/life conflict. I could help by giving her an easy-to-use framework to follow. I could make her aware of the things she needed to consider, but she had.to do the actual work. She nodded half-heartedly, and I continued with the workshop.

As we were all saying good-bye, Allison approached me. "After hearing about the steps and the creative ways others have resolved their work/life problems, I now see why it is up to me, because I can't go on like this much longer. That's for sure. But I'm not sure the answer is to leave my job." She laughed, "Are you sure you just can't tell me what to do?"

I grabbed her hand and responded smiling, "No, because we both know it wouldn't work. What I can tell you is that, with some effort, you *can* influence your work/life reality, and stop those tears. You are not at the whim of all of your current work and personal realities; you are not powerless to change them." And as she walked out the door, Allison seemed to be standing a bit taller and walking a bit more peacefully. I had hope, and I think she did too.

CHALLENGE YOUR THINKING

How do you feel about taking the initiative to create a better work+life fit?

- Does the concept make you feel overwhelmed or empowered? Why?
- Review the reasons why your manager, HR department, or prospective employer isn't able to solve your work/life conflict for you.
- Review the ways HR can support your efforts to find a better work+life fit. Spend some time researching what work/life supports your current or prospective employer offers that can help you in your efforts.

- Examine your loyalty to your employer. Is it blindly unconditional or appropriately conditional? Do you recognize that you have a right to find a better work+life fit?
- Assuming that your personal life and relationships are the only constant in this ever-changing globalized, high-tech work world, do you feel that you are making the appropriate investment of time and energy into these areas? If not, how would you like it to be different?

Seeing the 2 Possibilities

Misconception: *If I have a job, I must either work 100% of my current schedule or leave. If I'm looking for a new job, I must either accept what's offered or move on.*

Reality: *Between the extremes of 100% work and no work at all lay an infinite number of possibilities. Even the smallest change in the way I work can make a big difference.*

When faced with work/life conflict, it's easy to become extreme in your thinking about how to resolve it. It can indeed seem like you have to quit or walk away from an opportunity without asking for a change, no matter how small. However, the reality is very different. Hopefully, by now you understand that there are an infinite number of ways to creatively fit work into your life. Considering all of the options that lie somewhere in between the two extremes of all work or no work represents a new, more moderate "in between" way of fitting work into your life.

The trick is to choose a work+life fit that suits not only your work and personal realities, but also your comfort level. The beauty of having so many choices is that you can start out small and then, once you've tested the waters, perhaps make an even bigger change. Even the smallest change   leaving an hour earlier every Friday afternoon to visit your mother, or working from home every other Wednesday in order to paint during your lunch hour—can make all the difference. And this approach is much less overwhelming than the extremes of all or nothing.

That said, I do urge clients to, whenever possible, ask for the work+life fit they truly want up front; however, some people are more comfortable changing their work+life fit incrementally. Even though her ultimate work+life vision was to work three days a week, one client wasn't sure that either she or her boss could handle such a dramatic change. So, she initially proposed working from home one day a week. Six months later, she renegotiated her arrangement and began only working four days. One year later, she is now working three days, and she would say that going cold turkey with a three-day workweek up front probably would have failed in her situation. The reason was not only her manager's assumed discomfort (we don't know for sure because she never asked), but her own discomfort as well.

If you are someone who is currently searching for a new job and are interested in a work+life fit that differs from what is set forth in the job description, you also have options beyond the take-it-or-leave-it approach.

First, learn as much as you can about the potential position (e.g., its tasks and responsibilities, the corporate culture, etc.) and complete all Three Steps to ensure that the work+life fit you'd like is compatible with the realities of the job. Then, step back and reflect on your comfort level. Are you willing to compromise your work+life fit and propose an arrangement that more closely matches the job's current description with the idea that you would renegotiate later? Or are you determined to pursue the work+life fit you want even if the potential employer may consider it too much of a departure and choose another candidate?

Either choice is fine, of course. However, understand that depending upon how much you're willing to compromise, it may take you longer to find the right position. If you're able to be patient, persistent, and flexible, the benefit will be having a job that is compatible with the work+life fit you envision.

If there are so many possible ways to fit work into your life, why is it that people tend to see only the extremes of all or nothing? Well, it's human nature to be drawn to the black-and-white clarity of work or no work. And it certainly doesn't require as much effort and thought as completing the Three Steps to a Better Work+Life Fit. But there is a deeper social phenomenon at work here.

When faced with a challenge, what do you do? You look around to see how others have faced and resolved similar challenges. These role models may include family, friends, or coworkers, or come from the media.

If your parents faced child care–related work/life conflict, chances are they used the "dad works 100% and mom works 0%" model to resolve it, since 20 years ago a majority of mothers didn't work outside of the home as they do today. Or if your parents wanted to make a change in the way that they worked, they needed to leave their current employer and seek a different opportunity elsewhere.

Using your parent as a role model is particularly problematic for mothers ages 25 to 40. If a mom doesn't see the mothers who work in her company creatively combining work and family, they default back to the only other role model they have. And using their mothers as guides for how to handle child care usually means not working at all.

What do mothers want? They want to combine work and life in a more moderate, less extreme, flexible "in between" way. Specifically, when World WIT (Women in Technology) recently surveyed its 25,000 members in more than 20 countries asking "Which benefits would be most helpful in lightening the load of working mothers?"; 61% said flexibility, 15% said telecommuting, and 9% said onsite day care.[1]

A recent study of 8,000 members of the group Mothers & More, a national organization of formerly employed mothers who tend to be older, more educated, and more financially secure, found that a majority of its members felt that they had no other choice but to stay home (the "0% work" option). According to the organization's spokes person, Catherine Carbone Rogers, "(There was a feeling of) either take the career in which you've invested 10 years and chuck it, or never see your kids. So, it's not a choice. Many of us feel forced into staying home."[2] Sounds like they would have been open to an "in be-tween," more moderate way of addressing their work/life conflict if they had only known it existed. In fact, while a Whirlpool/Families and Work Institute study of U.S. women found that 59% of stay-at-home mothers are happy with their choice, 17% would prefer to work part-time, 6% would prefer to work full-time, and 17% would prefer to be volunteering.[3]

And that's just mothers. Fathers today expect to be fully involved parents as well and are willing to make financial sacrifices to achieve this goal. A recent Radcliffe Public Policy poll of men found that 80% of men 20 to 39 years old would choose a work schedule that enables them to spend time with family (the "in between" way) over chal-lenging work or high salary. While 70% said they actually would be willing to give up some pay to spend more time with their families.[4]

These fathers look to their own fathers and senior male managers as role models for combining work and parenthood. But twenty years ago, the answer for these fathers was 100% work. Remember, how-ever, this was at a time when corporate cultures often encouraged employees to leave work at 5 P.M., which is not the case in our 24/7 global economy. So fathers who chose 100% work still got home for dinner by six.

As we will discuss in greater detail in chapter 3, these scenarios aren't how today's mothers and fathers want work to fit into their lives. They want to choose from an array of more creative options, even though unfortunately many don't see that such options exist.

Previous generations aren't the only role models. You can also look to friends and colleagues who are currently dealing with similar work/life challenges. But be discerning. Make sure they aren't part of:

▶ The one-third of employees who "very often or often" allo-cate time and energy that they would prefer to give to their personal lives to work;

▶ The two-thirds of all employees who say that they would like to work less—on average 11 hours less per week;

▶ The 70% of fathers and mothers who say that they don't spend enough time with their children;

▶ The one-third of employees who often or sometimes experience minor stress-related health issues.

Hmmmm . . . looks like many of your friends and colleagues might be choosing the 100% work option, even though it's not the work+life fit that they want. I'm not sure that their suggestions will be helpful.

Then there is the media, which reflects the all-or-nothing paradigm of combining work and personal life. Why? In part, it speaks to the comfort the public seems to derive from their black or white solutions to the most multidimensional situations, as unrealistic as those solutions may be. But also it reflects the extreme terms which we as a culture use to describe our work and personal life choices, and these terms often do not reflect reality.

For example, the resignations of Karen Hughes, the former White House communications director, and Mary Matalin, the former assistant to Vice President Dick Cheney, to spend more time with their families have been widely reported. And in most if not all of the coverage their decisions have been presented as, "Karen Hughes and Mary Matalin have resigned to be with their families *instead* of working." When the truth is that both women found creative, more moderate "in between" ways to fit work into their lives.

In the case of Karen Hughes, yes, she telecommutes from Texas instead of working in an office at the White House. But she still works as a consultant to the president, often drafting communications strategies, traveling with him on many occasions, and consulting on various issues. In the case of Mary Matalin, she continues to work on special projects for the vice president and also consults to him on various matters. Not to mention the fact that she has a lucrative career as a writer and talk show pundit. Again, in neither scenario was the decision all or nothing—it was "How can I do this work I love differently so that I have more time and energy for my family?" Then they asked their bosses, and the two most powerful managers in the free world said, "yes." If you ask me, that's the story.

A cover of *Time* magazine read, "Baby or Work?" The story was about the struggles of professional women waiting too long to have a baby. But why does it have to be baby *or* work? Why doesn't the article focus on creative ways to do both? Not only would it be more realistic, but also more helpful to the millions of professional women who encounter this issue. Sounding extreme may sell more magazines, but it also perpetuates this all-or-nothing paradigm in our culture that then carries over into how we talk about our own work/life realities. Once a potential client explained to me that, "While I graduated from a top MBA program, I've been a stay-at-home mom for the past 13 years and am interested to get back into the workforce." Looking at her resume, she had spent the previous 13 years raising kids, *but* she'd also handled the day-to-day management and marketing for her husband's small business. She was an entrepreneur/mom, but didn't describe herself that way. And she is not alone.

This is the case as well for female authors who write books about the joy of giving yourself "100% to motherhood." Again, being a 100% mom is wonderful if it's your choice, but is that what the author is *really* doing? No, she is writing and promoting a book, which, trust me, takes a lot of time and energy. Now, she might be writing at night or when the kids are at school. Regardless, it's still work, and not the 100% motherhood and 0% work extreme the author is promoting. But as is the case with the supposedly stay-at-home Karen Hughes and Mary Matalin, the reality is that this author has found a creative way— an "in between," more moderate way—to fit work into her life.

And it's not just women. In a recent article in *Newsweek* about how more women are working while their husbands "stay home," one of the examples was a wife who worked for a company while her husband had primary care responsibility for their children *and* worked from home editing operas. But, the article described him as a "stay-at-home" husband, instead of someone who has an interesting and unique work+life fit.

If you can't look to the previous generation, your friends and colleagues or the media for role models, where do you look? Well, look a little bit closer at those around you. Who's happy and peaceful with the way work is fitting into their life? Now that you can see beyond the "100% or 0%" paradigm, you will begin to notice people with creative combinations of work and life. Even if they haven't made particularly big changes, they're still good role models. Look to the many examples in this and other work/life books, websites, and chat rooms. Throughout the rest of the book and in the Resource section, you will learn more about resources to support your search for a new work+life fit. Role models of the new, more moderate "in between" way of combining work and life are out there. Use their examples to inspire you. Again, don't necessarily focus on what they've done, but on how they did it. And, remember, you can start small. Make only the changes that feel comfortable. You can always do more later.

Let's look at Alan, a sales manager who shifted his all-or-nothing thinking to consider one of the many work+life fit opportunities that lay between the two extremes.

ALAN'S STORY

Alan, a sales manager for a paper company, is a 35-year-old father of three school-age children. He has worked at his company for seven years and likes his job, but because of his long commute, feels he is missing out on too much of his kids' young years.

When I met him, he had decided that he was going to leave his job and take a year off in order to "decide what my next move will be." You see, Alan thought that either he had to take his schedule as it was—in at 8 A.M. after an hour commute, then not get home until 7:00 P.M.—or he had to leave.

As we talked, I asked him if there were certain tasks that required him to be in the office every day from eight to six. After thinking for a minute, he said the only things were an 8:15 A.M. conference call every Wednesday morning, customer calls that required him to stay late a couple of nights a week, and travel two or three days a month. He also said that he tended to be in meetings all day and was more of a morning person, he got a lot of "thinking work" done in the first hour of the day. Given these work realities, it seemed that Alan had more flexibility to make a change in the later part of his day, with the exception of the nights he entertained customers or traveled.

I knew he liked his job and would like to stay if he could. I could see that the tasks and responsibilities of his job allowed for some flexibility. Plus, I knew he was valuable to the company and had many close relationships with big clients. He had built up a great deal of goodwill in the organization over the past seven years that would support his request for a change in his work+life fit. Remember, Alan was thinking of leaving only because he felt it was the *only* way he could figure out what job would allow him more time with his family.

But why not stay with his current employer—an employer he liked? And if he is willing to quit anyway, why not try to change his current situation first? What does he have to lose?

To jump-start his creative thinking, I gave Alan an example of a work+life fit that would allow him to adjust his current work schedule and give him time with his kids. What if he formalized an arrangement that took advantage of his being an early bird? Arrive at work a half hour earlier, but leave by 4:30 P.M. unless he had a customer commitment. And work from home every other Friday since most client-related activities take place earlier in the week. If necessary in order to do his job, offer to be available by cell phone. Perhaps this would satisfy his desire to eat dinner with his kids most nights and participate in their afternoon activities at least every other Friday, while allowing him to continuing doing a job he likes.

As is so often the case when people are presented with a reasonable alternative to their current work schedule—one that allows them to have more personal satisfaction while doing their job—Alan was stunned for a moment. Then he became very energized by all of a sudden having options when just a moment before there seemed to be none.

Thankfully, after our conversation Alan could see the possibilities that existed beyond quitting. He is currently taking a deep look at what he truly wants for both his work and personal life in order to come up with a creative solution that works for him, his family, and his job. Will he stay at his job? Maybe. The important thing is that he has a choice between a number of solutions—not just two.

CHALLENGE YOUR THINKING

1. Examine your own thoughts about finding a better work+life fit. Do you find yourself drawn to the extreme of all or nothing? Examine why that might be the case. Think about the language you use that describes work and life. Is it extreme? Consider your friends, family, and colleagues: Do they tend to describe work and life in extreme terms that may not reflect reality?

2. Think of role models that creatively found a better way to fit work into their lives in the following categories—even if they wouldn't describe it that way. Remember, they don't have to be extreme examples. Record aspects of their work+life fit that are particularly attractive to you:

   - Family members
   - Friends or colleagues
   - Media/books/magazine articles, etc.

   What lessons can you learn from the way in which they achieved their unique work+life fit?

Asking and Getting to Yes

Misconception: *I'm not going to ask for a different work+life fit because the answer might be "no."*

Reality: *I'm going to present my work+life fit proposal because most likely the answer will be "yes" to at least a six-month trial period.*

Don't let the fear of what your manager's answer *might* be keep you from seeking a new work+life fit. Because even though you think your proposal won't be supported, it most likely will be, assuming you have a well-thought-out proposal and are a good performer. At minimum, your boss will most likely agree to a six-month trial period for some variation of your proposed arrangement.

Will he dance a jig of joy over your request? Perhaps not. Your manager may not be overly enthusiastic about the whole thing, especially if it's his first time approving such an arrangement. But don't let the lack of enthusiasm derail you. Take the approval, no matter how begrudging, and do all that you can over the next six months to prove his hesitation wrong.

What if your manager does say "no"? Before answering this question, it's important to reiterate that chances are he will say "yes"—especially if you have taken your needs and the needs of the business into consideration. Or maybe the answer would switch to "yes" if you renegotiated the arrangement with your manager, making it more agreeable to him? Or, maybe the answer is "no" today because of concerns with your performance, but could be "yes" in a year once you've proven that you are trustworthy and a self-starter. In other words, "no" is not always the last word. It can represent the beginning of a constructive, ongoing conversation.

But what if "no" is the final answer? Then you need to look at "no" as a gift, because when in life are your choices ever clear? "No" does that—you either stay with your current work/life reality unchanged or you leave. Next steps become easier to see.

Here's something to consider. Seventy-five percent of employees say that their supervisors are supportive on a day-to-day basis.[1] Yet, these same employees, in focus groups and workshops, blame their lack of work+life fit on their unsupportive manager. When I hear this dissonance, I press people further. And when I ask if their managers ever said anything or behaved in a way that would indicate they wouldn't be supportive, they usually confess that the managers hadn't. They just *think* that their manager won't be supportive, even though they've never actually presented a work+life fit proposal themselves, nor have they seen their manager turn down a request from someone else. On the other hand, they've never seen their manager approve one either.

The reality is that more people don't have the work+life fit they want or need simply because they don't ask. And in the end, what do you have to lose by asking? Nothing. Especially if you are willing to leave your job anyway. Going into a negotiation willing to walk away if you don't reach an agreement is the strongest position from which to negotiate. *And, you have everything to gain.* Because the odds are that your manager will say "yes" to at least a six-month trial arrangement.

Recently, a workshop participant shared a story that supports this theory. People always tell me that Wall Street will *never* allow people to change the way work fits into their life (even though I've seen it happen many times). "People work crazy hours, for crazy money," they say, "and either you like it or leave." But Sheila works for a large, prestigious Wall Street firm, and she told the story of a friend who worked on a trading floor, which has a male-dominated, high-pressure culture.

Her friend wanted to work four days a week, and even though she had never seen anyone else propose anything like what she wanted, she gathered her courage and presented her proposal to her manager. To her surprise and to the surprise of many, he approved it. Later, another employee asked the boss why he had never approved such an arrangement before. He said simply, "No one ever asked." No one ever asked. And this is on Wall Street, where managers will *never* allow employees to find a better work+life fit. Add one more example to the list of people who made a change because they saw the possibilities and didn't buy into the limitations that were all around them.

How do I know that the chances are your manager will be supportive of at least some variation of your proposal for a six-month trial period? I know from working with managers who may have approved the first request from an employee with trepidation and from employees who found the courage to ask without knowing what the answer would be. Most managers will be supportive unless you are a consistent performance problem, which is an issue we will address in a later chapter.

Meeting "converted" managers is one of my favorite experiences. These managers admit that they often resisted approving their first work+life fit arrangement. But after seeing how both the employees and the business benefit, they are now some of the biggest work+life promoters.

BRUCE'S STORY

Bruce, the manager of a group of insurance analysts, arrived early to participate in a focus group I conducted. It was hard not to immediately notice his enthusiasm. He sat right next to me and extended his hand. He introduced himself and told me how excited he was to tell his story.

Once everyone arrived, I turned to begin the introductions around the table with those seated to my right, when Bruce, who was seated to my left, enthusiastically broke in, "Hi, my name is Bruce. I know you all know me, but I just wanted to tell you how much I didn't buy into this work/life stuff. Clearly, I'm from a different generation when this wasn't even an issue. So when I was forced by my manager to approve the request of one of my associates to work from home two days a week, I was not too happy. No way. But let me tell you, I have changed my mind. I now have three people on my team working various arrangements, and the work still gets done, and more important, I'm sure we would have lost them if I hadn't supported their requests. Sure, we review the arrangements every few months, but for now, it's been great."

Bruce made quite an impression on me that day. Here was a guy who admitted that his skepticism was a mistake and now enthusiastically saw the benefits of supporting his employees' requests for a better work+life fit. Think about it for a minute. What if the first brave employee to present his or her proposal had chosen instead to quietly leave the company? Bruce would never have "seen the light." It only took one brave employee to ask and open Bruce's eyes.

It's always difficult to support something—especially something new—until you try it for the first time. Again, make sure that your work+life fit proposal is well thought out by completing the Three Steps. It will make your manager more confident to at least give the arrangement a shot, and hopefully convert him or her to the benefit of helping other employees achieve a better work+life fit.

ELAINE AND JOHN'S STORY

When organizing focus groups, you try to find managers who are opposed to work/life practices and programs if you can. The goal is to take their views into consideration before making a final recommendation to the client. Thankfully, it's often difficult to find enough of these managers to justify holding a separate group. But when you do, they're often bold in stating their lack of support.

Elaine is a senior manager in her early 50s who wasted no time saying that she thought this work/life stuff was "nonsense." Elaine had been with the company for 20 years, and had sacrificed time with her family over the years "more times than I can even remember. That's just the way it is. Business is business."

As part of the focus group, we talked about how she ran her division and how she dealt with the everyday work/life conflicts of her employees. As the discussion proceeded, Elaine began to realize that she was more supportive of her employees than she thought. For example, she regularly allowed her employees to work from home, or change their schedule to avoid a long commute or to care for a child after school. "As long as they get their job done, I don't care" was her refrain. To her, it wasn't about work/life but about getting the work done.

As is the case with all "accidental work+life advocates" like Elaine, the issue is labeling. Neither they nor their employees label what they are doing as being "pro-work+life." It's just a smart way to do business, which is exactly what we have been saying.

John, a plant manager from a manufacturing company, is another accidental work+life advocate. In John's company, most teams operate on three rotating 8-hour shifts. He agreed to participate in a manager focus group because he was curious but "was never personally presented with a need to use work/life practices."

He listened to the other managers explain why they strictly adhered to the 8-hour rotating shift policy even though it sometimes forced parents to leave their kids in the car at night when they couldn't find child care. They felt that it was the only "fair" way to operate, even though many employees said that they preferred to always work the same shifts because it made coordinating personal responsibilities easier.

Jim sat listening to the logic of his colleagues with a puzzled look on his face. Finally he raised his hand and said, "My team came to me a few months ago and asked if they could be responsible for scheduling their shifts. I said okay, we'll try it for a bit, but if there's a lot of conflict, we're going back to the rotation. They said fine, and there haven't been any problems at all. In fact, now that you mention it, many of them do stay on either the night or day shift. I never thought about why, but maybe it does have to do with their kids." He then noted an interesting business benefit from this arrangement, "Since making the change, our accident rate and our defect rates have gone down. Maybe it's because the team isn't distracted by thinking about stuff at home."

Whether he knew it or not, his business decision was helping his employees resolve their work/life conflicts. Again, the only difference was the way it was labeled. Although still skeptical, I could tell the other managers were intrigued.

Maybe your manager has stated publicly that she would never allow an employee to have "one of those flexible work arrangements that HR is promoting." But, at the same time, like Elaine, she would approve a change in your work schedule if it didn't hurt the business. Again, this is why it is critical that you approach the change in your work+life fit as you would any other business proposal. Remember, implementing a work+life fit arrangement is not an "entitlement"; it's a smart way to do business, which is what these accidental work+life advocates unknowingly discovered.

Of course, there will be those few managers who, no matter how well crafted your proposal, will not support it. But I believe they are the exception and not the rule. However, as part of Step 3 we will prepare you in advance, so in case your manager doesn't support your request, you'll know what your next step will be.

CHALLENGE YOUR THINKING

1. When you think about asking your manager for a new work+life fit, how does it make you feel? Are you empowered to ask? If no, why? If yes, why?

2. Having read the chapter, review the reasons why you shouldn't let your fears keep you from presenting your proposal.

3. Could your manager be an unconscious work+life advocate? How could you present your work+life fit proposal in a way that would avoid the label "work+life" and keep it all about the business?

Believing You Add Value

Misconception: *Why would my manager approve my request? I'm lucky just to have a job. I'll have to leave the company if I can't find the flexibility I need.*

Reality: *I add value to the company; therefore, I will confidently present my work+life fit proposal, remembering that 60% of me is better than 0%.*

When conducting research in a company, you interview senior executives to gain a better understanding of the most critical strategic challenges they face. When asked, "What are your top strategic challenges?" they invariably include "recruiting and retaining the best and brightest employees."

After these interviews, I'd walk down the hall to one of many focus groups we'd conduct in order to learn about the work/life issues the company's employees faced. Typically, I'd walk into the room and find 20 people sitting around in a circle—20 of the very same employees whom the senior executive wants to attract and retain as one of his or her top strategic priorities.

With that kind of senior management commitment, you'd think I'd find a room full of men and women empowered to resolve their work/life conflicts by finding the flexibility they need. On the contrary, I often found a group of stressed-out, overwhelmed employees who felt powerless to do anything. Many were so overwhelmed that they were going to leave the company if they didn't find some relief.

For argument's sake, let's assume 20% were poor performers who wouldn't be missed if they left. That still leaves 16 valuable employees in the room.

Can you see the disconnect? The employees were completely unaware of their importance to the organization. And they also didn't know how to leverage their value in order to find a better work+life fit.

I often wondered how the group would respond if I shared what the executive down the hall had just told me—that attracting and retaining them was a priority. Would that give them insight into the value they offered the organization? Would it give them a new perspective and the confidence to ask for a new way to work? Unfortunately, my job was to listen and to gather data, not to inform. But now I can share this insight with you. *If you are a good performer, you are a valuable asset of your organization both in times of economic growth and contraction.*

I'm not advocating an arrogant, "I'm so valuable give me what I want or I'm gone" attitude. I'm simply urging you to view yourself as a valued equal partner in the negotiation process. You have something important to offer the organization. By trying to find a way to contribute and to have more flexibility, you are acting as an equal partner in that mutually beneficial relationship.

Even in the most challenging economic times, senior executives still want to find a way to keep and even attract as many of the best and brightest as they can.[1] If you are a good performer, you're adding important value. Feel empowered to leverage that value and ask for a work+life fit that works for you *and* the company. Make it part of your supporting business case.

Think of it this way: 60% of you is better than 0%. What does that mean? If you propose a work+life fit whereby you work 60% of your current work schedule, it is better for the company than having you quit—or having 0% of you. The percentage can be anywhere between 99% and 1%, but the point is the same. If you've ever been a manager, you know what it's like to lose a good person. You honestly would do anything to keep them. Consider the story of Gary, a manager, and Suzanne, one of his direct reports.

GARY AND SUZANNE'S STORY

Gary is the executive in charge of strategic planning for a large corporation. He has been with the company for more than 20 years, is married, and has three grown children. He readily admitted at the beginning of our interview that he has had limited personal experience with work/life conflict. When his kids were young and he worked long hours and traveled frequently, his wife was home full-time. And, so far, "knock on wood," his parents who are in their 80s seem to be doing fine. But, he can see that might change in the not-so-distant future. And his wife went back to work a few years ago, which leaves her less flexibility to fly down to Florida if his parents should require care. He admits this situation could bring work/life conflict into his life for the first time.

Our conversation moved from his personal experience to the prevailing business challenges facing the company. He thought for a moment and mentioned three, the second of which was, "finding and keeping the best people possible." Then he added, "For some reason, it seems to be getting harder to do that." As a follow-up, I explained to him the business case for using work/life initiatives for recruitment, retention, and leadership development. He was intrigued, but somewhat skeptical. So I took it a step further. I put forth the example of Suzanne.

Suzanne is a vice president of strategic planning. I'd met with her earlier, and I was impressed by her intelligence and her insight into a broad range of issues. She recently had gotten married and was considering starting a family. When I asked about her plans to address the inevitable work/life challenges that emerge when a high-powered career meets with a new baby, she shrugged her shoulders and let out a sigh (a common response to this question). "You know I honestly can't tell you. I'm such an organized planner by nature, but this issue has me stumped. I love my job, and Gary is a great boss. But, let's face it. It isn't exactly like he's been there and can empathize. Gwen, his wife, takes care of everything. I don't have that luxury. My husband works long hours. Plus, I don't want to have kids and never see them. That's not how I was raised."

I responded by asking her, "Hypothetically, off the top of your head, what would you want to do?" Without hesitation she said, "I would want to cut back on some of my responsibilities, but retain oversight coordinating the annual strategic planning process for the various divisions. If I did that, I know I could work four days a week, with one of those days working from home. But Gary would never go for it."

Remembering this conversation with Suzanne, I presented Gary with the following scenario. "Gary, imagine Suzanne has a baby and comes to you requesting that she work 60% of her former schedule or she might have to leave." He looked a bit puzzled and said, "But I want her to work her current schedule." I paused and patiently reminded him of the choices, "She would like to work 60% of her schedule or she may have to leave. What would you do?" He paused. "But I need her here." But, ultimately, it wasn't about what Gary wanted; it was about what Suzanne needed and whether she got it here or someplace else. Finally, the light bulb went off, and he said, "Well, 60% of her is definitely better than 0% of her. I think I'm beginning to see the business case."

Clearly, Gary values Suzanne. Yet Suzanne thought, "I can't change my schedule—I'll just have to leave." She needs to realize that it's better for Gary to retain 60% of her knowledge of managing the complicated strategic planning process than to start from scratch with someone else who needs to be hired and trained. And who's to say that Suzanne's replacement won't end up also experiencing work/life conflict? Wouldn't it be better for everyone if she recognized her value to Gary and the company and leveraged it in order to find a work+life fit that allowed her to stay?

There are as many ways to add value to a business as there are different types of jobs. We will specifically identify your source of added value in chapter 25. In the meantime, here are some examples to think about:

▶ Trustworthiness
▶ Self-starting, motivated work style
▶ Experience and maturity
▶ In-depth product knowledge
▶ Longstanding customer relationships
▶ Mechanical skills
▶ In-depth knowledge of a work process that makes you more efficient than a new hire
▶ Good customer service skills
▶ Computer skills
▶ Creativity
▶ Diverse life experiences
▶ A network of individuals throughout the company who help you get your job done efficiently
▶ Reliability

What if you can't honestly say that you add value? In fact, what if you can say that you probably don't because you've had past performance problems? We will discuss this in greater detail in chapter 20 as it relates to work style, because there are strategies to overcome the obstacle of poor performance and still find a work+life fit.

Believing that you are uniquely valuable will help give you the confidence you need to take the initiative and confidently proceed with the work+life fit process. Remember that it's good for you and your employer.

CHALLENGE YOUR THINKING

1. List the specific ways that you add value to your company or prospective employer. Be really creative!

2. Put yourself in your manager's shoes. Can you understand how retaining you, even at a reduced schedule, makes business sense for your manager (assuming that you are a good performer)? Try to articulate the reasons.

Making the 5 Business Case

Misconception: *My manager should approve my work+life fit proposal because it's "the right thing to do" for a loyal employee.*

Reality: *My manager should approve my work+life fit proposal because it works for the business as well as for me.*

If you want your work+life fit to fail, do the following. First, have your boss informally approve your request for a new arrangement because it is the "right thing to do." Don't have a formal proposal outlining the details of the arrangement or how you will perform the tasks and responsibilities of your job. Don't set a review date or clarify the business reasons upon which your manager can base his approval. Don't present the details of the arrangement to your work group, and don't have any official signatures.

Your reaction might be "Well, what's so wrong with casually working out an arrangement with my manager?" I agree that every situation is unique. And, yes, there may be certain situations where a casual arrangement may seem more appropriate, or times when just going ahead without permission is more appealing. But here's a rule of thumb. Formally document and negotiate your work+life fit if:

1. You would be working during different hours or in a different location from other employees. Reason: You can get full credit for all of the work you do; and/or

2. You are changing your job tasks, responsibilities, workload, or schedule in order to have the work+life fit that you want. Reason: Everyone is in agreement and on the same page.

It's best to approach changing your work+life fit in the same way you would conduct any other important business transaction—formally negotiating and signing an agreement listing the terms and conditions agreed to by both you and your manager. Why? Because it only benefits you. How? By doing the following:

- Lending credibility to your work+life fit
- Giving you credit for all of the work you do
- Clarifying expectations of all parties affected
- Supporting your manager's decision
- Ensuring your arrangement survives the peaks and valleys of corporate performance
- Allowing your work+life fit to continue despite management changes

Lending Credibility to Your Work+Life Arrangement

First, let's compare two business transactions. One is approved informally, without documentation. The other is formally negotiated and documented. Which one of the two is more likely to be taken seriously and respected by both parties? That's easy: the formal one. It's no different with a work+life fit arrangement.

Here's another way to think about it. When you formally propose your work+life fit arrangement as you would any other business deal, you present yourself as a partner with your employer, rather than in a dependent position. Remember, companies are in business to make money. Yes you, as the employee, are a critical part of that effort. In other words, the relationship between you and your employer is mutually beneficial. It is based on choice; the company chooses to employ you for a mutually agreed upon salary and benefits package, and you agree to perform a certain function in that capacity. If changes are made to this arrangement, they should be formally negotiated and documented. How would you feel if your employer wanted to informally increase your salary without any documentation, because it was "the right thing to do"? While you wouldn't refuse the offer, it would be a lot more credible and more likely to happen if it were formally on record. In fact, if it wasn't, you would most likely view your employer's approach as unprofessional, and you'd probably lose a certain degree of respect for your company and even for your work.

When you see your relationship with your employer as being mutually interdependent rather than dependent, it's easier to believe you are an equal partner in the negotiation for a new work+life fit. Draft your formal work+life fit proposal through a business lens, as you would any other business proposal. Keep asking yourself, "How does this make personal sense for me *and* business sense for my employer?" Taking this approach is the only way that your work+life fit will succeed.

Giving You Credit for All of the Work You Do

In addition to adding credibility to your request, an arrangement that is formally negotiated and documented ensures that you get credit for all of the work that you do.

Let's say that you have an informal agreement with your boss that you will leave every day by 5 P.M. (even though most people leave at 7 P.M.), and then you will work at home most nights from 8 P.M. to 10:00 P.M.

After a while, without formal negotiation or documentation to support it, all that your boss and coworkers see is that you are leaving at 5 P.M. Naturally they will begin to assume you are working less, when in fact you are working just as much only at a different time and at home. Remember that managers are too busy to make the minutiae of your workday their primary focus. In other words, if it's not formally documented, it never happened.

Now let's look at what happens with a more drastic change in flexibility. You've informally arranged with your boss that you will work four days a week and take a one-fifth cut in pay. For about three weeks you are able to take every Monday off, but then it becomes more difficult. People keep scheduling important meetings on that day and you find that you often have to come in. And you are getting paid less. I call these people the "grateful dead." Grateful just to have some flexibility, but dead because they are overworked for what they are being paid.

In this scenario, if you had a documented arrangement, the terms of your work+life fit would be clear to everyone—you work four days a week, with every Monday off, at four-fifths pay. Critical meetings would be scheduled, if at all possible, on your days in the office because your boss would have formally agreed and your coworkers would have been informed. Most important, on those days that you did come in, the extra effort would be viewed favorably as opposed to being "part of your job." You would get credit for the extra work you are doing.

Clarifying Expectations of All Parties Affected

In addition to giving you credit for your work, a formally negotiated and documented work+life fit clarifies, up front, the expectations of all of the parties affected by your new arrangement. These expectations are between you and your manager, and you and your work group. You need to show sensitivity about how your new arrangement could affect them and their respective workloads. We'll talk more about this as we move through the process; however, suffice it to say that the quickest way to undermine your new flexibility is to have a mismatch of expectations. It can lead to resentment and, ultimately, a lack of support. Think of your formal work+life fit agreement as a roadmap that will help everyone know where you are going and have an idea of where they fit in. And everyone can refer to it for clarification along the way.

Supporting Your Manager's Decision

What happens when your boss's supervisor questions him or her about the arrangement? How much confidence will there be when he says he approved it because "Joanne's a nice person"? Think about how much stronger his case would be if your manager could hand his boss a hard copy of the formal agreement. That alone lends an air of validity to your work+life fit. With the terms and conditions of the arrangement laid out in black and white, it will be easier for senior management to support your manager's decision. And, in turn, your manager will feel more confident.

Ensuring Your Arrangement Survives the Peaks and Valleys of Corporate Performance

A formally documented arrangement can also help your work+life fit survive the inevitable peaks and valleys of corporate performance. What happens when the company is having a difficult period and your boss needs to make some changes? If you have an informal agreement to work from home every Tuesday, or worse yet often just work from home on Tuesdays without saying anything, there is a chance your arrangement will be considered frivolous and something that needs to end. But, if your manager can refer to your formal agreement, he can review the terms and conditions of the approval. He can confirm how your job is getting done while you're working from home. Furthermore, he will be reminded of the formal review date, which will give him further reassurance. At the time of the review, your manager can consider whether or not to continue supporting your arrangement in light of the company's financial performance and your personal performance.

Allowing Your Work+Life Fit to Continue Despite Management Changes

Finally, a formal proposal provides you with security should there be a change of management. What happens if your manager is promoted to a new position, leaving you with a new boss who doesn't know your track record? Needless to say, your informal, verbal accommodation with your former manager won't continue for very long. However, a formally negotiated agreement would introduce your new manager to the underlying business rationale for the original approval. Moreover, the agreement's formal review date would give you and the new manager a chance to sit down and renegotiate once you've had time to get used to working together.

Why Wouldn't You Want to Formally Negotiate and Document Your Work+Life Fit?

If there are so many reasons to formally negotiate and document your work+life fit, why don't more people do it? First, until this book, I don't think many people had any idea where to begin creating, not to mention formalizing, a work+life fit agreement. Second, both companies and employees still get trapped in the paternalistic mind-set in which the employee is to be cared for by the employer. But there is another, more powerful reason both employees and managers avoid the steps of formalizing an arrangement: fear.

For managers, the fear falls into two categories (which we discuss at greater length in chapter 27). They're afraid that if they say yes to your arrangement, they will never be able to change their minds later. Therefore, the less formal and less defined, the easier it seems to just stop it at any time without formal discussion. And every manager has the "floodgate" fear, which says, "If I approve a new work+life fit for one employee, everyone is going to want it." This is why managers want to make arrangements informal and "just between you and me." They don't want the work group informed of details. But a formal arrangement gives the manager a six-month review date to change his mind. And, once the work group is informed, he will most likely be pleasantly surprised that the floodgates will not open because most people either can't or don't want to change their current work+life fit. *But* they do like to know that flexibility is there if they need it.[1]

We've talked about managers' fears, but what about your fears? Yes, asking for a better work+life fit can be scary, especially if you have never seen anyone else do it. But on some level, it must seem less scary to ask informally than formally. As if by not formalizing it, you aren't *really* asking. Maybe your manager won't even really notice if it isn't documented anywhere, almost like trying to fly your arrangement in under the radar screen. Sorry, it doesn't work. They do notice but usually for all of the wrong reasons that hurt you, like when you aren't sitting at your desk at three o'clock even though you are working at home. If you want a better work+life fit, you have to formally ask for and document the arrangement. Plain and simple.

CHALLENGE YOUR THINKING

1. How do you feel about formally proposing, negotiating, and documenting your work+life fit?

2. Review the reasons put forth in the chapter in the context of a formal approach to your own work+life fit goals.

Knowing That 6 Your Reason
Is a Good Reason

Misconception: *Working mothers have the most valid reason for seeking a better work+life fit.*

Reality: *I can seek a better work+life fit for any reason, as long as my proposal not only meets my own needs, but the needs of the business.*

I recently conducted a workshop comprised solely of young married and unmarried professional women, none of whom had children. When asked what brought them to the workshop, they all lodged a similar complaint, "My job is stressful and requires a lot of hours. I want to have a life outside of my job, but my company only gives working mothers a break. For them it is okay to have a life. Everyone else is stuck."

Clearly they were frustrated by what they perceived as an inconsistency in their employers' support of their needs just because they don't have kids. This belief underlies the phenomenon of the backlash against family-friendly corporate policies. Employees without children can feel that they are excluded from corporate work/life initiatives. But the problem lies in their perspective, not in reality.

What is the reality? First, it would be illegal for companies to offer a work/life policy, like flexible work arrangements, to one specific group and not to another. Second, I have helped many companies in many industries develop work/life strategies and never, not once, has either the underlying intention or the language of the strategy focused solely on mothers. If your company has a pamphlet describing its work/life supports, look at the language. Does it say that it's only for working mothers? Probably not.

"Then why are working mothers the only ones in my company who seem to find more flexibility in the way work fits into their lives?" you ask. "I don't have kids but I have aging parents, and I want to pursue my love of kayaking. That's just as important." Yes, it is important, but here's the difference between you and a working mother: It can be scary to ask for flexibility (we will address these fears in Step 2), but because a working mother has a helpless baby at home who *has* to be taken care of right now, she must put her fears aside. She needs to ask regardless of how scared she might be. Whereas, if you don't have children and are afraid to ask, you can put it off because it's easier to not visit your aging parent or skip a kayaking trip than it is to not care for your baby.

Think of it this way. Because they had no choice, working mothers paved the way for others. Their efforts have made corporate cultures more comfortable with the concept of flexibility. But, the ball is now in the court of all of the non-mothers who want to make a change. The challenge for you is to figure out the kind of work+life fit you want and then ask. You have little to lose by asking, and much to gain. Because, as the mothers discovered, chances are your manager will approve some variation of your proposed arrangement for at least a six-month trial period.

I must confess that when I hear people say, "Well, they only let working mothers do it," I wonder if it's an excuse to not take the risk and do the work to make a change in their lives. I've met too many people over the years who aren't mothers and who have found a better work+life fit for many different reasons. I know it can happen.

As you will see in Step 3, when you draft your work+life fit proposal, the reason for your request is not included. Why? Managers often say that they'd rather not know. Because if they do, then they feel forced to rank one employee's reason as more or less valid than someone else's. They would rather not be put in that position, because every employee must think that their reason is important or they wouldn't ask. And more important, a manager who doesn't know will decide whether or not to approve a proposal based solely on its business viability, which is the way it should be.

According to the research, non-mothers will increasingly propose creative ways to fit work into their lives, and companies will have to support their requests. Three specific demographic shifts are behind the trend. First, with their belief that "life is life and work is work, but life is not work," more and more Generation X employees (25 to 37 years old) will act on these values and seek more flexibility, especially as they face child- and elder-care challenges. This is particularly true for Gen X fathers who want to be involved in their children's lives and are willing to sacrifice professionally to achieve that goal.

Second, as the Baby Boomers continue to age, more men and women will face the challenge of finding the time and energy to care for an aging parent.

And, third, as more Boomers retire, many will want a "working" retirement whereby they have the challenge and financial benefit of work in their lives, but not full-time.

Add to this the growing shortfalls in the U.S. labor force projected as a result of Baby Boomer retirements. By 2011, it's predicted that the shortfall could total 5 million employees, and by 2031, grow to 36 million.[1] To retain and attract the best and the brightest in that type of environment, companies will be forced to partner will all types of employees—mothers, fathers, those caring for aging parents, working retirees, etc.—to keep them engaged and participating in the workforce. How? By helping them find the work+life fit that meets their needs and the needs of the business. And it will mean a significant increase in the number of people seeking unique work+life combinations.

Generation "X" Mothers and Fathers

Since the Generation X employees entered the workforce, researchers have attempted to understand the unique impact of their experiences, values, and expectations because they're quite different from those of the Baby Boom generation that preceded them.

Perhaps most profound: There are fewer Gen X employees than there were Baby Boomers at the same age. In 1997, employees between the ages of 18 and 32 made up 29% of the workforce, whereas 20 years earlier, employees in this age category made up 44% of the workforce.[2] This means there are fewer employees in the Gen X age group and, therefore, greater competition amongst companies to employ them, especially as Baby Boomers begin retiring. As a scarce resource, Generation X employees have even more leverage to change the workplace with their beliefs and expectations, especially in the area of work+life fit.

What are their work/life values? Generation X employees are more likely than their Baby Boomer colleagues were to experience the work/life conflicts associated with child-rearing as part of a dual-career couple. In fact, 75% of all employees between 18 and 32 who are married and have children also have a working spouse.[3] In contrast, 20 years ago, 61% of Baby Boomers who were married with children had a working spouse.

A recent study of Gen X employees conducted by Catalyst, a research and advisory organization, found that they place a greater value on personal life than on work. When asked what is "extremely important," only 21% said "making a great deal of money," whereas 84% said "having a loving family." However, when asked about how work is fitting into their lives, 72% said that job interference in their personal lives was "moderate or severe."[4]

Typically, when I work with Gen X employees facing work/life challenges, they are more likely than their Boomer counterparts to respond, "Well, I'll just quit if I can't find a workable solution to my work/life conflict." That's exactly what Brian, 35 years old and the father of three, did when he quit his job that required extensive travel. He went to work for Texas Instruments, which he felt gave him more of the flexibility he wants. "I left the other company because of the extensive travel they wanted me to do. I didn't want to be away from my daughters for six to eight weeks at a time. I don't need to make that kind of sacrifice just for a career."[5]

In fact, it was two Baby Boomer clients from Fortune 500 companies who first brought the impact of this Gen X perspective to my attention. I happened to have a similar conversation with these two clients at about the same time. Both had just begun their college-recruiting season, and they were amazed that the first question asked by many of the students wasn't "How much will I be making?" or "How long will it take me to advance?" Their first question was about their ability to work for the company and still have a personal life. In prior years, my clients noted, no one would have even asked these questions at all, much less asked them first.

Of course, my clients are Baby Boomers, both of whom often logged long hours at the office. They attributed this trend to a lack of work ethic. I, however, saw it as an important sign that a major shift in priorities was under way.

There has been much speculation as to why the values and expectations of Gen X employees toward work/life issues are so different. Some attribute the trend to Gen Xers seeing their Boomer parents get laid off in the late eighties and early nineties by companies to which they had devoted their lives, often at the expense of personal relationships. Others contend it's selfishness. Whatever the underlying factors are, employers will have to respond to these new expectations if they want to employ the best and brightest of this next generation.

I actually find it a bit disingenuous when managers express surprise and disappointment that younger employees aren't willing to give it all to the company. Why should they when there is so little job security—the same lack of security that these same companies created in order to compete in the global market? You can't have it both ways.

But I believe the biggest change is going to come from Gen X fathers who are now between the ages of 25 and 37 years old and are just beginning to have their children. These guys want time with their kids and they are willing to make the sacrifices, even financial ones, to make that happen. Plus, because a majority have working wives, making those sacrifices is easier.

As I mentioned in chapter 2, 80% of the men 20 to 39 years old surveyed by the Radcliffe Public Policy poll would choose a work schedule that enables them to spend time with family over challenging work or high salary. While 70% said they actually would be willing to give up some pay to spend more time with families.[6] That's huge. You may be saying, "They're thinking it, but they aren't doing anything about it." Perhaps not yet, but the intention and desire on the part of an overwhelming percentage of today's young fathers is definitely there. Hopefully, with the help of tools like the Three Steps, they will find a way to fulfill their goals and, in the process, change things profoundly for everyone. The good news is that some young fathers have already sought more flexibility and companies have responded. For example:

- ▶ Of the 1,900 employees who currently have flexible work arrangements (e.g., job-sharing, compressed workweek, and flexible hours) at Ernst and Young, 13% are men, some of whom are partners;
- ▶ Says Jeff Chambers, director of HR for SAS Institute, "One man who works for me, whose wife also works for SAS, works from 11:00 A.M. to 8:00 P.M. while his wife works from 7:00 A.M. to 2:30 P.M. That way, he gets their three boys to school in the morning and she covers them at the other end."[7]

But Gen X dads do have some hurdles to overcome. First, many of these fathers have male Baby Boomer supervisors who hold different beliefs about how time and energy should be allocated between work and personal responsibilities. Even today, Baby Boomers are more likely to feel that the "male sole-breadwinner and stay-at-home mom" model is the best. When asked "if it is much better for everyone if the man earns the money and the woman stays home with the children," only 36% of Gen X employees agreed, versus 41% of Baby Boomers.[8]

As James Levine, the director of the Fatherhood Project at Families and Work Institute, points out in his book, *Working Fathers*, there are many reasons fathers don't advocate more confidently for a better work+life fit. These reasons include, among other things, a lack of role modeling by senior managers (most of whom are male, with a stay-at-home wife) and a fear of not being seen as a "serious player."[9] Sylvia Ann Hewlett, the author of *Creating a Life*, recounted during a recent panel discussion that when she asked a group of men at a company why more of them didn't take advantage of paternity leave, one man responded, "When you ask, they look at you like you have lace on your jockey shorts."

Fathers in the workplace feel uncomfortable seeking a new work+life fit without fear of repercussions. They feel this way even though they are equally as likely as mothers are to say they want to work differently:

- ▶ Men are equally as likely as women to say they would like to work 11 hours less a week;[10] and
- ▶ Fathers are equally as likely to say they don't spend enough time with their children, and would like to spend more.[11]

As David Stillman, the coauthor of *When Generations Collide: Who They Are; Why They Clash; How to Solve the Generational Puzzle at Work* and father of two, points out, "The Boomer men were in a rat race to the top. But if Gen Xers leave work early to go to a school event, we're proud of that. We believe parenting is fifty-fifty, not just a woman's job. We're not going to pay the same price for success that we saw the preceding generations pay. The Boomers see us as wimps. So we pay a price for asking for the right to work at home one day a week or to flex our hours. A lot of us want it and are starting to demand it, but it's still a hard sell, which is what a lot of women have found already."[12]

With a value system that places more emphasis on family, an overwhelming desire to be involved, and a willingness to make sacrifices, I believe that Gen X fathers will gather their courage, overcome these hurdles, and seek a better way to fit work into their lives. The following story perfectly illustrates the conflict between a Gen X dad's values and his desire to succeed professionally.

STEVE'S STORY

In business school I had a friend named Steve who was smart and outgoing. He also had a great deal of international business experience. He was very happily married to a woman who was employed full-time in a career she loved. While we were in school, they had their first child. You could tell Steve was in love with this child. He often carried her around school slung in front of him in her baby carrier, and Steve even brought her on stage with him when he graduated with honors with a degree in finance.

I first became aware that Steve was struggling with how he was going to fit work into his life when I bumped into him in a crowded Manhattan supermarket. He was wheeling his daughter in her stroller and when he saw me shouted, "Cali, stay right there. I want you to meet my wife." With that he deftly maneuvered the stroller through the crowd and delivered his wife to me saying, "Jill, this is the woman I was telling you about. She's the one who is going to change things so that I can work and still find time to be with you and the baby." I was shocked. While I may have mentioned to him that I hoped to pursue a career in work/life consulting following graduation, I had no idea how much it meant to him that someone was going to try to address these issues.

On one hand, I was flattered by his confidence in me, but I was also sad. I knew that I wasn't going to be able to make a meaningful difference that would affect him in the near future, especially in his chosen field of investment banking. Investment banking is one of the most notoriously inhospitable industries with regard to having any kind of a personal life at all. Yet, it was his choice, and I prayed it would all work out for him and his beautiful family.

Fast-forward two years. I was now a senior research associate at Families and Work Institute, and a colleague of mine was searching for investment banking employees to interview for one of her projects. I immediately thought of Steve. I finally tracked him down and when I asked how he'd been, he said sadly, "Do you really want to know?" He proceeded to tell me that in his first year at the investment-banking firm he received outstanding ratings, but it put a real strain on his personal life. In order to succeed at the firm, he basically had to work day and night, during the week and on the weekends. At the same time, he and his wife had had another baby, and although his wife had cut back her hours, she was still working. He sounded very discouraged. He liked his work, but his family was too precious to him.

Although I knew this would be difficult in the workaholic culture of his industry, I suggested that he request reducing his hours or maybe even share his job with someone who also wanted more time with his family. There was total silence. Finally he said, "I can't do that. I think my only option is to leave." Again, I understood how hard it would be for him to propose such a work+life fit arrangement in his company, especially as a man.

Objectively, does this sound like good business? Clearly, this is an extreme example, but in my opinion it demonstrates all of the elements that make addressing the work/life needs of all employees so critical for companies. Obviously, his company valued Steve, but he was getting ready to leave because he needed more time with his family.

Alternatively, the company and Steve could have been creative. Perhaps there was another associate who would have liked to split Steve's workload as well as his compensation. In investment banking, such an arrangement would have given both people a 50-hour work-week as well as an annual income in excess of $100,000. In turn, the company could take the savings from combining two jobs and hire another person. Most important, a senior male would need to publicly support Steve and say that he was making a valid choice, for a professional, highly motivated man like Steve to feel comfortable seeking out such an arrangement in that culture.

Baby Boomers Caring for Aging Parents

While Gen X fathers are struggling with their need for a better work+life fit, Baby Boomers are not immune. This demographic is facing two trends that, I believe, will force them to creatively seek a new way to fit work into the rest of their lives. The first trend is the exploding growth of elder-care responsibilities.

The number of people with responsibility for an aging parent or relative will increase considerably over the next few years, and nearly all of these people will be Baby Boomers. How big is the potential impact? In 2002, 35% of all employees had significant elder-care responsibilities. That is a lot of employees, or 45 million to be exact.[13]

And, as we have already discussed, elder care is a gender-blind, "equal opportunity" responsibility affecting men as often as women. According to a study of 1,400 employed caregivers sponsored by MetLife and conducted by the National Alliance for Caregiving and the Center for Productive Aging at Towson University in 2003, men are as likely as women to report that they are the primary caregiver of an older or dependent adult. And, a majority of both men and women report having to modify their schedules and miss some work as a result of their caregiving responsibilities. The elder-care benefit that they most valued was flexibility in scheduling their work.[14]

While companies are aware of the trend, only a few have addressed it strategically. Therefore, if you are one of the 42% of employees who expect to face elder-care responsibilities in the next five years, you will not have much direct corporate support, not to mention the lack of community support.

If you think the availability of child-care programs is limited, elder-care programs are, by comparison, practically nonexistent. And, they are very expensive. This means that you can expect to be even more involved in the day-to-day responsibilities of caring for your mother or father with less outside support than you have for your child. And many of you will have to care for both an elder and a child simultaneously. It's pretty clear that the elder-care trend is going to force more Baby Boomer–age people to seek more flexibility. It's the only way that they'll find the time and energy to devote to these personal responsibilities.

Baby Boomer "Working" Retirees

And, finally, Boomers will face another catalyst for seeking a better work+life fit: retirement. We're all living longer, and as many maturing Baby Boomers face retirement they are finding that they aren't quite ready to give up working completely.

For many, this will be for financial reasons. According to a study conducted by the Senior Job Bank, a nonprofit senior job referral agency, by age 50, 75% of the U.S. population has less than $5,000 in the bank for retirement. And, at 65, only 2% of all people are self-sustaining.[15] For others, the choice to work will be based on the desire for camaraderie, structure, and the mental stimulation that comes from working. To do this, many preretirees are developing a new model of a "working" retirement. This model would allow them to work, but with more time and flexibility for other aspects of life outside of work, such as travel, grandchildren, and other hobbies.

Recently, Robert Samuelson dedicated his op-ed column in *The Washington Post* specifically to the need to transform work in light of a rapidly maturing workforce.[16] He wrote, "By 2010, there will be 79 million Americans 45 to 64 according to the Bureau of Labor Statistics (a 30% increase from 61 million in 2000). . . . Roughly one in three working-age Americans will soon be 'mature.'" He goes on to cite a recent study released by The Conference Board, which concludes that companies, "have a dearth of strategies to keep mature workers. The Conference Board did a survey of workers 50 and over. Nearly half (47%) said that 'more flexible hours' might delay their retirement. A similar number (43%) said they would like to work part-time, about two-thirds (68%) with their current company."

Samuelson echoes my belief that mature workers need to craft a creative way to fit work into their lives that departs from the historical definition of retirement, "More older Americans need to move gradually from work to full-time retirement. They need to mix jobs and leisure in ways that seem natural. We need more part-time jobs, we need more jobs with flexible working hours, and we need more jobs that engage people's interests even though promotion opportunities have faded." I would go a step further and say that mature employees need to *ask* for more part-time jobs and propose more flexible hours instead of waiting for someone to give those options to them. However, Samuelson does point out an important success roadblock that many mature workers encounter. If mature workers are going to succeed in this new type of hybrid retirement, they will need to redefine success as it relates to compensation, prestige, and advancement. They will be paid less. They may not manage people. They may not get the best assignments. They may lose seniority. But the benefits of finding a creative work+life fit in retirement can far outweigh what older workers give away in order to have it.

LESTER'S STORY

Lester is an excellent example of someone who stepped back and analyzed his skills to create a working retirement that kept him mentally engaged with the career that he loved while earning some extra income. In advertising for many years with a specialty in tourism, Les proposed to teach a class on tourism at a university that offered a hospitality major and was located near where he and his wife spent the winter. During the rest of the year, he used his skills to help a local university (pro bono) and continued to take on project work as a consultant to former clients.

THE BELLE COMPANY STORY

An example of a creatively structured work environment for working retirees is the Belle Company, a manufacturing company that primarily hires seniors over 65 years old to organize and package their cosmetic products for shipment. Because they have Medicare and don't require a pension, these seniors, some well into their 80s and even 90s, are an economical source of labor for the company. And the seniors say getting up and having to go to work a few days a week gives them the structure, a sense of purpose, camaraderie, and extra income that had been missing when they initially retired. Most of the seniors work a part-time schedule, and the foreman said they are the most respectful, conscientious workers at the plant. Sounds like a win-win for that company!

Other examples of companies supporting this new working retirement are:

▶ Monsanto, which launched its Retiree Resource Corps in 1991 with 60 retirees and now has 800 people in 24 locations;

▶ Deloitte and Touche, which offers a "phased retirement" plan in which employees gradually reduce their hours over time; and

▶ IBM, where there is no mandatory retirement age and some skilled retirees are encouraged *not* to retire.[17]

A better work+life fit is not just for working mothers. It's for all people—including fathers, retirees, and singles with no children—who, for any reason, want to find better ways to fit work into their lives.

CHALLENGE YOUR THINKING

1. Do you believe mothers are the only people who should be able to seek a better work+life fit? If yes, why? If not, who else should and for what reasons?

2. Do you believe your company's work/life initiatives overtly favor mothers? Review the company's work/life literature for confirmation that the supports are open to all employees.

3. Do you fall into any of these demographic groups—Generation X, those caring for an aging parent, or working retirees? Can you see how your values and responsibilities could cause you to want to find a creative way to fit work into your life? How might you want to do that?

Being Flexible 7

Misconception: *Now that I have my new work+life fit, I don't ever have to change it.*

Reality: *My work life and personal life will change over time, and therefore my work+life fit vision will evolve as well.*

Finding a better way to fit work into your life is a process that you will probably repeat a number of times in your life. In other words, you won't envision, negotiate, and implement a new work+life fit and never think about it again, although it's very human to want to address something and to check it off of your lifetime "to do" list: "changed how work fits into my life—check"!

As your personal life and your job grow and change, your vision will change and your work+life fit will have to adjust accordingly. The arrangement that works today may not be appropriate for you or your employer even a year from now. You will have to re-create your work+life fit to reflect and accommodate these changes.

Chances are that over the course of a lifetime you will reevaluate how you want work to fit into your life over and over again as your unique mix of work and personal realities evolves. This should take some of the pressure off to "get it exactly right" your first time around.

STEPHANIE'S STORY

Stephanie, a manager in the buying department of a retail company, worked four days a week, taking every Friday off to be with her daughters. Although she wasn't officially working, she was available by cell phone on Fridays if needed. And there have been many times she's ducked out of a play date to take a call.

She had this arrangement for about 18 months and loved it. But she also made it clear to her boss that she still wanted to be considered for advancement opportunities. A couple of months ago, an opportunity emerged. She was offered a promotion overseeing a department that was in trouble. Because this was a turnaround situation, she knew that she would need to be in the office every day.

She agreed to take the job and to come to the office five days a week with the understanding that once things turned around sufficiently she would like to negotiate a work+life fit similar to the one she had had. In the meantime, she proposed that her formal schedule would be working in the office from 8:00 A.M. to 5:00 P.M. and being available by cell phone until 6:30 P.M. Her new boss agreed and Stephanie made the necessary adjustments.

LAUREN'S STORY

Five years ago, when I first met Lauren, she was at the end of her rope. Since becoming a mother ten years earlier, Lauren had worked more than 50 hours a week at a job she loved and always felt like everything was fine with her work+life fit. That is until the health of her mother, who lived with them, started failing. And, then on top of that, her third-grade daughter was starting to have learning difficulties and needed extra attention. "For the first time I feel like much more of me is needed at home than at work. I'm going to quit." However, when she went to her boss to quit, he said, "I won't let you. Tell me what you want and we will make it work—whatever it is. Just don't quit."

Lauren gave it some thought and went back to him proposing to work two days a week. He agreed. Two years later, she was finding she no longer needed to devote that extra time and energy to her personal life since, sadly, her mother had passed away and, on a brighter note, her daughter was back on track at school. But when she thought about work, she realized she still didn't want to work full-time. She was enjoying the extra time to volunteer at her church and at the kids' school. But there were projects at work in which she wanted to be involved. Considering all of these work and personal realities, Lauren decided to propose working three days a week. Her boss approved her proposal.

Fast-forward two years later to today, and Lauren has decided that the time is right for her to once again go back to a full-time schedule. But when I talked to her about her new work+life fit, she smiled and said, "But I told my boss that one of those days I'm going to work from home." All he said in response was, "I don't care if you are working on the moon as long as you are working for me."

. . .

As Stephanie's and Lauren's stories illustrate, working through the Three Steps is not an endgame, but a way to allocate your time and energy between your work and personal responsibilities as they are today. Tomorrow's circumstances could require an entirely different allocation. You could revisit the process five years from now and many of the work and personal realities you address will be very different. Accordingly, your new work+life fit arrangement will reflect those changes.

Also, you may start with one vision and begin the process of making it a reality only to find that your original vision changes along the way and you need to shift your efforts. Be flexible.

CHALLENGE YOUR THINKING

1. As you begin the process of envisioning, negotiating, and implementing a new work+life fit, do you find yourself wanting to do it once and then not having to deal with changing it again for a while? And if so, why do you think that is? Is that realistic? Why would that attitude *not* be realistic?

Being Patient and Persistent

Misconception: *I need to find a better work+life fit, and I need to find it now.*

Reality: *I will be patient and take my time crafting a work+life fit proposal that not only meets my needs but also the needs of the business, and I'll try to enjoy the journey—however long it takes, I'll persevere.*

When you experience conflict of any kind, it's natural to want it resolved as soon as possible. Work/life conflict is no different. The problem is that unless you work through all Three Steps—shifting your attitude, avoiding the roadblocks, and taking as long as you need to create a work+life fit that is right for you and the business—chances are you will end up right back where you are now. You will have the same mismatch between the life that you want and the reality that you have.

People I work with tend to fall into two categories. The first category includes those who have no idea how they want work to fit into their life; they only know that they don't want what they currently have. Beyond that, they don't have a clue. If this sounds like you, be assured that you're like most people. But it means that you have some work to do clarifying your vision of a new work+life fit. And doing it will require some patience, but it's worth it. This is particularly difficult if you are a go-go, results-oriented businessperson. Also, once you've created your work+life vision, it may take time to make your work and personal realities compatible with that vision before it can become a reality. You'll need to persevere.

MY STORY

More than twelve years ago, I decided that I wasn't happy with my work+life fit, but beyond that, I had no idea what I wanted. It took almost a year to create a new work+life vision for myself, and I decided to transition from banking into work/life strategy consulting. But going from that vision to reality didn't happen overnight.

It took two years of full-time business school to get the education and credentials I needed. Three months of a low-paying internship before a full-time position became available for me in the field. In total, more than two years went by before Families and Work Institute hired me as a senior research associate and my original vision came to fruition.

A few years later, my vision changed again. I wanted to write this book to give individuals the tools to find a better way to fit work into their lives, and I wanted to spend time with my new baby. So I left work/life strategy consulting to work for myself from home. It took 18 months from the time I started writing the book proposal until an agent agreed to represent me. While I waited, I started my personal work+life coaching and workshop facilitation company, Work+Life Visions, Inc.

Then, it took almost another year for a publisher to buy the book. During that time I continued to write, to coach, to conduct workshops, and to have another baby.

After I found a publisher, it took two and a half more years until the final version went on sale. That is a total of five years from vision to reality. But I was patient and I persevered, and I can tell you that it has been worth it.

. . .

Now there are the rare few that fall into the second category. They begin the process knowing exactly what they want their new work+life fit to look like. And their work and personal realities are already compatible with that vision, allowing it to be implemented immediately without any alteration.

CECELIA'S STORY

Cecelia started our first meeting by announcing that she wanted to work from 8:00 A.M. to 3:00 P.M. in the office three days a week and work from home one day a week. She had the right can-do attitude and knew that this schedule would work with all of her relevant work and personal realities. Therefore, we reviewed the potential roadblocks in Step 2 and moved right into the implementation portion of Step 3. It does happen, but she is unusual.

. . .

Completing the Three Steps might be the first time you ever consciously considered how you want work to fit into your life. Look at it as an opportunity to learn new things about yourself, your job, your manager, your spouse, your work group, etc. Furthermore, remember that you always get a second shot. Give the Three Steps a try because it can't hurt and it very likely will help. And, if at first you don't succeed, you get as many do-overs as you need. Relax and enjoy the journey, and keep going.

CHALLENGE YOUR THINKING

1. Are you willing to take as long as necessary to find the work+life fit that is right for you, or can you see yourself rushing through steps in order to quickly resolve your conflict?

2. Review the reasons put forth in the chapter for taking the time that you need to find the right fit, rather than rushing to a solution and having it not work.

Step 2

The Work+Life Fit Roadblocks

HOPEFULLY, having completed Step 1, you've replaced some of your misconceptions about work and life with a new set of realities. It's important to pause now and look at some roadblocks that can derail your journey through the work+life fit roadmap that begins in Step 3. Roadblocks often emerge, even if you have the most thoughtfully crafted and implemented proposal. And they can appear at any time—in the beginning while you are first entertaining the idea of a new work+life fit, in the middle as you create the arrangement that you want to propose, and even after your manager has approved your proposal and you think that you are home free.

Learning how to recognize and bypass these roadblocks before you start the roadmap is critical because they can catch you off guard. And while they may seem insurmountable at first, they can in fact be easy to overcome with the right strategy. What are the most common roadblocks?

▶ **The success roadblock:** When your new work+life fit is incompatible with your definitions of success, in particular those related to money, advancement, prestige, and quality of caregiving;

▶ **The fear roadblock:** When fear—whether fact-based or speculation—keeps you from achieving your goal;

▶ **The resistance roadblock:** When you experience resistance to changing your work+life fit from within yourself, or from your partner, coworkers, or manager; and

▶ **The in-the-box-thinking roadblock:** When you have trouble envisioning a new work+life fit because you can't think outside of the standard "9-to-5, 5 days a week in the office" definition of work, or beyond the traditional flexible work arrangements of flextime, job-sharing, telecommuting, part-time, and compressed workweeks.

In Step 2, you'll learn what causes each of these roadblocks and how to recognize the red flags that warn you're about to hit one. And you'll learn how to bypass each roadblock and continue toward your goal.

It's also important to understand that when you encounter a roadblock, you do so on two levels: personal and cultural. Because you are the only one who controls your response to life's challenges, the focus here is on avoiding and bypassing roadblocks on the personal level. However, roadblocks are often grounded in broader cultural beliefs and behaviors. If you wait for these larger cultural beliefs and behaviors to change before you move forward with your new work+life fit, you may wait a very long time.

For example, the cultural beliefs associated with the success roadblock are pretty clear: Professionally, for both men and women, you are successful if you make a lot of money, have a prestigious job, and are advancing. Personally, if you are a woman, you're a successful caregiver if you are available at all times for the person for whom you care, be it a child or an elder. If you are a man, you are a successful caregiver if you devote all of your time and energy to the work by which you provide for your family.

So if you encounter a success roadblock, you might redefine success for yourself on a personal level by placing more value on the nonwork parts of your life. But that won't mean the prevailing cultural beliefs and behaviors related to success have changed. As a result, you'll be implementing a new work+life fit on a personal level that may be incompatible with what our culture says is successful. Again, you can't wait until the culture catches up before you find a better work+life fit.

Is it easy to pursue an arrangement that may be incompatible with a prevailing cultural belief? No, but if you've resolved the incompatibility personally, do you want an outdated belief to keep you from happiness today? Think about it.

Consider this. What is culture? It's a set of beliefs that we all buy into. And these beliefs guide our behavior and our values. But as society evolves, cultural beliefs must evolve as well. Unfortunately, there is often a lag between changes in the beliefs of individuals in a society and the beliefs of the broader culture.

I believe this is the case with work/life issues. One by one, as people start challenging the beliefs related to work+life choices, new, more productive beliefs will supplant the old and create a new culture. The trick, on a personal level, is not to be deterred by these larger, often outdated cultural norms. Be part of the effort to change things, not a victim of things as they are.

The Success 9 Roadblock

Definitions of success develop over time, forming the lens through which you interpret achievement in all areas of your life. As long as your vision of success is aligned with your current work+life arrangement, there's no problem.

Problems arise, however, when you change your work+life fit, but you fail to revise your definition of success to match. Through your old lens, the new arrangement will look to you like a failure. You become unmotivated and are likely to give up.

You've hit a success roadblock and have been derailed. That is, unless you circumvent the roadblock by redefining success in a way that affirms your new work+life fit. This shift of focus allows you to embrace your new arrangement as an achievement, rather than seeing failure.

The other option, of course, is to stick with your traditional definitions of success and not seek the flexibility you want given the realities of your life. Doing so may allow you to feel "successful" for a while. But the aspects of your life prompting you to combine work and life differently won't go away. In fact, ignoring them is a direct route to conflict and unhappiness. Wouldn't it be better to reexamine how you define personal and professional success and then make the adjustments necessary to have the work+life fit you want?

Success Roadblock Red Flags

Sometimes roadblocks will hit you out of nowhere—you're traveling toward your goal and, seemingly for no reason, you find yourself stuck and unable to move forward. Other times, however, there will be signs, or red flags, that will signal "roadblock ahead." These red flags come in the form of statements like: "Well, I guess you just can't have it all," or "I just don't feel like I am doing any one thing well."

If you hear yourself utter these words at any time throughout the Three Steps, stop and make one of the following choices:

> ► **"Redefine Success** Specifically, redefine what it means to "have it *all*" or to "do things *well,*" adjusting the meaning of *all* and *well*.
>
> Instead of *all* being a 60-hour a week, high-stress job plus 100% care for your aging father, maybe *all* can be four, 10-hour days with the fifth day off in order to take your father to the doctor and to visit with him. And having a home health aide care for him on the other four days.
>
> Or, instead of *well* meaning staying on the fast track at work while trying to become a world-class runner, maybe *well* means temporarily plateauing at your current level while participating in as many marathons as your remaining time and energy will allow.

> ► **Or keep your definition of success the same and stop pursuing a new arrangement.** If this is your choice, make sure it's

what you want. Again, while you may continue to feel successful by traditional standards, the danger is that the new realities in your life beckoning you to make a change won't go away. Continuing to ignore them may only result in work/life conflict and discontent.

The Four Most Common Causes of Success Roadblocks

When you see a red flag, or actually hit a success roadblock, one or more of the following four aspects of success will usually be to blame:

1. Money
2. Prestige
3. Advancement
4. Caregiver expectations

Understanding how each one contributes to your current definition of success *before* you begin Step 3 will reduce the likelihood of being unnecessarily derailed. I've found that very few people ever consciously say to themselves, "This is what success looks like to me." Here's your opportunity to alter the lens through which you see achievement before you start creating, negotiating, and implementing your new arrangement.

Money-related Success Roadblocks

We start with money because, in my opinion, it's the chief obstacle standing between most people and a better work+life fit. Money is something over which many people feel they have very little control. As a result, they often feel trapped not only in a job situation where they are financially successful, but trapped in a lifestyle that success enables. So as their work and/or personal realities change, they feel incapable of changing their successful lifestyle in order to adjust their work+life fit.

The truth is, not only do you have control over the choices you make with your money, but you can change those choices at any time. This is the primary strategy for moving beyond a money-related success roadblock. You implement this strategy, in part, by planning, budgeting, and making better, albeit sometimes difficult, choices with your money (we will cover this in more detail in chapter 21). But none of this will be effective unless you understand how you use money and lifestyle as a barometer of success.

If you believe that more money, and therefore more things, means more success, then by definition, if you make less money, you're failing. Even if by making less money you achieve the work+life fit you want.

Examining your relationship with money and assigning equal value to other areas of your life isn't easy. In our culture, money and the status it confers are king. And those who dare to replace it, even partially, aren't applauded. This is a perfect example of how you can change your definition of success on a personal level but can still encounter that same roadblock within the broader culture.

I'm not saying that money is an inappropriate measure of success. But it's only one measure. And it's fine as long as you're using it in a way that supports the work+life fit your heart desires.

When a client is stuck behind a money-related roadblock, it usually has two sources. It's either a valid financial difficulty, which with time and budgeting can be overcome, or it's an unconscious resistance to giving up part of his or her lifestyle and placing value on another nonmonetary aspect of life. How drastic that shift needs to be depends upon how dramatically your proposed work+life fit impacts your earnings. The larger the impact, the more your definition of success needs to encompass other parts of your life.

CLARK'S STORY

Clark, a highly regarded senior associate who is solidly on track to become partner, has been with his law firm for six years. Clark achieved this level of success by consistently billing more than the required number of hours every year. However, he does so by working long hours during the week and on weekends. It's a sacrifice he's been willing to make because it allows him to support a lifestyle that is important to him. And until last year, he considered himself a success both professionally and personally. That is, until his daughter was born.

Prior to his daughter's arrival, the time and energy devoted to work wasn't a problem. In fact, his wife also worked long hours. Both were committed to working hard in order to afford a nice house in a town with good schools, two new cars, and nice vacations. Then his wife decided to cut back on her hours at work, and he found himself increasingly resentful of what he was missing at home. Now she was pregnant with their second child.

Clark's anxiety increased when he and his wife started looking at bigger houses. Whereas before the kids, the prospect of a bigger house energized him, now all he saw was billing even more hours. And it wasn't even that his current house was too small, it just seemed that a bigger house was the next step.

According to the lens through which Clark viewed his life, a bigger house and the money needed to buy it were the next rung on the ladder of success. He was scheduled to make partner in the next two years and could handle a bigger mortgage. But it would mean the same long, if not longer, hours.

Suddenly, he started wondering if it was worth it. He wasn't feeling particularly motivated. In fact, he felt trapped. But finding a new work+life fit that gave him more time and energy for the kids meant less time and energy for work.

Clark liked his firm, and he liked the work he did. He knew of some female associates who had stepped off partner track and reduced their billable hours, which allowed them to leave by 6 P.M. and not work weekends. This schedule would be fine with him. But there were two problems. First, he hadn't ever seen any male associates change their schedules, so he wasn't sure it would be accepted. Second, reducing billable hours would definitely mean less income and might mean the extension of his partnership timetable.

Another option was to leave the firm and work for a company as an in-house counsel. Typically such jobs required fewer hours. But, in either scenario, the reality was clear. He would make less money. He knew that unless he shifted his definition of success, he would feel like he was failing. Clark had hit the money-related success roadblock.

Clark's Strategy:
Redefining Money-related Success

First, I asked Clark to clarify his vision of "having more time for my kids." After thinking a moment, he said, "You know, it would be fine if at least three nights a week I could get home in time to eat dinner with them, give them a bath, and put them to bed. I could even do work after that. Also, unless absolutely necessary, I'd like to keep weekend work to a minimum."

We tried to think of the best way to accomplish this with the least impact on Clark's compensation. Recognizing how much money played into his definition of professional success, he was afraid making too drastic a change wouldn't work.

He also decided to try staying at his firm. Having invested so many years of blood, sweat, and tears, he hoped some of that goodwill would create support for his proposal.

He considered his vision of a new work+life fit. He looked at the tasks of his job, and questioned whether, instead of working less, he could work more efficiently. He concluded that by shifting the hours he was in the office, setting aside specific times to return emails and calls, and eliminating a number of unnecessary tasks, he could achieve his goal without a large reduction in his billable hours. The corporate culture dictated a late start (10:00 A.M. for many) and late nights (10:00 or 11:00 P.M.), but he would propose coming in at 7:30 A.M. and leaving three nights a week by 6:30 P.M.

Because it wasn't a huge departure from his current schedule, he was comfortable proposing this arrangement for a six-month trial period. It would allow him to get comfortable with it, as well as see how much it would affect his earnings and his partnership timetable. At the six-month review, he'd consider how the arrangement was going—did he miss the money enough to switch back to his old schedule, or did he want even more time with his kids?

In the meantime he and his wife decided to refinish the basement and put off buying a new house. "We did see some really nice houses last weekend," he told me, "and my best friend in the firm just bought a gorgeous new home. But the kids are only little once, and it really isn't worth it."

· · ·

Clark's story illustrates how shifting away from an exclusively monetary definition of success can help you to move forward with changing your work+life fit. And he's doing it at a slow, comfortable pace so that his chosen work+life fit won't result in a drastic change in lifestyle. Remember, even the smallest change can make a big difference in your sense of well-being and feeling of success. Although Clark may have changed his personal definition of success, his colleagues haven't necessarily changed theirs. They're still making financial choices that place a primary emphasis on money and lifestyle—buying ever-bigger houses. But Clark is moving forward, knowing that his choices are right based upon his personal redefinition of success that expanded to value time spent with his family.

More Stories to Help You Redefine Money-related Success

Clark's story illustrates how changing the way you define success in terms of money can remove the roadblocks standing between you and the work+life fit you want. Here are a couple of additional examples to inspire you as you try to redefine money-related success.

ELLIOT'S STORY

Elliot attended a workshop that I conducted for men seeking a better work+life fit. At the end, Elliot approached me and said, "The point that hit me the hardest was when you talked about redefining success related to money in order to have the work+life fit you want." He continued, "There is a young father who works for me who clearly wants to reduce the number of hours he works by about five hours a week. He talked it over with his direct supervisor and with me, and we said fine. But he still hasn't done it and you know why? He can't deal with the fact that his bonus will probably be about 5% less than it would have been—5%!"

Elliot was astonished that such a small reduction in this father's overall compensation would cause him to not take advantage of an arrangement that he proposed and that had been approved. He concluded, "Now I understand what the problem is. This guy needs to change the definition of success that says if I'm making less money—even 5% less—I'm failing, even though I have the five extra hours a week that I wanted with my family." I encouraged Elliot to sit down with this young man and perhaps help him to see what he was doing. But we both acknowledged that at the end of the day only that young father would be able to do the work himself.

SHANNON'S STORY

Shannon called me after I'd helped a friend of hers implement a three-day-per-week work schedule. Having just had her second baby, she too wanted to cut back on her workweek. First, she spent some time creating her work+life vision whereby she would work three days a week with two of those days working from home to cut down on time lost from her long commute.

We then compared her vision to her work and personal realities in order to make sure that they were compatible. Everything was fine until we looked at personal financial realities and proceeded to run smack into a money-related success roadblock.

Because she would be working three-fifths of her full-time schedule, she would receive three-fifths of her salary and bonus. Now that she had two children however, her child-care costs had doubled. Plus, she loved the center that cared for her kids, but they charged the full-time rate even if she used the center part-time. It didn't take her long to realize that if she implemented this work+life fit, she'd essentially work for free.

Shannon looked at me and said, "This makes no sense. Is it worth it to work if I'm only breaking even? I should just quit if I want more time with the kids." This reaction is not uncommon when someone realizes that after covering child-care and elder-care costs with a re-duced salary you will have little or no money leftover. Even then, it isn't easy to answer the question "Is it worth it to work?"

Shannon and I talked about why she worked. She said that the ad-ditional income was helpful, but that with some budget cutting they would probably be fine financially. Beyond that, she'd been with her company for seven years. Her boss supported her professional devel-opment, and she could see that there were many opportunities for her to continue to learn and grow at this company. She added, "It seems like a lot to walk away from. I know that in a couple of years my older son won't be in day care and the baby will go to the toddler-level care which is less expensive. By that time if I'm still working three days a week, I will be making some money. So maybe it's worth it to work essentially for free for the next two years. It's enough that I'm being mom to two great little boys, and I'm finding a way to keep doing my job. I can see how it will pay off down the road."

Other Resources to Help You Circumvent the Money Roadblock

▶ *The 9 Steps to Financial Freedom* by Suze Orman. While this book includes wonderful traditional financial planning information, it also addresses your emotional attachment to money and changing the role it plays in your life. Her other books include *The Road to Wealth* and *The Courage to be Rich,* which are a continuation of those themes.
▶ Elaine St. James has written the *Simplify Your Life* series, which offers practical strategies for downsizing your life, both personally and professionally.

Prestige-related Success Roadblocks

Having a better work+life fit means making trade-offs. Sometimes the trade-off is between having more time and flexibility for your personal life or working for a prestigious organization or holding a prestigious position.

Does that mean you can't work for a well-known company and hold a high-profile position and have more flexibility? No, not necessarily. There are well-known, prestigious companies that embrace employee efforts to address work/life conflict. If your current or prospective employer falls into this category, they may support your proposal. And there are people in positions that others would define as prestigious who have creatively found ways to fit work into their lives. Hopefully, if you have achieved such a position, you will leverage your value and experience to do the same.

But what if you can't? What do you do if your prestigious company doesn't support your arrangement or your prestigious position simply requires more time and energy than your desired work+life fit would allow? You hit a prestige-related roadblock and are derailed. That is unless you consider working for a less well known, but perhaps smaller, more flexible organization, or you consider taking a less high-profile position with tasks and responsibilities that accommodate the time and energy you want for your personal life.

Prestigious, well-known companies are often larger. And according to research, larger companies tend to offer more direct and costly work/life supports (e.g., day-care centers or referrals to child-care and elder-care services), while smaller companies tend to offer more flexibility.[1] Therefore, if you are unable to find support for your proposal in a larger organization, perhaps you'll find the flexibility you need with a smaller, but perhaps less prestigious company.

Likewise, the more high profile the position you hold, the less time and energy you typically have to devote to your personal life simply because of the tasks and responsibilities associated with that type of job.

A senior tenured professor at a top business school once delivered a speech in which she stated, "You can be a tenured Ivy League business school professor and have a husband and a dog, but you can't have kids. You can have a husband, a dog, and kids, but then you will most likely not be a tenured professor at a Top Ten business school." In her opinion, attaining and maintaining a tenured professorship in an Ivy League MBA program requires so much time and energy that there is little left over for more than a dog and a husband. Let's assume for a moment that she's right. How could a person who wanted to be a business school professor while having a dog, a husband, kids, and, say, aging parents, redefine success in order to circumvent the roadblock?

Could she become an adjunct professor in the business program of a local college? Would that leave her with enough time and energy for her children and aging parents, and maybe even some for volunteering or pursuing an avocation? Again, it's all a matter of how you define success, and whether you would view anything less than a tenured professorship at Harvard as a failure.

But sacrificing prestige in terms of company or position can be difficult, even if doing it would give you the flexibility you want. It would mean replacing the prestige in your definition of success with other aspects of your life. The underlying cause of prestige-related roadblocks may differ, depending upon your particular work+life reality, but the strategy for moving beyond them is the same. For example, stay-at-home parents transitioning back into the workforce encounter a prestige-related roadblock when they put pressure on themselves to reenter work at the same level of prestige at which they left, even if that type of job would be incompatible with the work+life fit they want today.

CINDY'S STORY

After being a stay-at-home mom for the past couple of years, Cindy wants to work again now that the kids are in school all day. While many people in her position have no clue what they want to do, Cindy knows she wants to return to the retail industry. But she would also like to have enough time and energy to spend with her kids.

As we talked, she continually referred to her former job as a senior buyer for one of the premier retailers in New York City. In spite of the long hours and pressure, she clearly enjoyed the senior position she used to have at this prestigious company. I asked her if her goal was to find a similar job. She shook her head and admitted that the hours and the stress, not to mention the long buying trips to the Far East, wouldn't allow her the time and energy she wanted for her kids. Then she said angrily, "They would never let me work three days a week. And I just can't work the way I used to. It just seems so unfair, because I really liked that job and was really good at it."

Cindy's Strategy:
Redefining Prestige-related Success

Here was a woman with an unbelievable amount of experience in her industry. She knew that the tasks and responsibilities of a similarly high-powered job would not be compatible with a three-day-a-week work+life fit. Yet she was unable to see that there were many other opportunities to consider locally.

Finally I said, "What about a job at a local retail boutique? I'm sure that they would *love* to have someone with your experience. You certainly won't make as much money, but they would probably be more flexible with regard to your time and energy commitment." Her eyes squinted and her nose crinkled as she considered my suggestion. Clearly, the idea hadn't crossed her mind before.

Suddenly, I realized that being a senior buyer for a prestigious New York retailer was Cindy's definition of success. This was the bar against which she was measuring work. Anything less would be a failure. But this definition of success didn't affirm the type of work+life fit that she wanted. Cindy had hit a prestige-related success roadblock. No wonder she wasn't creatively considering any less prestigious, albeit more flexible, opportunities.

Cindy pondered my suggestion, and then she admitted that she wasn't even aware that she used her old career to set the standard for her job search. And she was intrigued by the idea of perhaps working in a small, specialized, high-end boutique. "I probably wouldn't make much money. But what matters more is that I find a situation that lets me ease back into work doing something I enjoy." Viewing success in those terms, clearly she was beginning to see the possibilities.

• • •

On the flip side, working parents or those caring for aging relatives want more time and energy for their *personal* life, but they may also have to sacrifice prestige in order to get it.

ALEXANDRA'S STORY

I recently met a research analyst who works for a large international bank. We talked about her desire to travel less often and to work four days a week in order to spend more time with her children. "The weekends just seem to be an unending race to get errands done," she sighed. But she laughed when I suggested proposing a new work+life fit arrangement to her boss. Clearly, she didn't think that was possible.

Alexandra's Strategy: Redefining Prestige-related Success

I suggested that she seek out a smaller, but perhaps more flexible, boutique research firm that would be thrilled to hire someone with her background and experience. Or, if she wanted to stay with the bank, maybe she would consider giving up some of her responsibilities in order to win support for her work+life fit.

She somewhat sheepishly confessed that it would be hard for her because the prestige of the organization was important to how she viewed herself professionally. And she would have trouble giving up some of the authority related to her current position.

I'd given it a shot, but I could see that she'd hit the prestige-related roadblock. If she didn't change her definition of success, what were her options?

She could keep things the way they are, but the realities in her personal life will remain unchanged, as will the associated work/life conflict.

She could try to find the extra time and energy she wants for her personal life by working more efficiently and changing her schedule (we will look at doing this as part of Step 3). But given her desire to cut down on travel and work only four days a week, I was skeptical that she could do this without proposing a more formal arrangement.

She could quit altogether. If financially capable, mothers, fathers, and elder-care givers will often make this choice rather than exchange the prestige of the company they work for, or the position they hold within a company, for more flexibility. To many it's easier to say, "I *was* a (prestigious title) at (prestigious company)," than to downshift in order to have the work+life fit they want.

In the end, none of these alternatives are as effective as Alexandra's redefining success related to prestige and making the necessary compromises in order to work and find more time and energy for her personal life. Hopefully, she will not let a title or a company name keep her from the work+life fit she wants.

. . .

More and more people want to work in retirement these days. But they resist the idea of working for a smaller, less well known but possibly more flexible company or the idea of staying with their current employer but in a lower profile position that may require taking a step back in terms of power, authority, title, responsibility, or seniority. One person who was considering a working retirement explained his hesitation this way: "I could work three days a week for my current employer, but I'd be reporting to people I hired 20 years ago, and I wouldn't have an office." Wouldn't it be better to redefine success and have a work+life fit that keeps your skills and contacts up to date while making some money?

GLEN'S STORY

Glen stepped down as foreman at a manufacturing facility after 20 years in the job. He started formulating a vision for how he wanted his retirement to look about a year ago. His wife had retired from teaching two years earlier after a cancer scare, and he knew he wanted more time to be with her. However, he loved the challenge of working and had a lot of experience to offer. And they could definitely use the extra income.

Glen's Strategy:
Redefining Prestige-related Success

In order to have the flexibility he wanted, he proposed to his manager that he remain with the company as a manufacturing consultant in the Southwest region. He would work about 60 hours a month, traveling to various plants training foremen, negotiating labor disputes, etc. Management was happy to retain his experience and skills and saved money by not having Glen on the books as a full-time employee with health insurance and retirement costs. Glen admitted it was strange at first to work in his old plant as a consultant to the new foreman, but he quickly got over that the first time he and his wife took off for a two-week trip to Mexico.

More Stories to Help You Redefine
Prestige-related Success

Cindy's, Alexandra's and Glen's stories illustrate how people with different work/life challenges experience and address prestige-related roadblocks. The following stories offer additional examples of how you can redefine success in order to find the work+life fit you want.

MARGGI'S STORY

For more than 20 years, Marggi worked at some of the most recognizable companies in the music industry, promoting some of the biggest performers in music, including Bon Jovi, David Bowie, and Tom Jones. And she will admit, while not always easy, it was an exciting life. It's not unusual for her to share stories from her past such as, "Oh yeah, there was the night that we met Elton John and some of his friends. We partied until the early morning. He was so nice and put us all up for the night in one of Paris's most expensive hotels."

She lived this life of high-profile people and international travel until the day her father became very ill. And, as she says, "Without a second thought, I found myself back in my parents' house in New Jersey, taking a year off to care for my father until he died. He was wonderful to me. I'm an only child, and I needed to be there for myself and also to help my mother."

After her father's death, she realized that her jet-set job was no longer compatible with the new realities in her life. Although her mother was still in relatively good health, it was clear that she would be better off with someone else around. So Marggi decided to change her work+life fit for the second time in a little over a year.

She used all of her savings to purchase a small commercial building in a neighboring town and opened a Pilates studio. Marggi had been studying Pilates for a few years and felt ready to devote her time and energy to this new, albeit far less glamorous, venture. She loved Pilates, and more important, she could set her own schedule and be available for her mother.

Five years later, memorabilia from the days when she worked with some of the biggest names in entertainment are scattered around the studio. While she looks back upon them with fondness, she doesn't regret her choice. Less than a year ago her mother also died, and Marggi got to spend every day of those last few years with her. "That time was worth more than sitting in the VIP section of a restaurant with Jewel. It was priceless. And I couldn't have done it if I hadn't been willing to place as much value on being there to care for the two people who took such good care of me all of my life as I did on being able to say, 'Hey, I'm with so-and-so big name rock star.'"

SARAH'S STORY

Sarah overcame her prestige-related roadblock and creatively fit work into her life after she had her first child. As a senior engineer for a large Fortune 500 company, Sarah was responsible for multimillion-dollar projects all over the world. But after Louise was born, she no longer wanted to spend months at a time away at a job site. Seeing no other appealing opportunities with her employer, she decided to consider other options.

But what? All that she had known was working for a large, well-recognized company in a senior position. After considering many different scenarios, she realized what she most wanted was to keep math in her life while having the flexibility to be with her daughter. So she went down to the local high school and signed up to be a tutor. Now, she tutors students in math in her home.

Is this a prestigious position? Absolutely not. But far from considering herself a failure, she sees her tutoring as a way to stay intellectually engaged and as she says, "get the pleasure of reading a math textbook." (Yes, that is a direct quote.) She changed her definition and judges her work+life fit to be a success.

BROOK'S STORY

Brook had a similar experience. She was the head of the graphics department for a multinational company, but then her husband became ill. They also had two small children at home. Brook decided to work for herself, and even though her husband regained his health, she continues to work with a small group of handpicked clients from her home-based office. When I asked her how it feels to no longer be associated with The International Corp., she said, "Fine. In fact, I don't miss it at all. I still do the part of the job I love the most, but on my time. And, most important, my husband and my kids are healthy and happy. It also feels good to know that I could go back if I had to, because I've kept up with all of the new technology and I still have great contacts in the industry. Who knows."

FRAN'S STORY

Having worked for Jones Manufacturing for 15 years, Fran didn't want to have to resign when her father's Alzheimer's moved into its final stages. She wanted to spend time with him every day if possible as long as he had some ability to recognize her, so she proposed changing her hours from 8 A.M. to 5 P.M. to 11:30 A.M. to 7 P.M.

She comfortably agreed to take a one-fifth cut to reflect the reduction in the hours she worked. But when it became clear that the tasks and responsibilities of her job as senior accounts receivable manager weren't compatible with this arrangement, she hesitated. Her manager was willing to promote one of the people who currently reported to Fran and allow her to take his place—to essentially swap positions.

"I would be reporting to Bob?" Fran wasn't sure. "You know I could afford to simply quit and be with my father full-time, especially if I sold my house and moved in with him." But then she reconsidered. "I'd be walking away from so much. It'll be nice to have the time with my dad in the morning, but then come to work where I know everyone and know the job." Then she added, "And who knows how long dad will live. After he's gone, if I'm uncomfortable not being the senior manager and reporting to Bob, I'll look for another position. But for now, I'm going to try it."

MADELINE'S STORY

Until she had kids, Madeline was the picture of prestigious success. She graduated from a Top Ten law school and clerked for a federal judge before settling into a high-profile law firm. But when her daughter was born, she knew something had to change. So she traded all of the prestige to work for a small, suburban sole-proprietor law firm four days a week, basically 9-to-5. Contrary to seeing this as a failure, she believes it's a gift. She gets to do what she loves to do, while having plenty left over to devote to her kids and husband.

ANDY'S STORY

For years, Andy worked for a multinational corporation arranging multimillion-dollar deals across the globe. He loved his job. But he loved his family more, and the travel was beginning to take its toll on not only the time but also the energy he had to devote to them.

He began to consider other options, but he hadn't settled on a particular vision. Until one day his in-laws announced that they wanted to reduce their involvement in the day-to-day management of the small private swim club that they owned and managed. After discussing it with his wife, Andy decided to step in and start managing the club full-time.

Two years later, he couldn't be more content. As we spoke, corporate jets from a local airport flew overhead. He looked up and laughed, "That used to be me. Sometimes I miss it, but this is where I know I should be. At least for now."

Advancement-related Success Roadblocks

Advancement=Success: Advancement is one of the cornerstones of our personal and cultural definition of success. As part of the FWI/ Whirpool New Providers Study, 1,502 women were asked "What makes you feel successful at work?" The answer with the highest percentage of responses by far was "quality of work/doing a good job/doing job right or well," with 51% citing it as their top measure of success.[2] How do we gauge how well we're doing our job? By whether or not we advance—whether we're given higher ratings, bigger titles, bigger offices, more money, more responsibilities, better projects, etc. It's not surprising then that the idea of plateauing or even stepping back is difficult, especially if you're a Type-A person who is used to always grabbing for that next rung on the ladder. If you aren't advancing, you must be failing. Right?

But this belief is built on myth. Avoiding the red flags and roadblocks caused by an attachment to advancement requires dispelling the following myths:

Myth #1: I need to be advancing or I am failing.

Reality: You can plateau at, or even step back from, your current professional position and *still* consider yourself successful.

Let me share a common conversation that I have with clients:

CLIENT: "I don't want this arrangement to put a red mark on my career."

ME: "What do you mean by red mark?"

CLIENT: "I don't want to be passed over for promotions or bigger responsibilities."

ME: "But do you *really* want to be promoted or take on bigger responsibilities right now?"

CLIENT (long pause): "No. I want more time with my kids. They're only little once (or more time with an aging parent, more time to travel in retirement, or more time to volunteer, etc.)."

ME: "Why isn't it enough—for a while, not necessarily forever— to simply continue to participate in and contribute to a job you like while being the kind of parent you'd like to be to your kids?"

CLIENT (another long pause): "You know, I guess it is—for now."

Why do we feel this way? It begins when we're born—life is a continuing series of advancements from crawling to walking to grades in school to college to jobs and on and on.

This up-and-up-always mentality is reinforced by corporate evaluation systems that rank you on a forced curve. How many people do you know who seek to be one of the average majority who "met expectations"? Not many. Most people shoot to be one of the few who "exceeded expectations." But why? If at this point in your life you can't give the extra time and energy it takes to reach that goal because of the work+life fit you want, what's wrong with doing a good job and meeting expectations for a while? And in the process, spend every other Friday taking your son to his away hockey games. Will you get 125% of your bonus potential if you meet expectations? Depending upon how your company's evaluation system is set up, perhaps not. But you'll get 100% of your bonus. Not bad.

Hitting the advancement-related success roadblock is one of the primary reasons people walk away from a work+life fit that, from the outside, seems to be succeeding. It happens the first time you don't get assigned to the hottest project or don't get offered a promotion. You view yourself as failing compared to your peers and lose motivation. And you either leave or discontinue your arrangement. Who first decreed that if you aren't trying to be the CEO at all times, then you're failing? What's wrong with being a solid contributor who has a full and satisfying personal life? And who's to say that after plateauing or stepping back for a while you won't ramp it up again—and maybe eventually become the CEO.

Unfortunately, as was the case with redefining success related to prestige, redefining success related to advancement is too difficult for some. And they decide it's simply less painful to quit than to stop advancing. When I talk to formerly employed mothers, I've actually heard the following, "I would've liked to have worked less than full-time or work for a smaller no-name company, but that would have hurt my career." Hurt your career? I have to resist the urge to say, "How does dropping out of the workforce altogether help it?" But I've heard this logic enough over the years to realize that on some level it makes complete sense to these women.

What would happen if instead you defined success differently? What if you believed that simply working at your current level while managing your personal responsibilities was success enough? You're no longer failing. You are succeeding—and motivated to keep going.

Here's an important reality check: There will always be people who, at one time or another, will want to devote more time and energy to work than you either can or want to. Because of this choice, they will have the extra time and energy that you may not have to pursue advancement opportunities. Neither one of you is better or more right. It's all about matching your definition of success with your current work+life fit.

In fact, a slower, less responsible track offers certain benefits, depending upon the way you want work to fit into your life:

▶ First, it allows you to "stay in the game" or to remain connected to work while fulfilling responsibilities outside of work; and
▶ Second, it makes it easier to ramp up again if circumstances change and you decide to reallocate more of your time and energy back to work.

It's a lot easier to go from working at a slower, less demanding pace to seeking more responsibility and advancement than it is to start from scratch. Just like it's easier to go from 35 mph to 60 mph than to go from 0 to 60 mph. You have less ground to cover and less energy to expend. Why? Because you've kept your skills up to date, and you have more confidence. You also have current experience and contacts in the field to draw upon.

Myth #2: Once I stop advancing, I can never advance again.

Reality: You can start advancing again *any time* you want.

A few months ago, I listened to a panel of distinguished female executives discuss strategies of career advancement. As is often the case, a young woman in the audience asked the panelists how their decisions about work and family affected their careers. A woman who was president of a large, well-known company responded as follows: "I will be honest with you, my career has suffered because of some of the choices I made. A few years ago, I faced some serious health challenges and decided to take a six-month leave. And then a couple years later, I decided to take six months off to spend time with my child before she left for college. And each time I did suffer a career setback. You can't have it all." Rather than describing her work/life journey as a triumphant success—"Look, I am healthy, I spent precious time with my child, *and* I am the president of this prestigious company"—sadly, in her mind, she felt her career had fallen short of expectations because of those decisions. At least that is how it sounded. Taken in a more positive and inspiring context, her story illustrates a very important point: You *can* plateau or even step back professionally in order to have a different work+life fit and still advance at a later date—even to the level of president.

Studies prove that employees mistakenly believe that there is a much greater career penalty for using flexibility than there really is in the eyes of employers. The 1998 Business Work-Life Study of 1,057 companies formally dispelled the myth that flexibility hurts your future advancement opportunities. When asked if the use of flexible times and leave policies jeopardizes employees' opportunities for advancement, only 10% of the company respondents felt it did. In contrast, 40% of the employees surveyed in a comparable study felt that those who used flexible schedules and took time off *did* impede their job advancement.[3] Clearly, there's a disconnect between employee perceptions and the employer reality. Employees are letting this misperception keep them from asking for the flexibility they need. When in reality, 90% of employers say it will *not* keep them from advancing in the future.

As you pursue a new work+life fit, keep asking yourself, "Do I want to advance?" If the answer is no, fine. But someday the answer may change and you may feel that you once again want to advance professionally. Then you need to let the powers that be know that you would like to be considered for future opportunities and are willing to make the necessary adjustments to your work+life fit to accommodate. It may take time to get back on the fast track, but if you are a solid performer, it can be done.

Myth #3: If I have a work+life fit that differs from the traditional in-the-office, 9-to-5, full-time work schedule, I can't advance.

Reality: You *can* advance even if you have a schedule that changes where, when, and how you work. It's a matter of whether you *want* to take on the additional tasks and responsibilities that often go along with advancement.

Catalyst, a not-for-profit research and advisory firm, conducted a 10-year follow-up study of 24 executive women with part-time work arrangements (defined as anything less than a full-time schedule) and found that:

- ► Almost all of the women still worked for the same company;
- ► 50% still worked part-time, while the rest now worked full-time by choice;
- ► Almost all of the respondents now held either middle or senior management positions, with more than half being promoted over the past 10 years when they were working less than full-time; and
- ► All reported satisfaction with their choices.

"How did these women work less than full-time and still advance?" you ask. It depends in large part on how drastically your work+life fit differs from a typical full-time schedule in your field and at your level. If you are working a full-time, or almost full-time, schedule but telecommute two days a week or have a compressed workweek, there should be no reason that you shouldn't continue to advance if you *want* to.

However, let's say that you are part of a job-share team, whereby you work two and a half days per week in partnership with another person. Now you can tell your manager that you would still like to be considered for all advancement opportunities, but you may need to change your work+life fit to accommodate the new tasks and responsibilities that come with it. This may jeopardize your job-share, and you need to ask yourself if that's what you want at this point in time, and your answer may be "no."

CHRISTINA'S STORY

For six months, Christina enjoyed a work+life fit that allowed her to work from home three days a week and in the office one day a week. Even though she wasn't always included in every meeting or given the most high-profile assignments, she still felt successful both personally and professionally. Everything was fine until the day that two of her peers were promoted. And to make matters worse, she now reported to one of them.

She wasn't sure why their success affected her so deeply. Maybe it was the first time the reality of her choice not to seek more responsibility for a while hit her in the face. Or maybe it was that she knew she could've had the job if she'd wanted it. In fact, a senior manager had asked her to consider it. But she passed, knowing it would require more time working in the office than she was willing to give right now.

Clearly, whether she knew it or not, Christina believed if she wasn't advancing, she was failing. She began having second thoughts about continuing her arrangement. Maybe she should just leave? Or maybe give up a couple of the days she worked from home and apply for the next promotion? Christina had hit the advancement roadblock.

Christina's Strategy:
Redefining Advancement-related Success

Not surprisingly, Christina ended up applying for the next advancement opportunity. And, as expected, she got it. But when faced with the reality of giving up the three days that she worked from home, she had a change of heart. She finally gave herself permission to admit that maybe, just maybe, not advancing beyond her current level was okay for now. And maybe, just maybe, continuing to perform well in a job she loves while raising a family is indeed a success in and of itself.

In fact, the more she thought about it, the prouder she became. Instead of quitting, she'd found a way to stay in the game, while still having enough time and energy for her family. She also knew that someday she would probably go for that promotion, get it, and run with it. But for now, she was not only content, but genuinely happy for her colleagues who were promoted. She realized that just because they want to pursue a work+life fit different from her own doesn't mean that she failed.

Choosing to put yourself on a path of less responsibility for a period of time is only a failure if that's how you choose to see it. Otherwise, it can be a great way to succeed at fitting work into your life when time and energy is needed for other responsibilities, and not necessarily only those that are child-care related.

More Stories to Help You Redefine Advancement-related Success

Christina's story illustrates how she redefined success related to advancement. The following stories offer additional examples of how you can do the same in order to have the work+life fit you want.

MARGARET'S STORY

Impressive is the word you think of when you meet Margaret. In addition to being articulate, she has a razor-sharp analytical mind that thinks through and solves any challenge. And Margaret was now setting her sights on solving her work/life conflict.

As a consultant with an international consulting firm, Margaret was used to long hours and lots of travel. She loved it, but could see that the pending arrival of her first child would make this schedule difficult. Especially since her husband also traveled with his job.

After our initial discussions, Margaret was convinced that she would have to leave her company even though her manager encouraged her to consider proposing an alternative arrangement, and her company had a culture that supported this type of negotiation. "I just don't see it working long term," she told me. "The people here are just too high achieving and intense. I really need to find someplace where people don't work very hard." When she said that sentence, I stopped in my tracks because finally I understood that she had hit an advancement roadblock.

I challenged Margaret, "I've consulted to a lot of companies, and yes, some do have less intense work cultures than others, but even in those companies there is still a group of hard charging, '100% work,' A-list employees. I would guess that no matter where you worked you would automatically associate yourself with those high-achieving people, which is what you are used to being. That is unless you decided beforehand to simply contribute as much time and energy as your chosen work+life fit will allow. Even if that contribution would be considered good, but average." She thought for a minute and said, "You know, I had never thought about it that way, but you are probably right."

We agreed that after the baby was born it would be a good idea for her to try to reduce her work schedule at her current employer. Take some time to see how it feels to redefine success related to advancement in a culture that so highly values continual achievement. If she can do it there, it will be much easier not to fall back into the 100% work trap if she does ultimately decide to leave for another job.

GAYLE'S STORY

After a number of coaching sessions, Gayle was ready to negotiate her new work+life fit proposal with her manager. She set the date, and all went well until her boss started to discuss how her reduced schedule would affect where she fell on the forced-curve evaluation system the company uses. In this system, every manager can rank only a very few employees as "exceeds expectations," the majority as "meets expectations," and a couple as "performs below expectations."

Even though he supports Gayle's work+life fit proposal to work three days a week, he wanted her to know that she most likely would not rank an "exceeds expectations," which is what she typically received. He assured her that it was fine to rank as "meets expectations," but he felt it was important for her to know because it would have bearing on her bonus and on her development plan within the company.

With that, Gayle hit the advancement-related roadblock. "Meets expectations! That's it." We talked about why she was having this reaction. Her boss had approved her request and gave her the courtesy of telling how it would affect her rating, but she was still angry. Finally, she admitted, "I know I'm still going to work hard on the three days in the office, but the truth is I won't be there two full days, which does limit what I can do when compared with someone working full-time. I have to get used to plateauing for a while because it really is more important to me to have those extra days off."

Other Resources to Help You Circumvent the Advancement Roadblock

▶ *Coming Up for Air: How to Build a Balanced Life in a Workaholic World* by Beth Salvi
▶ *Downshifting: How to Work Less and Enjoy Life More* by John Drake

Caregiving-related Success Roadblocks

Work-related definitions of success are not the only ones that cause problems. Personal definitions of success, especially those related to the quality of caregiving, whether it's caring for children or an aging parent, can cause just as much difficulty, particularly for women.

From the time women are very young, our families and our society dictate what it means to be a "good" mother to a child or a "good" daughter or daughter-in-law to an aging person. For many women, the only role models of motherhood populate two extremes: either women who devoted all of their time and energy to caring for their children or women who devoted most of their time and energy to work. What if a young mother finds the 100% work extreme unappealing? She naturally defaults to the only other role model she knows—100% mom. That becomes her definition of success, which is then reinforced by our culture's definition of a good mother.

Again, I believe that as more women become inspired and empowered to pursue an in-between, more moderate way of creatively combining work and their personal lives, beliefs will change both personally and culturally. But for now, this is the reality for many.

Let me be clear. I'm not saying that choosing a work+life fit that devotes 100% of your time and energy to caring for your children or an aging parent is wrong. If it's what you want and you can afford it, great. But what I see and what the research shows is that most women want to work in some way, whether for the mental stimulation, the feelings of camaraderie, or the money. Specifically, even if money weren't a consideration, 54% of women who were currently employed and 23% of those who were currently stay-at-home mothers said that they would prefer to work either full-time or part-time.[4] But they want to do it in a way that leaves enough time and energy for their personal responsibilities, including children and elders.

The woman with child- or elder-care responsibilities who decides to work—however much or little—will succeed only if she clearly defines for herself, in advance, exactly what "enough time and energy for her kids or aging relatives" means. She needs to establish a definition of quality caregiving that matches the time and energy she has to give to personal responsibilities in light of her new work+life fit. And she will *not* have 100% to give to her children or her aging father if she works. If she doesn't establish that new definition, she will most likely hit a caregiving roadblock, as she doubts the quality of the care she's providing to those she loves and for whom she feels responsible.

In other words, if 100% mom or daughter is your definition of success and you try to work, you will fail even before you begin. Because even if you are working part-time, you still won't have 100% to devote to caregiving. What mother or daughter is motivated by a sense of failure? So they give up, quit, or never seek another opportunity.

Interestingly, the opposite definition of successful caregiving is what causes men to hit a roadblock. For most men, the role models that influenced their definition of a good father were men who devoted most of their time and energy to work. A father's traditional role was that of provider. As a result, when a dad wants to reallocate time and energy from work to his kids, the standard of success built upon this 100% work definition of fatherhood tells him that he's a failure. He hits the caregiver-related success roadblock too, just from a different angle.

ALICIA'S STORY

Alicia is typical of new moms who attend my workshops. Six months ago, she had her first child. Since she returned from a three-month maternity leave, she's been sharing a job with one of her colleagues who is also a new mom. Although they're technically each supposed to work three days a week, overlapping one day, they both usually end up working four days a week and overlapping two.

Up front, Alicia acknowledged how fortunate she was to have her job-sharing arrangement. And she was happy because it allowed her to stay with the company in a job that she likes, make money, and have time with her son. The problem is that she can't seem to get past these feelings that she's letting him down by working at all. And to make matters worse, her job-sharing partner, Nancy, doesn't seem to have any guilt.

As hard as she tries, she can't seem to figure out what her problem is, but it's making her consider quitting. In fact, if she didn't want to let Nancy down, she probably would have quit two months ago.

First, I asked her the most important question: In her heart-of-hearts, how did she want work to fit into her life? Did she want to devote 100% of her time and energy to her son? Because it would be fine if she did. She thought for a moment and responded, "No, I really don't think so. I was actually a little bored during the last part of my leave, and really liked the thought of getting out of the house three days a week. Not to mention liking the extra money. For the first month, I was able to stick to my three days per week schedule. I really loved being with my son on the two days at home, but was ready to get back on the days I had to work."

I asked how her son was doing. She shrugged, "He seems to be just fine. He's happy and I really like my sitter. Clearly, it's got nothing to do with his care. It's just that I'm afraid I'm not being a good mother to him by working. But when I ask my job-share partner if she ever feels this way, she almost looks confused. She feels like we have the perfect situation. And when you get down to it, we do. I like my job. My boss is really supportive. What's wrong with me? I can't go on feeling this much guilt."

Alicia's Strategy:
Redefining Success Related to Quality
of Care as a Mother

First, I asked Alicia to take some time and make sure that work was part of her vision for her life right now or if it was just something she thought she *should* do. I reminded her that a new work+life fit really only works if it is solidly based upon your heart's desire. A week later we got together and she had a clearer idea of what she wanted and a clearer definition of what it meant to her to succeed as a mother.

Even though her arrangement required her to come in only three days a week, she usually worked four because "that's what 'real' work is." But after being really honest with herself, she knew that anything more than three days was too much. "That leaves me two whole days a week to do activities with my son and to get my errands done. And then I'm much less likely to feel like I'm failing as a mother."

She reviewed her arrangement with her supportive boss and made it clear that she didn't want to come in more than three days a week, unless of course there was an emergency. Since she had been his assistant for more than four years, he was happy to have her even if it was only three days a week, especially since the alternative was not having her at all. Plus, Nancy more than adequately covered for Alicia on her days off.

By challenging her extreme definition of not only successful mothering but also of work, Alicia was able to identify and then finally embrace a unique, more moderate combination of work and life that made her feel success both professionally and personally.

*   *   *

Regardless of whether you are male or female, if you face the prospect of caring for an aging relative, you may encounter a similar conflict. Sons and daughters develop their definition of successfully caring for aging parents from watching how their parents did it. And in many cases, their parents cared for their aging relatives by relocating them into their homes. But this was during a different era, when a majority of women were able to devote 100% of their time and energy to elder care because their kids were grown and they didn't work.

Times have changed. Not only are people living longer, which creates an increasingly large population of aging parents, but a majority of women now work. And more often than not, men are expected to carry equally the responsibility of caring for aging relatives. Not to mention the fact that many people who care for an aging parent have young children to care for as well. There isn't 100% of *anyone's* time and energy to give. But if that's your definition of successful elder care, then you are going to hit the caregiving roadblock.

HAL'S STORY

I met Hal while conducting a focus group of senior executive men at a Fortune 500 company. Hal didn't say much for most of the discussion until the subject turned to elder care. Then his hand shot up. "I need to share a personal story with the group." This was unusual because few of the executives had personal stories of work/life conflict to share. While they could refer to experiences of more junior colleagues, their own experiences were relatively conflict free, primarily because their wives didn't work when their kids were young. But clearly, when it came to elder care, this guy was expected to pitch in and it was causing a problem.

"Three weeks ago my elderly father came to visit," Hal began. "He lives far away and has to fly, so his visits are few and the trip is taxing for him. My plan was to take the day off to take him to the airport and get him on the plane. Well, wouldn't you know it, I get a call saying there's an urgent meeting that morning. I thought fine, I should be done in time to stick with my plan for my dad. Of course, the meeting runs long, and when I get up to excuse myself to take my elderly father to the airport, someone says half-jokingly, 'Isn't that what taxis are for?' For a moment, I actually found myself considering staying at the meeting and calling a car to take him. When my dad was my age, he and my mom cared for various aging relatives in different ways. In fact, my grandmother lived with us. Yes, my mom didn't work and my wife does after years at home. But really, I should be able to leave a meeting without feeling guilty in order to do the right thing and take my dad to the airport. In fact, it's the least I can do. It makes me wonder what's going to happen if he really needs me, especially given the fact he lives so far away. Will I find myself choosing a meeting over him?"

Hal's Strategy:
Redefining Success Related to Quality of Care for His Aging Father

As for Hal, he too needed to determine what percentage of his time and energy should be appropriately devoted to caring for his father. While a trip to the airport isn't a life-or-death issue, the issue clearly caused him to question his values and how he envisioned his involvement with his father's care—even if it meant he had to leave a meeting early.

In my experience, the people who most successfully redefine caregiver success are the ones who analyze their situations as objectively as possible. They research and learn as much as they can about child care and elder care: how to get the best, most affordable care, and the effects that different forms of care may have on their loved one.

They also talk to other people who seem to have successfully cared for a child or an elder while working in some capacity. When I say "successfully," I mean the children are happy and thriving, and the elder is content and comfortable. They try to learn from the experiences of others. As one client told me, "I stopped feeling guilty about working after I talked to other moms, some who worked and some who didn't, and I realized that there were just as many nice kids with moms who worked as there were troubled kids with moms who didn't work. It's seems to be a matter of what works for you and your family. For us, that means we're fine as long as I don't work more than about 30 hours a week."

Finally, and most important, you need to consider how much time *you* want with your children or elder. As another client observed, "My kids would probably be fine if I worked five days a week, but it's me who selfishly wants time with them."

More Inspiring Stories of Redefining Caregiving-related Success

As Alicia's and Hal's stories illustrate, you can redefine success related to your definition of what makes a "good" parent or child of an aging parent. Here are some additional examples of others who've faced this challenge.

LUISA'S STORY

I ran into Luisa about six months after I'd helped her envision and implement a work+life fit that transitioned her from stay-at-home mom to part-time social worker working three days a week. I asked her how things were going, and she hesitated. "Okay, I guess." I asked her to explain. "I'm enjoying being back at work. I had forgotten how much I liked being a social worker and helping others. And the extra income is great; but, I just can't seem to get everything done. Cup-cakes go unbaked, and Halloween costumes are purchased last minute at Party City whereas before I was organized enough to make them. I guess that I feel a little bit out of the loop whereas before I was involved in everything. I don't know."

We spent a few minutes reviewing her definition of a "good mother" that we established before she went back to work. I asked her to repeat what she remembered: "A good mother is there to listen to her kids when they need her. She supports them when they need her support and makes sure they are clean, fed, happy, and loved." I followed up, "Let's look at how you're meeting your own criteria. Do you feel like you spend enough time listening to your kids?"

"Yes," she said, "my hours are such that I can take them to school every day, and then on the two days off, I make sure we spend extra time after school catching up. In fact, it's funny, I'm almost more conscientious about making time to talk and listen to them now that I'm working than when I was home."

I continued, "Okay, next one, are you supporting them if their Halloween costumes and their cupcakes aren't homemade?"

She laughed, "You know they really couldn't care less about those things. And as far as supporting them, I have my cell phone on even at work. And they know that they can call me at any time. When I'm with a client, I put the phone on vibrate and call them right back. So far, none of the calls have been urgent, and we have more than enough time to deal with issues when I'm home or on my day off. As far as sports and activities, my working has actually forced my husband to rearrange his schedule, and he really likes being in charge a couple of evenings a week."

"Finally," I said, "are they clean, fed, and happy?"

"Well, there may be a few more mac and cheese nights than before, but, yes, they are clean, fed, and happy, especially about the extra fun stuff my salary allows them to have. For example, I bought my boys the new X-Box game they wanted because they did well at school. I could never have done that before. I guess according to my own definition of being a good mom, I am one." Before we departed I suggested that she might want to write that definition down and look at it frequently. "Not a bad idea," she said as she smiled and waved good-bye.

Other Resources to Help You Circumvent the Caregiving Roadblock

▶ *Ask the Children: The Breakthrough Study That Reveals How to Succeed at Work and Parenting* by Ellen Galinsky. The author interviews dozens of children to understand how *they* feel about their parents working and provides an invaluable picture of what does and doesn't matter to kids with regard to their parents' work+life fit. It really helps parents to sort out what they should and shouldn't worry about when considering the best way to fit work into their lives.

▶ *Working Fathers* by James Levine and Todd Pitinsky. Their book offers stories and insights into the work/life conflict from a working father's point of view.

▶ *Another Country: Navigating the Emotional Terrain of Our Elders* by Mary Pipher. A wonderful book that looks at the issues related to caring for a elder from an emotional and cultural perspective.

Hopefully, the stories in this chapter will help you recognize the typical triggers of success roadblocks along your own journey to a better work+life fit: money, prestige, advancement, and caregiving. As you pursue a new work+life fit, you know now that "Well, I guess you can't have it all," or "I just don't feel I am doing any one thing well," are red flags that you've hit one. But you also now have the strategies to bypass success roadblocks and continue down the road toward your goal. All you have to do is step back and shift your definition of success, thereby changing the lens through which you view your work and life. Then you too will see success instead of failure.

Complete these exercises prior to moving on to Step 3. The goal is to be aware of any potential conflicts in an effort to avoid being derailed by one of the success roadblocks. Then, if you hit a success roadblock while working through Step 3, come back and review the exercise to help circumvent the roadblock and to keep moving forward:

- Draw a picture of what "success" looks like to you today; not what you *think* it should look like, but what it really does look like.
- Describe this picture in words: What is your definition of success? Be as detailed as possible. (When answering this question, be as honest as you can.)

Money-related Success

1. Before you begin Step 3, reflect upon what role money and lifestyle play in your definition of success.

   - What aspects of money and lifestyle are particularly important to your definition of success?
   - What portion of your definition of success is dedicated to money and lifestyle? A lot / Half / A little/ None

At this point, do you think the role that money and lifestyle plays in your definition will help or hinder your ability to find a better work+life fit? Why?

   - Who or what influenced the roles money and lifestyle play in your definition of success?

- How open are you to redefining the role that money and lifestyle play in your definition of success if it meant having the new work+life fit you currently want? Very open / Maybe / Not open
- Why?
- How would you feel if you made less money or scaled back your lifestyle?
- How would you have to redefine success related to money in order to achieve the work+life fit you want? On what other parts of your life could place more emphasis?

Prestige-related Success

2. Before you begin Step 3, reflect upon the role prestige plays in your definition of success.
   - What specific aspects of prestige are important in your definition of success (e.g., working for a prestigious company, having a prestigious title, working on prestigious projects, being included in prestigious meetings, etc.)?
   - What portion of your definition of success is dedicated to prestige? A lot / Half / A little/ None

   At this point, do you think the role prestige plays in your definition will help or hinder your ability to find a better work+life fit? Why?

   - Who or what influenced the role prestige plays in your definition of success?
   - How open are you to reducing the role of prestige plays in your definition of success if it meant having the work+life fit you currently want? Very open / Maybe / Not open
   - Why?
   - How would you feel working for a less well known company or taking a less prestigious position?
   - How would you have to redefine success related to prestige in order to achieve the work+life fit you want?

Advancement-related Success

3. Before you begin Step 3, reflect upon the importance of advancement in your definition of success.

   ■ What aspects of advancement are part of your definition of success (e.g. more responsibilities, higher rankings, bigger title, salary increases, etc.)?
   ■ What portion of your definition of success includes advancement? A lot / Half/ A little /None

At this point, do you think the importance of advancement in your definition will help or hinder your ability to find a better work+life fit? Why?

   ■ Who or what influenced the importance of advancement in your definition of success?
   ■ How open are you to reducing the importance of advancement in your definition of success if it meant having the work+life fit you currently want? Very open / Maybe / Not open
   ■ Why?
   ■ How would it feel not to advance or to step back? How would it feel if someone else you know advanced and you didn't or if someone were assigned a high-profile project and you weren't?
   ■ How would you have to redefine success related to advancement in order to achieve the work+life fit you want?

Caregiving-related Success

4. Before you begin Step 3, reflect upon your definition of a successful caregiver, whether it's caring for children or an elder.

   ■ What portion of your time and energy is required to be a "successful" caregiver (approximately what percentage)?
   ■ How do you define being a successful caregiver?

- Who or what influenced how much of your time and energy you believe is required to be considered a "successful" caregiver?
- At this point, do you think your definition of a successful caregiver will help or hinder your ability to find a better work+life fit? Why?
- How would you have to redefine success related to caregiving in order to achieve the work+life fit you want?

Any Other Definitions of Success

5. Are there other aspects of your definition of success that we haven't examined?

   - If yes, what are they?
   - Take each of these aspects and complete the same exercises that helped you define money-, prestige-, caregiving-, and advancement-related success above.

6. At this point, list all of the ways that you have redefined success. Refer frequently to this new definition of success as you start Step 3 and begin creating, implementing, and negotiating your new work+life fit. If you find yourself stuck, go back to your definition and make sure that you are embracing your new belief and that it matches the work+life fit you want.

7. Compile stories, articles, and anecdotes of people who redefined success and achieved their unique vision of a better work+life fit. Use this as a source of inspiration if you are finding that you need to redefine or expand your definition of success in order to achieve your goal.

EXERCISES TO COMPLETE *DURING* STEP 3
WHEN YOU HIT A SUCCESS ROADBLOCK

Remember, you can hit a success roadblock at any time throughout Step 3, so don't be discouraged if you have to revisit these exercises as well as the exercises above numerous times.

1. Review your work+life vision as described in your workbook. Now compare your vision to your picture and description of success from the beginning exercise.

   - Does your vision match your definition of success as depicted in the picture and the description?
   - If not, where is the mismatch? What aspect of your definition of success do you have to redefine in order to circumvent this road-block?
   - Depending upon which aspect of success is causing the problem, revisit the appropriate strategy sections in this chapter.

2. Draw a new picture of success as you are defining it in order to match and affirm your new work+life vision. To reinforce and remind you of this redefinition, post your picture prominently in your office or home.

3. To further clarify your redefinition, describe your picture in detail in writing. Compare your definition to your vision to confirm their compatibility.

4. Go back to the new definition of success you compiled in Exercise #6 and make sure that it's compatible with your vision.

The Fear Roadblock

10

I was once part of a corporate work/life consulting project in which more than 100 employees who successfully found a better way to fit work into their lives were interviewed. We asked them what advice they would give to others. Much of their advice reinforces the strategies put forth in this book, such as redefining success, making the business case, and taking the lead on your own behalf to find the work+life fit you need. But many also added, "Tell them to just go for it." Go for it. Sounds like something you'd say to someone who's about to jump off the high dive or climb a mountain for the first time. What exactly were these people trying to say?

Well, they've been in your position—wanting a better work+life fit, but feeling very afraid. And they know that it feels like a leap into the unknown. But they also know that once you have a well-thought-out proposal, then you have to "get past the fear and just do it." They want you to know that it's worth taking the risk.

Now, I'm not saying the fears you encounter throughout the process aren't very real. They are. But if those 100+ employees, and countless others I've met and worked with are an example, fears can be overcome. And hopefully it helps to know that others were fearful before they achieved their goal, but they did it anyway.

It takes courage to seek a better work+life fit because it means saying "no" to certain things, such as "no" to a certain lifestyle, to a promotion, to a project, or to a meeting. And that can be scary, especially when no one else around you is doing anything similar. But as Mark Twain so wisely counseled, "Courage is the mastery of fear, not the absence of fear." An arrangement that resolves your work/life conflict and makes you—imagine this—actually happy is indeed worth mastering your fear. Again, it may not be easy, but the goal of this book is to make it manageable.

The primary work+life fear is the fear of the unknown, because in many cases you may not know anyone who has pursued a work+life fit like the one you want; therefore, it's tough to visualize an outcome before you begin. For example, if you're a father, a childless employee, or someone who wants to work during retirement, there may not be many visible role models for you. Historically, the role models have been working mothers. While I can assure you that role models do exist in all of these categories, they aren't common enough to reassure you that "oh if he/she can do it, then so can I."

For many, seeking a better work+life fit *will* be a bit like jumping off the high dive or climbing a mountain. But those who went before you charted their course without the benefit of any guide or framework to assist them. You have the Three Steps put forth in this book. I've included as many role models as possible, and a wide variety of work/life circumstances, so perhaps you will see yourself somewhere in these pages.

Fear Roadblock Red Flags

Fear roadblocks can take many forms and emerge at any time along your work+life fit journey. But the red flags that signal roadblock ahead fall into two categories: "what ifs" and "yes, buts." Sound familiar? And sometimes they're actually said together as in, "Yes, but what if my manager says 'no'?"

Fear is not always a negative. It can be a helpful gauge of how ready you are to make the changes necessary to achieve your goal. Bob Greene, the author of *Make the Connection* (better known to many as Oprah's personal trainer) always interviews his new clients. If he hears "yes, but" three times, he will question whether or not they're ready to do the hard work neccessary to achieve their goals.

As you embark on the work+life fit journey, if you find yourself mired in "yes, buts" and/or "what ifs," you might step back and reconsider whether you're ready to gather your courage and take the risks. If the answer is "no," that's okay. Maybe you aren't in enough work/life conflict to make it worthwhile. I've found the following to be absolutely true: no pain, no change. While it's better not to wait until your work/life conflict becomes too painful to ignore, some people wait to make a change until they have no other choice. But if you truly aren't ready at this time, step back from the process and take a break. Revisit it when you are ready.

However, if you *are* ready to do whatever is necessary, you know you're going to encounter fear roadblocks along the way. The question is how do you bypass them?

Strategies to Bypass the Fear Roadblock

Strategy #1: Create a solid, well-thought-out proposal in which you can have confidence.

This is the work of Step 3. By completing the process, you emerge with a work+life fit that's compatible with the work and personal realities most critical to its success. The confidence comes from knowing that you've created a work+life fit with the greatest likelihood of succeeding.

Strategy #2: Challenge the fear to determine if it's based on facts or assumptions.

Challenging your fears involves answering the following questions:

- ► What is your fear?
- ► Is this fear based on facts or on assumptions? In other words, do you have concrete facts to back up your fear or do you only have assumptions based on gossip, rumor, or conjecture?
- ► If it's based on unsubstantiated assumptions, gather your courage and move forward continuing toward your goal.
- ► If it's fact-based (you have solid facts to support your fear), challenge it again by asking how might the facts of your situation make the outcome different and more positive for you?
- ► If you can identify a difference that works in your favor, gather your courage and move forward.
- ► If you can't, challenge the fear once again. Ask yourself if it's worth trying to have a better work+life fit even if someone else may have failed or is there a more appealing alternative you haven't considered? That alternative may include leaving.

Strategy #3: Dig down deep into yourself, find the courage, and go for it.

Recognizing that you've hit a fear roadblock is the first step. Do I hear a "what if" or a "yes, but" from you? Once you've hit it, complete strategy #1, creating a solid proposal that you can confidently propose, and then follow strategy #2, challenging the fear to determine if it's based on fact or assumption. But that may not be quite enough. In the end, it often comes down to courage. Courage to be the first to ask. Courage to risk having to make another change someday when your circumstances change. Courage to look inside yourself, learning all that you can and honoring it.

Ask yourself, "Is it worth it to spend even one minute of life miserable, not living the life I was meant to live?" But no one is going to roll out the red carpet and hold your hand. I hope the information in this book will help, but you need to make it happen. Don't wait until you feel no fear, because you will wait forever. Gather your courage, challenge your fear, and continue on your journey toward a better work+life fit.

LINDA'S STORY

Linda, a young married woman without children, came to my workshop because she was searching for a better way to fit her very demanding finance job into her life. Not only did she travel but she worked long hours.

We talked for a while and she admitted that the tasks of her job would accommodate leaving the office earlier a couple nights a week, and she could still easily meet her goal for billable hours. She also admitted that most of the long hours were due to a corporate culture that said long hours equaled hard work even though people spent a lot of time goofing off.

I then asked her, "Do you really want to be doing this job?"

And she answered, "You know, I'm really afraid to ask myself that question, because I'm not sure I know what the answer will be and I'm afraid of where it might lead and of the changes I may have to make."

Linda's Strategy: Moving Beyond Fear

Linda's fears are not unusual. Believe it or not, the fear of introspection is a big roadblock for many people. You hit it at the very beginning of Step 3 when you must ask the most critical work+life fit question: How do I want work to fit into my life?

Answering this question requires a level of introspection that's new for many people. It might be the first time you ever asked yourself how you consciously want work to fit into your life as a whole.

You're probably more accustomed to unconsciously letting work be what it is, then jamming and cramming your personal life in where you see tiny openings of time and energy. Looking inside for your answer is a completely different approach and it can seem scary. What if you find out something you didn't know—or maybe knew deep down and didn't *want* to know?

But let's look at how you might use the fear roadblock bypass strategy if you encounter this fear of introspection and where it might lead.

► What is your fear?

Your fear is that if you start to think about the work+life fit you really want that you will discover something that you didn't know. And this discovery will force you to make life-altering changes.

► Is this fear based on fact or assumptions?

Until you actually start the process and begin to see where it leads, this fear can only be based on assumptions about what *might* happen. How can you know the facts until you begin? Plus, you are unique. Some choose to make drastic changes after reflecting upon how they wanted work to fit into their lives. But it doesn't necessarily mean you will. However, let's assume you still fear the outcome of introspection.

► Ask yourself whether there are mitigating factors that would make your situation different.

There are a couple of very important points to be made here. First, you *always* have 100% control over the choices you make. You may not be able to control your circumstances, but you do control your choices. What does that mean? For Linda, it meant that after a period of long, hard thinking about her true work+life vision, she realized that she really wanted to be a self-employed artist who paints murals in people's homes.

This realization scared her because it was such a big leap from her current situation, and seemed so completely overwhelming. But here's the reality: She doesn't have to leap into that new scenario right now.

She can take her time and implement a work+life fit to-day that's more comfortable and less scary knowing what her ultimate goal is down the road (remember Work+Life Fit Fundamental #2). Maybe for a year, she cuts back her week-end hours and uses the time to paint and build up her port-folio. Again, she has 100% control over her choices.

My second point is that self-reflection and self-knowledge are *never* bad. You can't ever know too much about yourself, especially if your goal is happiness in all areas of your life.

In Step 3, you'll learn more about using the mind, body, spirit tools in order to listen to your internal guidance and find your desired work+life fit. Unfortunately, the process of looking inward for answers rather than outward is new for many people. And the information you unearth about what you really want, what you love, and what your strengths and weaknesses are can almost seem like meeting a stranger. But remember, how you choose to respond to it is up to you.

Work/life-related fears are so varied and particular to each situa-tion and experience that it's difficult to use them all to illustrate how the three bypass strategies work. But let's look at three of the most common fears to see how this process might play out for you.

Fear #1: I'm afraid they will say "no."

Hopefully, Work+Life Fit Fundamental #3 empowered you to at least ask your manager for a six-month trial period. But, because this fear is so pervasive, let's use it to walk through the bypass strategy just to reinforce the concept.

▶ What is your fear?
My manager will say "no" to my request for a new work+life fit even though I made sure the arrangement takes my needs *and* the needs of the business into consideration.

▶ Is this fear based on facts or on assumptions? Do you have concrete examples of your manager either turning down a request or specifically saying he or she wouldn't support a change in work+life fit?

In some cases, the answer will be "no, I haven't actually seen anyone turned down. I just assumed the answer would be 'no,'" and you'll gather your courage and continue on to the next step in the work+life fit process.

If the answer is yes, can you identify any facts that would make your work+life fit different from that of the colleague who was turned down, making your proposal more worthy of support? For example, did your colleague have an equally well-thought-out, business-oriented proposal? Or was it presented as an informal, "right thing to do"? If the answer is "no, they didn't have a formal proposal," then gather your courage and, again, move on to the next step having confidence in the strength of your proposal.

What if the answer is "yes, my colleague did have a solid proposal and was still turned down"? What do you do? Well, this presents a more difficult situation.

▶ Ask yourself whether any *other* factors might make your proposal more palatable than your colleague's: Is your work+life fit more applicable to your type of job? Are you a better, more experienced performer than your colleague, and thus more valued by the company?

Hopefully, you will find a way to differentiate your request and continue toward your goal. But let's assume that you can't. What do you do? We will cover this in detail in Step 3, but you need to consider your alternatives. Will you leave if you can't find a better work+life fit? If the answer is yes, that brings us to the crux of the fear roadblock:

Why not ask if you are going to leave anyway?!

What do you have to lose? The worst-case scenario is that you end up doing what you had planned to do anyway—leave. Being willing to walk away if you don't get what you want is the strongest negotiating position you can be in.

Long ago I lost count of the number of people who have said to me, "Oh, I just left instead of asking for a better work+life fit." Wouldn't it have been worth taking a chance and asking? Most likely your manager would have surprised you and said "yes" to a six-month trial period. If you like your job, like your manager, like your colleagues, like your company, and like making money, wouldn't it be worthwhile to find a work+life fit that allowed you to stay? It's definitely easier than starting all over at a new organization. Think about it.

That's why you need to ask. Again, the worst thing that your manager can say is "no." And even then, "no" might not be the end of the negotiation. It might simply mean you have to adjust some aspect of your proposal, and then your manager will approve it.

But let's assume that "no" means "no" and the discussion is over. Then your manager has given you the gift of "no." Yes, that's right, the gift of "no."

As we've already discussed, "no" is a gift because it allows you to know exactly where you stand. Your options become clear. You either keep things the way that they are, or you move on. You can't get much clearer than that. And clarity of any kind is a gift.

Fear #2: What if my commitment is questioned or I lose my job because of my work+life fit?

This fear is another common one, because you wouldn't be human if you didn't question the potential impact of changing the way you work. But this fear can have a positive effect. It can motivate you to make sure that your job and your work+life fit are compatible because you don't want your commitment questioned and you definitely don't want to lose your job.

But left unchallenged, this fear can keep you from pursuing your goal; therefore, you must also ask yourself the following questions:

▶ What is your fear?

I'm afraid that if I propose a new work+life fit, my commitment to the company will be questioned or worse, I could lose my job.

▶ Is this fear based on fact or on assumptions? Do you have concrete evidence to suggest that your commitment would be questioned or that you could lose your job if you asked?

If the answer is "no, I don't have any evidence that my commitment will be questioned or that I could lose my job," then gather your courage and skip to the next step in the process.

If the answer is "yes, I've actually seen the commitment of others who have sought more flexibility questioned, and I've seen someone lose their job because of it," then face that reality. Unfortunately, especially in organizations where flexibility is rare, it's not unusual to initially have your commitment questioned, particularly if you want to work less than full-time.

Thankfully, I've never seen a request for a new work+life fit result in an immediate termination. If after the arrangement is implemented it happens, usually there are other problems with personal or corporate performance that prompt the dismissal.

However, if there were a need to end the arrangement, most likely what would happen is that you would be asked to resume a regular, full-time, in-the-office schedule. And you'd then face the decision whether or not you want to stay under these new terms.

But the best thing to do is face these realities up front and ask youself if you can think of any mitigating factors that would make your request less likely to cause your commitment to be questioned or make you less likely to lose your job.

If the answer is "yes," then continue with the process and incorporate those strategies to make your work+life fit different. For example:

I will communicate more effectively with my boss and colleagues than others with a similar arrangement may have in order to avoid misperceptions about my commitment. I will demonstrate that I'm not only doing my job but am still engaged, and will make sure to go that extra mile from time to time—e.g., come in on my day off for a meeting—in order to reinforce my commitment.

I will emphasize my excellent performance history and the way that I add value to the business. Because even though the person who lost his job telecommuted two days a week, he had other performance problems that most likely caused his termination. I do not.

What if the answer is "no, I can't think of any mitigating factors; therefore, chances are that my commitment will be questioned and I may lose my job"? Again, there are unfortunately still companies where, in spite of your best efforts, any deviation from the culturally sanctioned work schedule immediately calls into question your dedication and puts your job at risk. If you've determined that this is your reality, you still have a couple of choices:

Decide that it's good enough that *you* know you're committed and propose your arrangement anyway. This is especially true if you are willing to leave if you aren't able to resolve your conflict. Then spend the first six months of your arrangement proving that having a different work+ life fit doesn't mean your commitment to the company changes. In fact, it means just the opposite. You are even more committed because you are trying to find a way to stay at the company while meeting your personal responsibilities.

If you fear losing your job simply because you *ask* for a better way to fit work into your life, do you really want to work at your company or for your manager? You need to seriously consider this point. I know it's tough to hear, but maybe you need to first change the company and/or the manager for whom you work, and *then* change the way you work.

Fear #3: What if my new work+life fit fails?

Another common fear is that your new work+life fit will fail in some way. Challenging this fear requires the following steps:

- ▶ What is your fear?

  Your fear is that your work+life fit won't work and you'll have to give it up.
- ▶ Is this fear based on fact or on assumptions?

  The answer to this question is simply that until you actually implement some sort of new arrangement and see how it goes, this fear can only be based on untested assumptions. Just like the saying goes, you never know until you try.
- ▶ But again, because this fear is so pervasive, let's assume that you believe this fear is real. "Yes," you say, "I saw a colleague implement a new arrangement and then give it up. Clearly, it failed."

Remember, what may look like failure to you may not be failure for someone else. As you learned from Work+Life Fit Fundamental #7, the realities in your work and your personal life will change, and as a result your work+life fit will have to change too. Maybe that person didn't fail, but instead, unknown to you, his circumstances simply changed and the arrangement he had was no longer viable.

Time and again, I've seen people implement one work+life fit and then a year later decide they want something different even though their arrangement was technically succeeding. You just don't know what's really going on in someone else's life.

▶ Can you think of any mitigating factors that would make your work+life fit less likely to fail? Is your proposal better suited to the type of job you have? Can you identify some of the reasons the other person's work+life fit may have failed (e.g., they didn't manage the arrangement responsibly, didn't discuss it with the work group, didn't communicate well with the manager)? Perhaps you can learn from the mistakes of others and do things differently.

▶ If the answer is "yes," then gather your courage and move on.

▶ However, what if the answer is "no, I can't think of anything that differentiates my request or would make it more likely to succeed"?

Then you're back to the tough decisions about whether or not your job is worth sacrificing the rest of your life for. And again, if you decide to leave if you aren't able to find a better work+life fit, then ask anyway. You have nothing to lose.

EXERCISES

1. As you proceed through the Work+Life Fit Process in Step 3, use the bypass strategy to challenge the fears that you encounter:

■ As you begin to clarify and implement your desired work+life fit, keep track of any fears that emerge in your workbook. What is your fear?

■ Is this fear based on concrete fact or unproven assumptions? In other words, do you have concrete facts to back up your fear (not assumptions based on gossip, rumor, and conjecture)?

■ If it's based only on assumptions, gather your courage and move forward.

■ If it's based on solid facts, challenge it again by asking how your situation might differ in ways that could result in a more positive outcome.

- If you can identify a difference that works in your favor, gather your courage and move forward.
- If you can't, challenge the fear again. Ask yourself if it's worth trying to move forward even if someone else may have failed, or is there a more appealing alternative you haven't considered? That alternative may include leaving.

2. Use the mind, body, spirit tools in chapter 14 to help you identify fears, to discern whether they are real or imagined, and to bypass them.

3. If you need additional information and exercises to help you overcome fear, read *Fight Your Fear and Win* by Don Greene, Ph.D.

The Resistance 11 Roadblock

Finding a new work+life fit means change. Change not only for you but also for those around you, both personally and professionally. And it's the odd person who loves change. Most of us resist it. You never hear anyone say, "Yeah, change!" This is the source of the resistance roadblock: You don't seek or continue with a new work+life fit because you experience resistance from within yourself and from others.

Resistance Roadblock Red Flags

As is the case with the other roadblocks, certain catchphrases can be red flags that you're approaching or you've hit a resistance roadblock. In this case, beware of: "This can't be done," "What do I think I am doing?" and "Am I nuts?" These are the kinds of things you may find yourself—or others—saying when comparing your new, well-thought-out work+life fit with what is considered rational. Again, you—and others—are seeing limitations instead of possibilities.

Can you change your work+life fit? Yes. Should you think of doing it? Yes. Are you nuts? No, as long as you put in the time and thought to make sure your arrangement benefits you and the business. Resist the resistance.

External Resistance

How likely is it that you will experience resistance to your work+life fit from your manager or coworkers? Of the more than 100 employees interviewed as part of a corporate work/life consulting project who successfully changed their work+life fit, a majority felt supported by both their manager and their coworkers. Their experience mirrors that of countless others I've worked with over the years who say with surprise, "You know I've been leaving at 4:00 P.M. (or working from home or not working one day a week, etc.) and no one has said a word."

The fear that someone, either your boss or coworkers, will challenge your work+life fit is greater than the reality it will actually happen. I'm going to repeat this important point: Most likely no one will have trouble with your work+life fit. So don't let this fear keep you from moving forward.

That said, if you do experience that rare case of external resistance, it's usually attributable to one of two things: jealousy or feeling out of the loop. We'll call the source of the resistance "the resister." He may not even know it, and may deny it to his dying day, but when someone comments on your work+life fit it usually means that person would like to do the very same thing. However, for whatever reason—fear, laziness, apathy—he's unwilling to do the work.

SHERI'S STORY

Sheri is a manager for a large retail company and a mother of three children. When I met her for the first time, she was about six months into a new work+life fit arrangement. She arrived at 7 A.M. and left work at 4 P.M. Monday through Thursday, and she took Fridays off but was available by phone in case something came up.

She had done everything right. She sat down with her team prior to starting her new hours to discuss whether they had any concerns. She shared her schedule with her internal clients *and* with her external clients. Despite all this, there was still one colleague who, every day at 4 P.M. when Sheri walked out the door said, "Half day?" She'd hit a resistance roadblock.

Sheri's Strategy:
Resisting the Resistance

How does Sheri handle this? She has a couple of options for resisting his resistance. First, ask the person why he has the problem. If he will admit that it's because he too would like a better work+life fit, then she could offer to share with him the process she went through.

If he thinks her arrangement is negatively affecting his ability to get his job done, then she should offer to sit down and try to resolve the oversight.

If neither of these approaches works, ignoring the resister is the best strategy. As long as you, your manager, and the rest of your team are on the same page, that's all you need to be concerned about. Who knows, maybe someday the success of Sheri's work+life fit will inspire the resister to get past his roadblocks and implement his own vision.

Sheri knew the only way around this roadblock was to look at the resister's possible motivations and challenge them one by one in order to embrace and to reaffirm her new work+life fit. She decided the reasons for his resistance were:

▶ On some level, he doesn't think mothers should work, but also I think he's jealous because he does talk about wanting to spend less time at work but doesn't have the nerve to ask.

▶ He thinks that my arrangement will make his job more difficult.

Then she challenged them:

▶ It doesn't matter what he thinks about working mothers because my boss and the rest of the team support my arrangement. As far as wanting more flexibility himself, if the opportunity ever arises, I'll try to engage him in a conversation about how and why I found a different work+life fit.

▶ He was at the meeting where our boss and I presented my arrangement to the team and I asked if they had constructive concerns about how it may affect their ability to do their jobs. A couple of concerns were offered and I addressed them. But he said nothing, so I need to assume that his work is not negatively affected until he says something.

The exercise helped her to depersonalize his comments and to bypass the resistance the comments created. Thankfully, Sheri is also the type of self-confident person who isn't willing to let someone else's issues derail her. In fact, when I asked her recently how she was handling it, she laughed, "Oh, I've started to tease him when he arrives two hours after I do at 9 A.M., 'Sleep late?' I realize as long as my boss is fine with what I'm doing and as long as I'm open to my teammates constructive concerns related to their work, I need to ignore his comments. Because I know they have nothing to do with me."

The second type of resister emerges when you haven't considered the feelings of your team or your partner in the formulation of your arrangement. A colleague in your work group has every right to comment about your work+life fit if she wasn't given the opportunity to voice any concerns about your arrangement's affect on her workload.

And if the terms and conditions of the arrangement were never discussed, she's bound to feel justifiably out of the loop.

Your partner or spouse also has every right to resist your work+life fit if it conflicts with his or her work or personal reality in a detrimental way. Combining the goals of your work+life fit with those of your partner is a critical, yet mostly overlooked, step. Historically, efforts to resolve work/life conflict focused on the individual, and never considered the needs of the business or the partner. All that mattered was that *your* personal realities and expectations were compatible with your new vision. But the truth is that your plan must also be compatible with your partner's expectations and realities if you want it to succeed. Again, the trick is to acknowledge the differences and work through a compromise with your partner.

This is why Step 3 of the Work+Life Fit process considers all of the relevant parties potentially affected by your arrangement—work group, clients, spouses, or partners. The goal is to avoid any mismatch of expectations and thus reduce the likelihood you will experience any external resistance.

Internal Resistance

Many people think the resistance that they experience from others is the most challenging, when in fact I believe that the resistance from inside yourself can be more insidious and create the largest roadblocks. While external resistance occurs less frequently than you might imagine, it's easier to identify because it's more overt; you hear the words or you see the actions. But your internal resistance is stealthy and sneaky, cloaking itself in the cape of rationality.

In other words, when you start to make a change, you search for ways to confirm that your path is "rational." But maybe by comparison to what other people are doing, it isn't. Maybe no one else you know is seeking a work+life fit just like yours. Does that mean you shouldn't do it? No. As long as you've carefully thought through all of the relevant work and personal realities, your decision is rational. What you're really resisting is a change in the status quo. You're seeing only the limitations rather than the possibilities.

The other source of internal resistance can be the feeling that you don't deserve a better work+life fit. In other words, you buy into the myth that life and work are hard. "Work is what it is, and I just have to deal with it." When the truth is that you do deserve to find the best way possible to fit work into your life. Will it mean some hard work, some risk, and some difficult choices? Yes, but remember you can take as much time as you need to work through the process. And you *do* deserve it.

BILL'S STORY

One of my responsibilities at FWI was coordinating the program for the Conference Board's Work and Family Conference. Every year it was an opportunity to bring together some of the world's leading academics and work/life practitioners.

As we were putting together the list of potential speakers, I happened to read an article on the front page of *The Wall Street Journal* about one of President Clinton's top domestic policy advisers. His recent resignation in order to "spend more time with my son" was causing quite a commotion. The adviser's name was Bill Galston.

Thinking that he would be perfect for our fatherhood panel, I decided to track him down. While he was thrilled to be asked, he confessed that he was shocked by how much attention his very personal decision was receiving.

He explained that his position in the Clinton administration represented the culmination of years of hard work, as well as an opportunity to influence policies that were meaningful to him and would hopefully help a lot of people. But it also required long hours and a tremendous amount of energy both during the week and often on weekends.

He would sometimes bring his son who was about 12 years old

back to the office after dinner to "visit" while he worked. Although he knew the situation wasn't optimal, he had no idea how badly it was affecting his son until he received a letter.

The little boy had written to his dad about their mutual love of baseball and how "baseball just isn't as much fun without a dad." As he read his son's words, Bill knew that as much as he loved his job, work wasn't fitting into his life the way he wanted it to. He needed a better work+life fit because his son was only going to be young and want to play baseball with him once. That was too precious to miss.

Bill's Strategy: Embrace Change

The strategy for bypassing the resistance roadblock is simple: Embrace change. Embrace all of its ambiguity, embrace all of its discomfort, embrace all of its possibilities and challenges, especially if the status quo is making you unhappy.

So how do you do it? If you know in your heart of hearts that your work+life fit is right, then you resist the resistance and embrace the change that you've chosen.

The story of Bill Galston is a perfect illustration of how embracing the change enables you to overcome even the most overwhelming resistance—mostly from within yourself but also from others.

At first he considered trying to reduce his hours but changed his mind after determining that the workaholic culture of the White House precluded such an option.

So after much soul-searching, he decided to take a faculty position at the University of Maryland. While it did not offer the prestige or power of his White House job, it was interesting work and it gave him the time and energy he needed for his son. Bill emphasized that his decision was not easy, but he knew that it was right.

Now, think for a moment. Imagine the resistance roadblocks that someone like Bill Galston encountered when he made this decision to leave his prestigious, once-in-a-lifetime, powerful position as economic policy adviser to the president of the United States in order to spend more time playing baseball with his son.

He admitted that he experienced tremendous resistance from within himself. Not only was he walking away from a position that he had worked his entire professional life to achieve, but he also was making a choice few if any of his colleagues in similar positions had ever made. He spent a lot of time thinking, "I must be crazy to do this."

Then there was the external resistance. Probably because "no one in their right mind would walk away from a White House job for his kid," news of his decision filled the front pages of national newspapers like *The Wall Street Journal* and *The New York Times*. Imagine if the wisdom of your decision to work four ten-hour days instead of five eight-hour days was challenged in the national media? Talk about a resistance roadblock the size of Mount Everest. That's on top of the resistance he must have experienced from his colleagues and from the President himself. Do you think you would hold up against a resistance roadblock in the form of the President of the United States?

But with the courage of his conviction, Bill Galston left the White House and is now a professor and ball-playing father to his son. Ironically, he told me the attention his story received had made him a symbol of working fathers, and he was flooded with requests for interviews and conference appearances. These new demands had the potential to keep him as busy as he had been in the White House. The irony made him laugh, but he had resisted resistance, embraced change, and knew in his heart that the work+life fit he'd chosen was right for him.

* * *

You now have two examples—one extreme, but very inspiring, and one more common but also thought-provoking—of not only the types of resistance you will experience, but also how to bypass them.

The best response to resistance is to assume it most likely will not come from others but from within yourself. And use it as a way to reflect upon your work+life fit, embracing the change you've worked so hard to accomplish and reaffirming your commitment to your choice. "Yeah, change!"

More Stories to Help You Move Beyond Resistance Roadblocks

As Sheri's and Bill's stories illustrate, you can resist the resistance and embrace change. The following stories hopefully will inspire you to do the same.

ANNA'S STORY

Anna is a mother of two small children. After her first child was born, she continued to work full-time even though she would've preferred to reduce her schedule or to telecommute part-time. Frankly, she didn't think she had any other option, because her boss, Joan, essentially worked 10-hour days, six days a week. And even though she never made Anna feel like she had to work more than the 45 hours a week she put in, Anna just felt that she would never support any type of flexibility.

Then Anna had her second child and decided that if she had to, she would leave in order to have more time for her now expanded personal responsibilities. This is when a friend suggested that Anna meet with me before she quit.

We talked, and Anna admitted that she would like to find a way to work three days a week if she could. However, she explained, "Joan will never go for it. You see, Joan has basically worked over 60 hours a week for 20 years. During that time she raised two sons and willingly sacrificed a lot of her time with them. I'm just not ready to make that same sacrifice."

I challenged her thinking. "Anna, do you *know* that Joan won't support it or do you just *think* that? And, if faced with the choice of either losing you completely or helping you work three days a week, which option do you think she would choose as a smart businesswoman?"

She thought for a minute. "You know, I don't know that she won't say yes, and I don't think she wants to lose me because I do know my job cold."

I added however, "Don't be surprised if, as part of the discussion, Joan brings up the fact that she sacrificed a great deal to get where she did in her career. If this happens, don't get defensive thinking it's a lack of support, because most likely she's simply stating what her reality was. Acknowledge it and then directly ask for her support to help you do it differently."

The next week Anna presented her proposal. Joan looked it over and paused. "Gosh, I would never have dreamed of asking for anything like this when my boys were little. It was just unheard of. You either worked or you didn't, and I guess on some level, I chose to make the sacrifice but basically we had no choice." Anna thought about what we discussed and instead of interpreting Joan's comments as a lack of support, she listened respectfully and said, "You know Joan, I can appreciate the sacrifices you've made. It must have been really hard. But it paved the way for women like me to have the ability to do things differently, and I would really appreciate your support for this proposal because it makes sense not only for me but for the business."

Joan reflected for a moment. "Okay, let's give it a shot. You seem to have accounted for all of the changes in your tasks and responsibilities. However, I would feel more comfortable if I knew I could reach you on cell phone during the two days you were out of the office in case there were any problems."

Anna nodded. "Sounds fair."

As she was leaving, Joan said, "You know I'm glad you decided to ask instead of just quitting."

"I am too," replied Anna.

JAMIE'S STORY

As more fathers begin to make work+life choices that are different from the traditional work/life paradigm, they will have to deal with resistance from within themselves and from others who will question what they are doing. I met Jamie when he took his daughter to a dance class that I attended with my daughter. As the only dad in a group of twelve moms, Jamie was hard not to notice, especially since he was one of the parents who seemed to be having the most fun. Curious about the work/life reality that allowed him to attend this class, I introduced myself and asked him about his story. He explained that, two years ago, he had been laid off from the graphics firm that he worked for full-time for seven years. "I was devastated," he said, "but after a couple of months, I realized that I was getting the same amount of money freelancing four days a week as I had working full-time. Plus, I was spending one day a week on average with Mariah. And I loved it. My wife works three 12-hour shifts a week as a nurse; therefore, she gets benefits so I didn't have to worry."

He continued, "Then about six months ago, a former colleague called to invite me into a partnership with three other people from my old firm. I thought it about it for a couple of days, and even though I thought it was crazy, I passed up the opportunity. I called and said 'no thanks,' because I knew that it would mean going back to long hours and I would miss my day with Mariah. I just wasn't interested in that right now. You know, it's funny, but my former colleague still can't believe my answer. He called the other day just to say, 'Are you sure?' I said 'yes' but I am always interested in any freelance work you may have. And the next day he sent me a project. The best of both worlds!" With that, he grabbed Mariah's hand, and they headed to the playground.

EXERCISES

1. Create a file of articles or stories about people who made changes in their lives despite resistance from within themselves and from others. Take special note of the strategy they used to resist the resistance.

2. Reflect back on a time in your life when you faced another major change. On a piece of paper, write the following:

   - What was that change?
   - What resistance did you experience related to that change?
   - What would your life have been like had you allowed the resistance to keep you from making that change?

- What was the strategy you used to bypass the resistance and continue toward your goal?

3. As you complete Step 3, use this exercise any time you need help resisting resistance—whether it's internal or external.

  - Describe the resistance you're experiencing (e.g., I am feeling that this can't be done; I am crazy to do this; I can't do this).
  - Divide a piece of paper into two columns. On top of the first column, write a description of the resistance from above (e.g., I am crazy to do this).
  - On top of the second column, write "Embrace Change."
  - In column one, list all the reasons that you are crazy for seeking a better work+life fit. For example:
    I am crazy because . . .
    - no one ever does this on my team;
    - I won't be able to find a nanny part-time;
    - I'll never get my company to cover all of the expenses of telecommuting.
  - In column two, challenge each of the reasons you listed in column one. For example:
    I am not crazy because . . .
    - no one may have done it before, but there's always a first for everything. The worst they can say is "no";
    - I've looked in the paper and I see plenty of ads for part-time caregivers so there must be some out there somewhere;
    - I will propose a business case to support my request, and if any company doesn't pay for all of it, I will consider paying for part of it.

4. As you experience resistance at any point in the process, refer back to the mind, body, spirit tools in chapter 14 to help reconnect to your internal guidance and bypass the roadblock.

The In-the-Box-Thinking
Roadblock

C ali, it can't be done in my job. It's too closely related to the stock market to allow any schedule other than in the office, five days a week, from 8:30 A.M. to 4:00 P.M. It just can't be done any other way." For the past four years, I've had the same conversation with Suzanne. On her quest for a better work+life fit, she is constantly thwarted by the same thing: the in-the-box-thinking roadblock.

You hit the in-the-box-thinking roadblock when you find yourself unable to think beyond either the traditional definition of "work," or the five standard definitions of flexible work arrangements in order to create a new work+life fit.

By the traditional definition of "work," I mean the in-the-office, five-days-a-week, eight-hours-a-day model upon which corporate America was built. Yes, you need to consider the tasks of your job and how they can be done with a new work+life fit. But there are 24 hours in every day and there are seven days in every week. Use them.

It isn't only the definition of work that gets in the way. Ironically, it can also be the definition of flexibility. Companies have made a lot of headway over the past 10 years implementing policies defining and supporting the five standard flexible work arrangements:

- ▶ **Part-time:** a schedule less than the standard 40-hour work-week
- ▶ **Flextime:** hours that differ from the standard 9 A.M. to 5 P.M. workday
- ▶ **Job-sharing:** sharing a 40-hour workweek with someone, whereby each person works either two and a half or three days a week
- ▶ **Compressed workweek:** either working 80 hours in nine days (nine-hour days) and taking the tenth day off or working 40 hours in four days and taking the fifth day off
- ▶ **Telecommuting:** working from a remote location

Unfortunately, when trying to think creatively about how you want work to fit into your life, it's easy to get stuck thinking that you have to pick one of those five options exactly as they are defined. But, as we discussed earlier in the book, that contradicts one of the key findings of the work/life research, which is that many of the most successful work+life fit arrangements are a creative combination of two or three types of flexibility.

In-the-Box-Thinking Roadblock Red Flags

As with the other roadblocks, if you find yourself saying the following words, it's a red flag that either you are approaching or have hit an in-the-box-thinking roadblock. The words of warning are: "My job just simply will not allow me to work differently."

You are convinced your work can only be done within the traditional schedule. Or you think you can only use one of the five traditional flexible work arrangements exactly as they are typically defined, but the tasks and responsibilities of your job won't accommodate it.

Suzanne's difficulty is a perfect example. Contrary to her annual protestations, people with jobs tied to the financial markets can have flexibility. I've witnessed it. They just have to be creative and think outside of the box. Her challenge is the same as it is for everyone else: to put one foot in front of the other. Test one option; if it doesn't work, try another until you find one that makes sense. But first she has to see the possibilities, rather than the limitations.

WENDY AND LESLIE'S STORY

Wendy and Leslie work on the trading desk of a large financial institution. They are both mothers of young children and want at least one day at home per week. While eating lunch together, they started talking about how much they would like to share a job, *but* the policy defines the arrangement as "two individuals working two and a half or three days per week" sharing the responsibilities and tasks of one job. Given the realities of their jobs as salespeople, they knew that they couldn't be off of the desk two days a week. So they dismissed the option as impossible. Wendy laughed, "We're smart women. There's got to be a way to attack this problem creatively."

Wendy and Leslie's Strategy: Out-of-the-Box Thinking

In order to bypass an in-the-box-thinking roadblock, you need to seek all possible combinations of hours, days, and locations in which your job can be done so that it fits into your life the way you need it to while meeting the needs of the business. There are a couple of key points to remember when you are doing this:

1. There are an infinite number of work+life fit possibilities between the extremes of 0% work and 100% work. Even the smallest change can make a difference;

2. Start small and make only a minor change in your work+life fit, if that's more comfortable for you, and build up to a more drastic work+life fit over time. Once you experience one way of changing how work fits into your life, you may begin to see more possibilities; and

3. Don't worry if it hasn't been done before. It can be harder to figure it out if you've never seen it done, but if you analyze all of the relevant work and personal realities and find they work with your proposed arrangement, go for it.

Wendy and Leslie sat down together and looked at the tasks and responsibilities of their jobs as well as the other work and personal realities that would influence the success of any arrangement they proposed. Then they formulated an unconventional job-sharing arrangement, whereby instead of each working three days a week (the standard job-sharing arrangement) each one of them works four days. Then they cover for each other on the one day each takes off.

Fast-forward six months after they implemented their new arrangement: Not only were they successful, but they are consistently ranked as two of the top producers on the floor. What makes their situation even more remarkable is that often people with jobs in trading cite the antifamily, macho corporate culture as the reason that they don't make a change. But Wendy and Leslie managed to overcome that too *and* prosper.

So, contrary to the traditional workweek of their job *and* contrary to the standard definition of job-sharing, these two women found a creative solution that worked for them.

* * *

To reinforce the importance of creativity when envisioning a new work+life fit, it helps to study situations that fail. In pursuit of "fairness," some companies try to implement one type of flexibility across an entire work group. A majority of time these arrangements are discontinued, simply because every individual's work and personal realities are unique and require creativity in terms of combining work and life.

ONE TEAM'S COMPRESSED WORKWEEK FAILURE

A team of 25 people implemented a compressed workweek schedule whereby employees could work from 9 A.M. to 6 P.M. for nine days, then take every tenth day off. While people could opt out, they weren't individually allowed to then implement a different arrangement that might work better for them.

While the intentions underlying this effort on the part of management were noble, not surprisingly the initiative was discontinued after three months. First, a number of people immediately opted out because their child-care arrangements didn't support the schedule. They needed to be at the caregiver to pick up by 6 P.M. Second, a number of people felt their jobs were better suited to being available at least part of every day. These people would have easily been able to shift their hours or work from home a day or two a week.

Again, the problem wasn't the concept of giving people access to flexibility. It was the lack of creativity associated with the creation of each individual arrangement to accommodate everyone's unique work and personal realities.

The saddest part of this situation is that now, not only do the individual employees believe "they'll never let us have flexibility," but management has lost confidence in the concept as well. Had management encouraged each employee to create an individual work+life vision rather than only offering a one-size-fits-all approach, the outcome would've been different.

More Stories to Help You Get Beyond an In-the-Box-Thinking Roadblock

Wendy and Leslie are just one example of how thinking creatively can help you get past the roadblock of in-the-box thinking in order to find a better work+life fit. Here are a few more examples of work+life creativity.

LUIS' STORY

Luis is a customer service representative for an insurance company. His desire for a better work+life fit led him to implement an arrangement whereby he arrived at 6 A.M. and left the office by 3 P.M. four days a week. On the fifth day, he worked from home.

The standard hours at his company are 9-to-5, but he looked at the tasks of his job and realized that many of his overseas clients would love to have access to him before 9 A.M. when their day is almost over. But he also wanted to have a day when he could avoid the long drive to his office, so he proposed telecommuting every Wednesday to break up the week. He creatively combined flextime and telecommuting to create a workable arrangement that met not only his needs but also the needs of the business.

Here are some creative ways that other people fit work into their lives:

- ▶ In order to meet her son after school, one woman worked 9:00 A.M. to 2:30 P.M. in the office and then 6:30 P.M. to 9:30 P.M. at home.
- ▶ The staff editor of a magazine worked from home Monday and Tuesday from 9 to 4, and in the office Wednesday, Thursday, and Friday from 10 A.M. to 11 P.M. because the workload was the greatest and most time-sensitive at the end of the week.
- ▶ A senior manager in a company took a cut in responsibilities and seniority in order to work from 8:00 A.M. to 6:00 P.M. Monday and Friday, and 1 P.M. to 7 P.M. on Tuesday, Wednesday, and Thursday in order to enjoy his young twins in the morning before they took their naps.
- ▶ A technology engineer for a large company works a compressed workweek (40 hours in four days) and telecommutes two days of the week, in order to have every other Wednesday off to attend business classes at a local college.

▶ A senior editor for a large New York-based publishing house proposed telecommuting full-time from her new home in North Carolina. She works out of her New York office one week every other month and travels to New York at other times for critical planning meetings.

EXERCISES

1. As you did with the resistance roadblock, compile stories of others who have creatively combined work and life as a source of inspiration. Newspapers, magazines, and chat rooms are full of stories of people with all different types of work/life realities. Keep a file of these stories and refer to them as a creative "jump start" if you find yourself having a hard time seeing the possibilities for resolving your own work/life conflict.

2. Test your comfort with work+life fit creativity. When you think about working in a way that is different from your standard schedule, or in a place other than your office, what's your initial response? If your initial response is "it can't be done," then you run the risk of hitting the in-the-box-thinking roadblock as you start the Work+Life Fit Process in Step 3. Spend some time before you begin Step 3, creatively thinking about work and how it might fit into your life. Answer the following question:

   ■ Imagine that you are alone in a room and no one can see or hear anything you say or do. Without censoring yourself, write down the first *three* answers that come into your head to this question: "If I could have any work+life fit I wanted, I would . . ." (List your responses in your workbook.)

If you had trouble coming up with three examples or if you feel your answers still weren't as creative as you would like, try again. And continue the exercise until you feel that you are really thinking outside of the box with regard to your work and life.

3. Exercises to complete *during* Step 3 if you find that you hit the road-block:

   - Describe your desired work+life fit as best you can at this point.
   - What part of your job do you believe conflicts with this goal?
     - Work hours
     - Days in the office
     - Tasks of your job

   - Assuming that you could change any aspect of your job, how might you creatively change the parts that you think conflict with your work+life fit?
   - Understanding the definitions of the five standard flexible work arrangements, can you see a creative combination of any of them that would give you the work+life fit that you want?

4. To jump-start your creative thinking at any point in the process, refer to the mind, body, spirit tools in chapter 14.

Step 3

The Work+Life Fit Roadmap

THE WORK+LIFE FIT ROADMAP will guide you, step-by-step, through your journey:

- ▶ First, you will create your work+life vision by figuring out exactly how you want work to fit into your life;
- ▶ Next, you'll answer the question, "Is this vision compatible with the realities in my work life and my personal life?" To do this, you'll reconsider your vision in terms of each relevant aspect of your job, then in terms of each relevant aspect of your personal life. You reconcile any incompatibility by either changing the reality or by changing your vision. The result is a final work+life fit with the greatest chance of success;
- ▶ And finally, the journey culminates with the negotiation of your proposal with your manager and the implementation of your new work+life fit.

Let yourself systematically work through the roadmap from beginning to end, and try to avoid the urge to skip ahead. If you skip ahead,

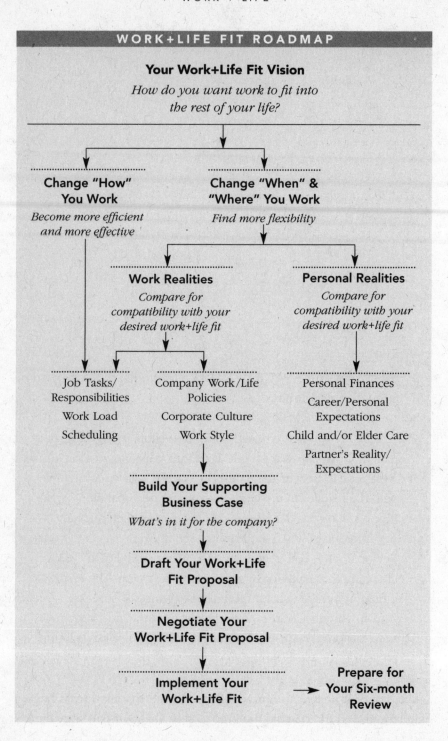

WORK+LIFE FIT ROADMAP

Your Work+Life Fit Vision

*How do you want work to fit into
the rest of your life?*

**Change "How"
You Work**

*Become more efficient
and more effective*

**Change "When" &
"Where" You Work**

Find more flexibility

Work Realities

*Compare for
compatibility with your
desired work+life fit*

Personal Realities

*Compare for
compatibility with your
desired work+life fit*

Job Tasks/
Responsibilities

Work Load

Scheduling

Company Work/Life
Policies

Corporate Culture

Work Style

Personal Finances

Career/Personal
Expectations

Child and/or Elder Care

Partner's Reality/
Expectations

**Build Your Supporting
Business Case**

What's in it for the company?

**Draft Your Work+Life
Fit Proposal**

**Negotiate Your
Work+Life Fit Proposal**

**Implement Your
Work+Life Fit**

**Prepare for
Your Six-month
Review**

you risk overlooking a reality that, unbeknownst to you, isn't compatible with your vision. And, again, having a work+life fit that is compatible with all of your relevant work and personal realities is key to the ultimate success of your final arrangement. Even if you think, "That doesn't apply to me," read the chapter anyway and review the questions at the end. Indeed, maybe that particular issue doesn't apply, but it's better to know than to be surprised and unexpectedly derailed later.

Approach each part of the Work+Life Fit Roadmap as you would any journey. You don't want to skip over any spots that lie between your starting point and your ultimate destination, because you might miss an experience that could mean the difference between a trip of a lifetime and one you can't wait to forget.

EXERCISE—THE "YES, BUT" THREE TIMES TEST

As we discussed in the fear roadblock chapter, when personal trainer Bob Greene works with a new client, if he hears "yes, but" three times during their initial discussion, he asks them to reconsider whether they're truly ready to address their diet and fitness issues. Success depends not only on effort, but also on commitment and belief. The same holds true for achieving your desired work+life fit.

- Set aside a page in your workbook entitled "yes, but."
- As you work through the roadmap, keep track of when and how often you find yourself saying "yes, but."
- Reflect upon what's making you hesitate. For example, "Yes, but my husband won't support me," "Yes, but I have too much work," "Yes, but we can't afford to do this," "Yes, but I don't have a home office," "Yes, but I don't know anyone in that field who could give me a job."
- Review these reasons, and if you aren't willing to try to work through them, then consider whether this is the right time for you to proceed.

But, assuming that you are ready, let's follow the roadmap that will ultimately lead you to a better work+life fit.

13 Creating a Vision

What Is a Work+Life Vision?

By definition a vision is "an imaginative insight into a subject or problem" (*Oxford American Dictionary*). Therefore, by creating your work+life vision, you are *creating an imaginative insight into how you want work to fit into your life as a whole.*

In other words, your vision is not how *someone else* sees work fitting into your life, but how *you* see it. It's not how work *should* fit in, but how you *want* it to fit in. And it's not how does your *life* fit into your *work*, but how do you imagine *work* fitting into your *life*? This is your work+life vision.

And that vision needs to encompass work as well as the rest of your life if you want to resolve your work/life conflict in a way that optimizes both your personal and professional success. To just focus on one—work or personal life—presupposes that they are two distinct spheres without any reciprocal influence. As we discussed in the beginning, this is the illusion under which so many people operate today and it's the reason for the work/life conflict they experience in the first place.

Why Is Creating a Vision So Critical?

Everyone's vision is unique. It's like snowflakes. In all of my years in this field, I have yet to have two people describe the same work+life vision. This is important to understand as you begin the roadmap. Your vision is your secret weapon for resolving your work/life conflict. Why? Once you know where you want to go, your efforts will not only be more effective, but also more efficient because you are the only person on the road that leads toward that particular vision.

Efficiency of the Work+Life Fit Roadmap

Going back to the travel analogy, can you plan a trip without an initial destination in mind? Yes, but how efficient will that be? Think about how much time and energy you would waste hitting dead ends, getting into unnecessary traffic jams, etc. Not to mention the frustration and disappointment that could easily cause you to pack it up and head home without accomplishing anything.

With a destination in mind, you can avoid detours, pick the least traveled roads, and more easily identify important landmarks that will lead you to your goal.

The same is true for the Work+Life Fit Roadmap. A clear work+life vision enhances your efficiency by:

▶ Giving your efforts a focus. In other words, "This is where I want to end up, so this is how I'm going to get there." Otherwise, you scatter your energy everywhere with no guarantee of any positive results.

▶ Helping you discern more quickly and clearly whether or not a particular choice, situation, or opportunity brings you closer to your goal. If it does, you can pursue it with confidence and conviction. If it doesn't, you can move on without wasting any time.

Effectiveness of the Work+Life Fit Roadmap

You measure the success of the Work+Life Fit Roadmap by how effectively it helps you resolve your conflict. However, without an imaginative, insightful vision as a beacon throughout your journey, you are more likely to fall prey to the roadblocks that will keep you stuck. Without a clear vision of where you're trying to go, what will guide you around limiting beliefs and influences that you encounter along the way?

A work+life vision will also give power and passion to your pitch: "I know this can work for me. Here is why and here is what makes it worthwhile both professionally and personally." A powerful argument that is full of conviction is more effective than one that is not grounded in a particular goal.

Again, your unique work+life vision is a secret weapon, because it's yours and yours alone. And when vision meets opportunity, watch out. Even if that opportunity is something you need to create and propose yourself, the power of the work+life vision supporting it will make your pitch more persuasive.

That power will also help you to persevere when you inevitably hit one of the roadblocks. With your vision as a guide, you'll be better able to quickly and effectively navigate around the roadblock and continue toward your goal.

After you've created your vision, you will compare the realities in your work and personal life to see if they are compatible. To resolve an incompatibility, you will have to try to either change the reality or change your vision. With your original vision as a guide, you will more effectively determine which short-term compromises you're willing to make without undermining your ultimate goal. Without that vision, there is a greater chance that a compromise to resolve an incompatibility could take you farther away from ultimately resolving your work/life conflict rather than bring you closer.

For example, you have a vision that allows you to work three days a week, but when you compare that vision to the personal financial reality of having a child going to college next year, you realize that your vision and this reality are incompatible. You can't change the fact that your child is starting college, so you decide to compromise your original vision in the short term. You will work full-time for the next two years to save money. But, in the meantime, you will begin to lay the groundwork for ultimately achieving your original vision of a three-day workweek.

Or, perhaps you want to work from home every Tuesday, but there is a weekly meeting on Tuesdays you need to attend. Can you change that reality by either having someone else attend the meeting or could you perhaps attend via conference call? If neither of these options is viable, you may need to adjust your original vision. Maybe instead of working from home on Tuesdays, you compromise and try Wednesdays.

LAUREN'S STORY

Lauren's original vision of a better work+life fit was to reduce her work hours from 40 to 25 hours per week in order to care for her aging mother. Unfortunately, as she worked through the roadmap, she realized that certain realities in her personal life weren't compatible with this vision, specifically her personal finances. She couldn't afford to work less than 40 hours per week, which meant she couldn't pursue her original vision for at least another year until she saved some money and/or changed her lifestyle.

So, she decided to adjust her initial vision to accommodate this reality, but still allow more time with her mother. She ended up with an arrangement whereby she worked four ten-hour days a week and had

Wednesdays off to take her mother to the doctor. Perhaps in a year—when she has saved some money—she may revisit the Work+Life Fit Roadmap to see if her original goal has become possible. But, for now, she's content.

If Creating a Work+Life Vision Is So Important, Why Don't More People Do It?

If creating a vision is critical to resolving your work/life conflict, why don't more people do it? In my experience, people aren't used to stepping back and consciously envisioning how they would like work to fit into their lives as a whole. Historically, individuals who experienced work/life conflict moved right to implementing a solution that was usually one of the standard, one-size-fits-all arrangements offered by HR. They did this without reflecting first on the outcome that they hoped to achieve. So when it didn't work, they either resumed their full-time schedule or quit.

Part of the problem has been that work/life experts (myself included, for many years), HR professionals, and managers tend to start with the assumption that you already know what you want and that it's just a matter of giving you the policies and programs to achieve your goal.

However, in my experience most people don't have a clue. They only know that they *don't* want what they currently have. If this sounds like you, then you're in good company. Just remember, a vision enhances both the efficiency and the effectiveness of the Work+Life Fit Roadmap, allowing you to target your efforts, and enhances the probability that you will reach your goal. Now that you understand the importance of having a vision, the next chapter will give you the tools to create your own.

The Tools You Need

In the definition of work+life vision—*creating an imaginative insight into how you want work to fit into your life as a whole*—the most important words are *imaginative* and *insight*. Why? These are the words that describe the importance of looking within in order to see the possibilities for your life. This is how you create your work+life vision.

Ground Rule: Leave All "Reality" at the Door, Now It's Time to Dream

The only way you're going to create a vision that truly reflects how *you want* work to fit into your life is to check "reality" at the door. You'll have plenty of time to worry about reality later. But for now there are no limits, no "shoulds," "can'ts," "oughts," "yes, buts," or "what ifs."

There are only possibilities and dreams. Only "why nots." To help put you in the correct frame of mind, take a moment to complete the following exercise, and repeat it every time you find yourself drifting back into the land of limitation.

EXERCISE—REALITY CHECK

- Take a moment to get comfortable in your chair.
- Close your eyes and take three deep, slow breaths in and out.
- Now, imagine standing up and walking to the nearest door. Visualize yourself physically throwing all of your limitations and "realities"—all your "oughts," "shoulds," and "can'ts"—out that door.
- Now, visualize shutting the door and walking back to your seat.
- Next, look around and imagine that the walls of the room are gone and that light and air, which are symbols of all things that are possible, surround you.
- Open your eyes and continue with the chapter.

Where Does Your Work+Life Vision Come From?

There are two parts of the mind, the conscious and the unconscious. The conscious mind is your "rational" side. It's the source of all that is considered "realistic."

While your unconscious mind also recognizes reality, it isn't encumbered by it. Therefore, it's the source of all that is possible. Your unconsciousness speaks to you in dreams, but it can also speak to you while you're awake through your internal guidance. It's sometimes referred to as "that still small voice" or "your gut." Regardless of what you call it, your internal guidance is the source of your work+life vision.

If you remember only one reason for listening to your internal guidance, it's this: *Only your internal guidance dreams bigger dreams for your life than your "rational" mind could begin to imagine.* And it dreams visions for you that take into account all aspects of your life. It knows and values all parts of you. It knows what you love, it knows your strengths, it knows your weaknesses, and it even knows your "realities." But unlike your conscious mind, which latches onto those realities as excuses not to make changes in your life, it's able to see beyond them. In other words, your internal guidance is simply what you *know* is right for you. Not what someone else thinks is right, but what *you* know.

Everyone knows on some level how they want work to fit into their life. Whether or not they'll admit it, that's another story. Much of my time with clients is spent simply moving someone to the point where they'll say, "Okay, what I really want to do is (fill in the vision), but . . ." When I hear those words—even with the "but" at the end— I know we've hit the visioning jackpot.

Unfortunately, very few people take the time or exert the energy to connect with their internal guidance and all the possibilities it sees. Instead, we allow our choices to be ruled by our conscious mind with all of its limitations. From the time we're small, we're taught to look outside of ourselves for affirmation of "How am I doing?" instead of reflecting inward and checking with our internal guidance to determine if our choices feel right.

This external checking process begins in school where grades, test scores, and GPAs tell us whether or not we're smart. Then in the world of work, titles, promotions, bonuses, raises, and stock options take the place of grades as the indicators of success or failure. And, in our adult life, our address, the cars we drive, and the people with whom we associate tell us whether or not we've made it. It's how we learn to define success and build the success roadblocks we discussed in chapter 9.

Therefore, it's understandable that you are dumbstruck when I tell you to "follow your internal guidance to create your work+life vision." I can almost hear you saying, "What did she say again?" Your internal guidance is like a muscle you've never exercised.

It's there but it isn't very strong and requires some effort initially to work.

Tools to Help You Listen to Your Internal Guidance

If accessing and trusting your internal guidance is a new concept for you, the remainder of this chapter may take longer to work through than others (in fact, it might be a good time to review the Work+Life Fit Fundamental #8 regarding patience and perseverance). Or, perhaps you are part of the unusual minority who already has a vision. Then, you'll move through more quickly. But remember, if you don't have a clue, you're in good company—trust me. It's a lot like an archeological excavation. But rather than digging through layers of dirt, you are digging through layers of "shoulds," "can'ts," and "oughts" to unearth your internal guidance and its vision for your life.

What Does Your Internal Guidance Sound Like?

Years ago, when I decided to move from banking into the work/life field, I didn't have the first idea where to begin either. At that time, a very smart person gave me the following advice: "Just start to pay attention. As you read a book or talk to someone, see what grabs you or makes you pause for a moment, and then continue in that new direction." It's the very same advice I give my clients today.

That "catch" or "pause" is what it feels like to hear your internal guidance prompt you to follow a particular path. So as you read this chapter, if something catches your attention or makes you pause, highlight it and come back to it. On the other hand, if something holds no interest, just let it go. Chances are your internal guidance knew that particular piece of information wasn't relevant for you right now.

This may be your first opportunity to be led by that "catch" or "pause." Use it to help you and your internal guidance to become better acquainted with one another.

Two Approaches:
Head-based and Heart-based

There are two approaches you can take to help you tune into your internal guidance. The first approach is more logical and from the head. The second approach is more internally focused and from the heart. You'll need to decide which one you feel most comfortable with. But before you do, please look at what they both offer in terms of the greatest access to your work+life vision.

Both the head-based and heart-based approaches use the same tools of mind and body to achieve their goals. The difference is that the heart-based approach includes the powerful, reflective, inward-looking tool of spirit. By spirit, I don't mean religion. I mean understanding that which is uniquely you—your values, your priorities, your beliefs—and how they are expressed in all parts of your life.

The head-based approach will indeed give you insight, but insight primarily into the "work" piece of your time and energy pie. The heart-based approach, thanks to the extra tool of spirit, will help you see the bigger picture of how you want the "work" pie piece to fit into your life as a whole.

The head-based approach may lead you to a new job, a new company, or a new career, but you run the risk of remaining unsatisfied with the way work interacts with the other parts of your life. Why? Because the logical, head-based approach often discounts the silent wisdom of your internal guidance, precisely because it often isn't logical by definition.

Imagine the mind, body, spirit tools working together like a computer. The mind is the software, taking in hard data from the outside. That data gives your internal guidance the raw material of the "who, what, where, when, and how" it needs to create your vision.

Your body not only physically houses your mind, but it's the vehicle through which you experience and interpret your world. The body is the hardware—the model and speed of the computer. A well-maintained computer with a hard drive free of viruses is going to process the mind's data for your internal guidance more accurately and with greater efficiency. And, if you stop there, this head-based approach would give you a logical, work-focused idea of how you want work to fit into your life.

But add spirit to the equation, and the possibilities expand. You see, spirit shifts the process from the external data-gathering of "what is" to an internal vision of "what could be." It provides the context within which your internal guidance interprets the hard data, considering all aspects of your life as part of your work+life vision.

That context is the magic of spirit. Without this context, the data is just that—data. It isn't truth informed by your internal guidance. Again, your work+life vision is all about discovering your heart's desire, not your head's. Remember that your logical mind can't dream as big as your spirit. That said, without the facts and the ability to analyze them clearly, your internal guidance will not be adequately informed to create your vision.

In other words, the tools of mind, body, and spirit are equally important and are most powerful when used in concert. These tools can also help you access your internal guidance in order to bypass the Work+Life Fit Roadblocks you experience along the way.

By now, it's probably clear that I favor the heart-based approach. From my own experience and the experience of my clients, it's the best way to create an imaginative insight into how you want work to fit into your life as a whole. But I also know there are some who may continue to be uncomfortable with the concept of spirit as a tool and its relevance to this particular issue of work+life fit.

I've been there, and I respect how you feel. Therefore, recognizing its limitations, if you want to follow the head-based approach, concentrate primarily on the following sections titled mind and body. If, however, you are open to exploring the heart-based approach, read the information in all three sections: mind, body, and spirit.

Tools for Creating Your Work+Life Vision: The Mind

As we've said, the mind is the tool that gathers the facts—the "who, what, where, when, and how" of your work/life-related choices. You may be caring for a child, changing careers, volunteering in the community, planning partial early retirement, or pursuing an avocation. Regardless of your challenge, books, articles, websites, testing, working with counselors or coaches, and talking with others are great places to start gathering as many facts as you can.

Books, Articles, and Websites

Books, articles, and websites may seem obvious, but they are some of the most important sources of information. Again, the nature of the problem currently driving you to seek a better work+life fit will determine which book, article, and/or website will be most helpful to you.

Try online searches using key words describing your particular work/life challenge: child care, working mother, working father, caregiver of an aging parent, elder care, working retirement, changing careers, etc. Go to the library and review the books and articles available using a similar keyword search.

Websites with special interest forums include: About.com (fatherhood, motherhood, elder care, child care, retirement), iVillage.com (motherhood, child care), Women.com, ThirdAge.com, and AARP.com (retirement, elder care). Others can be found in the resource section (page 363).

Self-Assessment Tests

Testing is a great way to objectively understand yourself a little bit better in order to find a work+life fit you love. Aptitude and personality testing can be particularly helpful.

The Myers-Briggs personality test, for example, will explain whether you're more likely to process information through your five senses or through your feelings and intuition. It also tests whether you are energized from within yourself or by being with others. A person who is energized by others would enjoy working in an office environment and find it difficult to work from home, whereas someone who draws energy from within may find telecommuting appealing. These are important aspects of yourself to understand if you want to be happy with your final work+life fit.

There are many related occupational tests that are administered by career counselors, graduate-level education departments at your local university, or websites. Some examples of work-related testing websites include:

- Myers-Briggs Personality Test and Strong Interest Inventory (www.discoveryourpersonality.com).
- The Johnson O'Connor Research Foundation, which offers a comprehensive battery of aptitude testing—offices can be found in 11 major cities across the U.S. (www.members.aol. com/ jocrf19/).
- The Keirsey Character Sorter is a free test of personality traits, similar to the Myers-Briggs (www.keirsey.com).
- CareerLeader assesses your interests, tests what's important to you, and evaluates your abilities. Charges a minimal fee (www.careerdiscovery.com).

Counselors/Coaches

In addition to writing this book and consulting to companies, I coach individuals one-on-one and in workshops. Work+life is my particular expertise, but there are as many types of counselors and coaches as there are topics about which to be counseled or coached. For example, if your issue is caring for an elder, there are counselors trained specifically in helping with elder-care options. There are coaches who specifically target time management skills or organization skills. There are financial counselors. Or perhaps you are stuck because you can't redefine success; a psychologist can help you to change your relationship with money, with a prestigious job, with advancement, or with clarifying your definition of a "good" caregiver.

How do you know when you need some extra help? Perhaps you feel stuck and no matter how many books you read or people you speak with, you can't quite move closer to envisioning and achieving a better work+life fit. At this point, you may want to consider enlisting the aid of a counselor or coach, especially if you find yourself unable to circumvent a roadblock, like my client, Christine.

CHRISTINE'S STORY

Christine sought counseling to address issues related to her parents, after I suggested that these issues might be keeping her from resolving her work/life conflict. Christine, a single woman, prided herself on the fact that before the age of 35 she was making more money annually than her parents ever did. She lovingly describes them as "free spirits." The problem was that she was on her tenth "stable" albeit high-paying job in as many years, and she was miserable. Like her parents, she too found herself drawn to a more freestyle way of living and had even taken some time off to work for a charity organization abroad. She loved this experience, but forced herself to set a deadline to get back to "work." Even though in her heart she longed for a less structured life, she kept taking 9-to-5 jobs that she found unfulfilling. It seemed to be how she defined "success." Perhaps a counselor could help her to figure out why and move beyond the roadblock.

●　○　●

To find someone with the expertise you need, once again, talk to people. Ask them if they've needed to address similar issues or know of anyone else who has. Then ask them who they worked with and if they were pleased with the experience. You can also contact a national professional organization for recommendations of certified coaches or counselors in your area, such as CoachU (www.coachu. com). Career coaches aim primarily at helping people to find a career they love and are passionate about, and they usually also offer a number of the aforementioned aptitude tests. For psychologists or therapists that can help you with emotional issues, try websites such as www.4therapy.com.

Talking to Others about How They Fit Work into Their Lives

Talking to others, especially those who face a similar conflict, is another means of gathering data and finding role models to whom you can relate. Remember, focus as much on *how* they achieved their goal as on *what* they achieved. The work+life fit you want may be different, but it doesn't mean that you can't learn from their experience. The more people you talk to the better, because not everyone facing the same issues will offer advice that you find appealing.

There are national organizations dedicated to providing information and support to specific demographics, such as mothers, fathers, those caring for aging parents, and retirees. For example, the mission of the National Association of Mother's Centers (www.motherscenter. org) is to offer information and support while breaking the isolation of motherhood. Through a network of community-based centers and its website, NAMC offers information on a range of issues mothers are interested in, from childrearing to working to other matters.

Maybe you are one of the 54 million employees who will care for an aging relative in the near future. Contact a local social services agency for the elderly or someone at your place of worship to get ideas about how to fit work into your life while caring for an elder. You could try posting an email message on your company's bulletin board seeking out others who have dealt with caring for an aging parent or relative. Online support groups offered by AARP, or one of the other national caregiving organizations listed in the resource section at the back of the book, are another easy-to-access source of information.

Maybe your issue is finding the time and energy to volunteer in the community while you work. Visit various local not-for-profits or schools. Ask them if any other volunteers work long hours and then ask if you can speak with them. Online chat rooms are another great way to connect with others who have similar work/life issues and experiences.

Tools for Creating Your Work+Life Vision: The Body

At first, it may not be clear why your body is an important tool to access your internal guidance. But, if you think about it for a minute, you'll see why getting enough sleep, eating well, and exercising are critical to your success.

Whether you are an archeologist "digging" to unearth your vision, or a computer processing data with maximum efficiency, your physical well-being is critical if you want to have the endurance and clarity to get the most out of the Three Steps. Why? Although the amount of energy we have to expend in a given day is fixed, taking care of your body gives you access to as much of that energy as possible. When you're run down physically, you deplete some of that precious energy.

Listening to your inner guidance takes time, concentration, and reflection. And as we discussed earlier, if you're like most people with work/life conflict, you steal time and energy formerly available for sleeping, cooking healthy meals, and exercising and give it to work.

You will most likely *not* be able to set aside two weeks to sit in a room and do nothing but reflect on your work+life vision. You'll have to go to work, take care of the kids, or attend classes at night.

Precisely because you still have to work and take care of your personal responsibilities, you have to make the time to take care of yourself.

Okay, don't worry. I'm not a nutrition fanatic or a physical fitness nut. What I'm simply saying is:

- ▶ Get up and move your body for at least 20 minutes every day;
- ▶ Eat at least three healthy meals and drink six glasses of water every day; and
- ▶ Get at least eight hours of sleep a night.

From my own experience and the experience of my clients, I know that if you're eating poorly and not exercising, you won't have the energy or clarity to distinguish your inner guidance from the buzz of everyday life all around you. The word "buzz" accurately describes how life sounds when you aren't taking care of yourself—it's like TV static.

Perhaps the stress from work/life conflict is making you physically ill, as is the case with 38% of employees.[1] Maybe you have stomach problems, back problems, or headaches. Or maybe you eat unhealthy food as a way to manage the stress and make yourself feel better, which ultimately leaves you feeling less energized. All of these issues can be relieved at least in part by resting, eating well, and exercising. And feeling better will allow you to concentrate on resolving the work/life conflict that is making you sick in the first place.

To help you understand more about how stress and unhealthy habits affect your physical body, as well as to learn about steps to take for a healthier life, I suggest you read the books listed in the resource section.

Tools for Creating Your Work+Life Vision: The Spirit

Again, spirit simply means understanding that which is uniquely you—your values, beliefs, and priorities, as you define them—and how they are expressed in your life as a whole, not just in work. And then using that understanding to create an imaginative insight into how you want work to fit into your life.

As the opening line of this book states, I believe that we are all put on the earth with a specific set of skills and talents that we are to use to fulfill our life's purpose in all areas of our life—not just work.

While I believe that the logical, head-based approach to your work+life vision can help you identify your skills and talents, only your spirit provides the context for how and where to use them to fulfill your life's purpose. And this purpose can change, depending upon what stage of life you're in.

By using the tool of spirit, your internal guidance will help you with the answers to those big life questions:

▶ Who am I, as a whole, not just as a worker?
▶ What is my purpose, not just at work but in my life as a whole?
▶ What do I love to do at work and in my personal life?
▶ What are my unique talents and gifts?

The answers to such questions form the context within which your internal guidance analyzes data from the mind and body. This is why spirit is such an important tool for creating your work+life vision. It considers all of who you are and not just your "work-self." Again, with the tool of spirit, you are able to dream and achieve much bigger things than your more limited logical mind could ever conceive.

Unlike the rest of the book in which I've illustrated concepts with stories of other people, to illustrate the experience of using the spirit tool, I will use my own story. Why? The use of spirit as a tool is a very personal and multifaceted experience. Therefore, I only feel qualified to accurately portray the details of my own journey and how the spirit tool facilitated it.

FROM WORK/LIFE MISERY TO WORK+LIFE CLARITY

My journey took me from being a person who didn't even know her internal guidance existed to someone who never makes a decision, large or small, without first checking in with the wisdom of the "stillness within the silence."[2]

As I climbed the corporate ladder in my banking career, I seemed to have it all. By all external measures of success, I was doing well. But I was miserable. So I began the logical, head-based process of finding a new job because it was the only thing I knew how to do. I had offers from two other banks, and I even decided to go back and get my MBA in finance to become a corporate comptroller but backed out at the last minute.

You see, even though it never "felt" right, finance and banking were all I knew. Everyone I talked to about careers outside of banking only reinforced my doubts, telling me it was almost impossible to change careers. And besides, if I didn't work in the finance industry, what *would* I do? I had no idea what alternative career I wanted to pursue.

With my family and business background, I thought anything to do with spirit was just a bunch of mumbo-jumbo. That is until I became so unhappy with my career in banking that it made me physically ill—stomach problems, headaches, and anxiety attacks. I had exhausted all of the head-based approaches that I knew of to solve my work/life conflict. I was at the end of the line and was willing to try anything—even things that I thought were a little flaky.

Out of this newfound openness, I learned about various practices to access my internal guidance. I started reading spirit-related books, meditating, journal writing, and connecting to something greater than myself; all things that I had never done before.

Eleven years ago, if you told me, as I sat in the bank, that I would be reading spiritual books, meditating for 15 minutes daily, keeping a journal, and reconnecting to something greater, I would have said you were nuts! They were certainly not activities in which professional businesspeople like me engaged. Ironically, of course, businesspeople like me need these activities even more than monks.

And after a few months of consistently using the mind, body, spirit tools, I began to notice that I felt more peaceful and aware during the day. I felt more present and I paid closer attention to conversations or experiences I had. And I began to understand the information, or data, these conversations and experiences offered.

It was at about this time that I had my life-changing conversation with the CEO that I described in the introduction. Also, I realized I had amassed a six-inch-thick folder of work/life-related articles in my desk. But I still didn't know what all of this meant for my vision. Then one day, I finally understood.

As part of my morning routine at the bank, I ate my bagel, drank my coffee, and read *The Wall Street Journal*. Those of you who read the *WSJ* know that periodically they publish a special fourth section entirely devoted to one particular topic. On this morning, the *WSJ*'s Sue Shellenbarger devoted the entire fourth section to the field of work and family.

I sat at my desk in plain view of everyone well past 9 o'clock, devouring every word. When I had finished, I walked over to my boss's desk, sat down, pointed to the work/family section, and said to her, "This is what I want to do." She politely, but haltingly, responded, "Well . . . okay." I knew this was the vision that my internal guidance had for my work+life fit.

Now, from a purely logical perspective, this made no sense. But because I was reading, meditating, journal writing, and so forth, I had slowly started to understand what my internal guidance sounded like, and it was saying, "This feels right." Now, people sometimes ask me,

"What do you mean 'you knew' it was your internal guidance? What did that knowing feel like?" The following words most accurately describe the feeling: clarity, focus, and peace.

For a moment, I had a sense of clarity and focus that *this* was it. Everything else in the room seemed to disappear—people, sounds, everything. It was so powerful; I can still feel it today. But, as powerful as it was, it wasn't scary or anxiety-producing. In fact, that's how I knew it was different from the other paths I thought were "it," such as taking the other banking jobs or getting an MBA in finance. In each of those cases, I was anxious and full of doubt. There weren't any moments of pure clarity and focus, or what many psychologists call "flow."

Flow is when all aspects of who you are—intellectual, psychological, physiological, and spiritual—seem to align and work in perfect harmony, almost making time stand still. Good examples of flow are when you seem to complete a work project effortlessly or read a good book without realizing the entire afternoon flew by.

Practices to Help You Use Spirit as a Tool

The following sections highlight some of the practices that can help you to use spirit as a tool to access your internal guidance. They include reading, meditating, journal writing, and connecting to something greater. I chose these four practices because they are the spirit-based practices with which I have the most positive experience both personally and from working with clients. Hopefully, you will find them as helpful as I have in staying connected to your internal guidance and what it has to tell you about your heart's desire for all areas of your life.

Reading

Books related to spirit—searching inside for the answers about your life—are written from such a wide range of perspectives that you're sure to find at least one or two that you feel comfortable with. These perspectives range from religion to nature, from poetry to music. Regardless of the differences, the common theme in all is honoring that which is uniquely, sacredly, you.

The first book I read was the classic *The Road Less Traveled* by M. Scott Peck. It was the first time I considered the vision-expanding questions he raises, and I will never forget how that felt. Other helpful books, some more "spiritual" than others, are included in the resource section. But as you learn more about the process of using spirit to access your inner guidance, you will be led to other wonderful books that give you even more insight and knowledge.

Meditation

I have described how, after months of using various spirit-based practices to connect to my internal guidance, I felt more peaceful and aware. Well, of all of these practices, meditation is the chief contributor to these feelings of peaceful awareness and well-being.

When I first heard about meditation, it conjured up images of a yogi in an ashram somewhere in the Far East with his legs crossed, chanting, burning incense, and levitating. Nothing against levitating yogis, but I saw little application to my world.

My introduction to meditation came from a somewhat surprising source: my mother. She had been meditating for years, but as is often the case with something that your mother does, I never gave it much thought. All I knew is that Mom went in her room and "meditated" for 20 minutes after work, and that my sisters and I thought it was hilarious.

When I told my mother that I was learning more about spirit-based practices, she gave me a book called *Minding the Soul, Mend-*

ing the Body by Joan Borysenko. Now, Joan Borysenko is by no means a levitating yogi. In fact, she is a Harvard-educated doctor. And, I must admit, at that time in my life I found that very comforting. I also related to the fact that she was drawn initially to meditation in order to deal with her own stress-related illnesses, as was the case for me.

In addition to relieving my headaches and stomach problems, unexpectedly, meditation gave me something else; something that has proven much more important. For me, meditation is the most important spirit-based practice for hearing the prompting of my internal guidance—what some people call "that still small voice."

In the stressful, chaotic world in which we live, the buzz of everyday life easily drowns out that voice. No wonder you aren't able to hear what your internal guidance sounds like. You never slow down long enough to hear it. Slowing down and paying attention is what meditation is all about.

Meditation also gives you something I call a split-second "choice point," which is the ability to consciously decide in the moment how you want to react to, and in, situations you experience throughout the day. Why? Because meditation quiets the static, and that quietness allows you to be less reactive and more discerning of the people, places, and things you encounter as you move through life.

This choice point was probably the reason I paid attention to the strong reaction I had to my conversation with the CEO, to the work/life conflicts of my employees, and to the bulging folder of articles in my desk, as well as to that special section of the *WSJ*. Who knows, if I hadn't been meditating, those experiences might have come in and out of my life without a conscious thought, as was the case with many experiences in the first 25 years of my life. Instead, they all led me to realize the vision my internal guidance had for my life, and it was in the work/life field.

Even though meditation is now an integral part of my life, when I first started, I almost gave up 100 times. In the beginning, my typical type-A goal was to meditate for 45 minutes without a thought in my head. Imagine my disappointment and frustration when my mind wandered almost 95% of the time. I was sure I wasn't doing it right.

Years later, I now meditate about 15 minutes every day, and my mind still wanders probably 95% of the time. But now I know that it doesn't matter, because having clarity and focus 5% of the time is enough. Yes, there are days when I am particularly focused and peaceful and my mind actually will be still a whole whopping 15% of the time. That's it, but believe it or not, that 5% to 15% is enough to change your life.

In *A Path with Heart*, Jack Cornfield uses a helpful analogy. As you meditate, imagine that your mind is a puppy you're trying to train. You put the puppy down in one place and tell it to sit, only to have it wander off two seconds later. So you lovingly and peacefully bring the puppy back to its original place and start the process again. This analogy helped me to get over my Type-A approach and to enjoy meditation more. As I became more forgiving of my ever-wandering mind, I stopped putting pressure on myself to "get it right." There is no right way to meditate. It's truly whatever works for you.

SOME QUICK TIPS TO HELP YOU GET STARTED

1. Find a comfortable, quiet place in your home where you can sit without being disturbed for at least 20 minutes. Sit, don't lie down. Sitting up with your spine straight is the best way to meditate. If you lie down, there is a very strong possibility you'll fall asleep.

2. Dim the lights. Some people, including myself, like to light beautiful-smelling candles. Others like to play peaceful music. I prefer silence. But it's whatever works for you. Now, close your eyes.

3. Place your hands on your belly and breathe in deeply through your nose so that your belly expands and lifts your hands. Then exhale deeply through your nose, releasing your belly, which should lower your hands. This is what it feels like to breathe correctly. Most of us breathe incorrectly by expanding our chests. Now, breathe in and out slowly and deeply 10 times. Then return to a normal belly breath and

try to empty your mind while you concentrate on your breath—in and out, in and out, and in and out. Some concentration tips:

- Imagine your breath flowing in and out of your nostrils.
- Create a mantra to repeat over and over, such as "Peace, peace, peace." It can be anything that is meaningful to you and gives you focus.
- If you do light a candle, with your eyes closed, imagine the candle flame and concentrate on it.

4. Starting at the top of your head, with each in and out breath, relax all the muscles in your body all the way down to your toes.

5. Then breathe normally, concentrating on either your breath, your mantra, or candle flame for at least 20 minutes every day. Set a timer so you won't think "Has it been 20 minutes yet?"

Keeping a Journal

As you learn more about yourself and about honoring your internal guidance, you'll probably find that you need a place to sort out your thoughts. For example, as you read a book, you may get interested in an idea you want to explore further. Or you might gain an awareness during meditation that you can't quite understand until you write it out. A journal is a perfect place to do this. Keeping a journal helps you become familiar with what your internal guidance sounds like and also helps discern the messages of clarity and possibility from the "shoulds" and "oughts" inherent in your more head-based approach.

Not only does a journal help you to hear your own voice and understand what you want, it also serves as an archive of your journey over time. I can look back at the entries during the time when my internal guidance was leading me to the realization that I wanted to go into the work/life field. As I read through the days, I can see how all the individual pieces fell together over time.

Initially, keeping a journal may be more difficult than you expected. Like my initial forays into meditation, at first I thought I wasn't doing it right. That is, until I met a seasoned journal-keeper (a good example of "when the student is ready, the teacher will come"). She suggested writing three pages every day, even if all I wrote was three pages of "I have no idea what to write."

I took her advice and persevered, but those first few mornings of journal writing were still brutally difficult. Looking back, my first entries seem so formal, as if I was trying to impress myself in my own journal. But, as promised, it did get easier and the later entries reflect that ease. Slowly but surely the wisdom of my internal guidance began to emerge on the page.

There are no particular rules about keeping a journal, although there are helpful books written on the subject. The book *The Artist's Way* describes a journal-keeping process called "morning pages," which is similar to the practice I just described. I, however, take the basic approach. Although I've been given a number of beautiful journals over the years, my tried and true favorite is the cardboard-bound, black-and-white-speckled notebooks of lined paper I used in elementary school. I don't know why. I just like them. Other journal-keepers prefer the computer. Personally, I find I receive more clarity through the physical process of putting pen to paper.

Although I did force myself to write three pages a day when I began, today the time I devote to it daily varies. When I'm facing a critical issue, I will journal a great deal. On other days, I devote my entries to things I'm grateful for. This is an idea I learned about in Sarah Ban Breathnach's *Simple Abundance*. If my time is limited, I just list five quick things. If I have more time, I expand the list. As a mother with kids who take up much of my time, the gratitude journal allows me to continue to engage in journal-keeping that is helpful in so many other areas of my life.

SOME QUICK TIPS TO HELP YOU GET STARTED

1. Find a blank notebook of any kind and a pen that you like to write with. If you prefer a computer, find one that's located in a quiet environment and that you can comfortably type on.

2. Find a place where you won't be disturbed, and where you can write easily. As with meditation, some people find it helpful to light candles and to play music.

3. At the beginning, make yourself write at least three full pages a day, even if it's just "I don't know what to write." Keep this up for at least a month or until you feel comfortable putting your feelings down. Then proceed daily as you see fit to support your heart-based journey.

4. Here's another tip to help you feel more comfortable writing about your true feelings. Get a book of daily inspirational passages (I often recommend *Meditations for Women Who Do Too Much* by Anne Wilson Schaef or the companion edition, *Men Who Do Too Much*). Try reading the daily passage, and begin your journal-writing session by reflecting on how that passage made you feel.

Reconnecting to Something Greater

I seriously debated whether or not to include this as one of the practices for accessing your internal guidance. I debated because it's a concept that means different things to different people, and sometimes, depending upon your history, those meanings are not positive.

By something greater, I mean simply a power greater than, or outside of yourself. And it's an important practice if you want to use spirit as a tool to resolve your work/life conflict. Why? Because sometimes the vision put forth by your internal guidance can seem so far out of the realm of possibility that if you don't feel connected to or supported by something greater than yourself, you're likely to give up. The path from vision to reality can be long, lonely, and fraught with roadblocks. Sometimes it helps to have something besides yourself to hold on to.

When I went from being a banker to a career as a work/life strategy consultant, and then, a few years later, decided to write this book, both of these visions had to be connected to something greater than I am. Why? Because there is absolutely no way my rational, conscious mind would have entertained these seemingly impossible goals. Had I not felt guided by something greater than myself, I definitely would have succumbed not only to the resistance from others, but also from myself! You know the voice that says, "Are you crazy? There's no way!"

I'm not advocating a connection to organized religion. What I am advocating is sitting back and reflecting on your place and purpose in the universe. How are you supposed to use your unique experiences, gifts, and talents in some combination and context to make the world a better place?

Your unique contribution may be different at different points in your life, and work may play a greater or lesser role in these various stages. This is why you might revisit the Three Steps over and over again.

I believe a greater power works through your spirit, which informs your internal guidance. Helping you not only see your work+life vision, but also guiding you on how to make that vision a reality. You just have to trust. Then move forward, putting one foot in front of the other.

Religious faith may not inform your belief in a higher power and greater purpose for life at all. Perhaps your connection will be made through nature, art, music, literature, or poetry. In fact, I carry a poem with me that I think beautifully articulates the true meaning of success in work and in life. It reminds me more than any other passage of all the various combinations and possibilities a successful life can encompass.

In Step 2, we discussed overcoming the Work+Life Fit Roadblocks. Hopefully, you can see how all of the spirit-based practices are important tools to help you to bypass these roadblocks, but connecting to something greater is perhaps the most important of all. Why? Because redefining success, overcoming fear and resistance, and seeing all of the creative possibilities for your work+life fit are easier when you feel connected to and supported by the universe. It makes the roadblocks seem much less formidable.

Serendipity and Coincidence: Signs That You're Moving in the Right Direction

I'm consistently amazed that once clients start to listen to and follow the prompting of their internal guidance, the universe begins opening doors to facilitate their progress.

I'm not saying that they don't have to work hard and be conscious of the often subtle cues. Walking through an open door still takes effort. But if they stay the course, they will find inevitably that a coincidental discussion or a serendipitous encounter with the right person gives them confirmation and confidence that they're on the right track.

As I've said, deciding to try to get into the work/life field was a leap of faith. But, over and over I had experiences—some would call them coincidence, or serendipity—that confirmed my belief that something greater was supporting my journey. And it kept me believing and moving forward through the inevitable work+life roadblocks I encountered along the way.

Here are some examples of these serendipitous moments:

► I was accepted to Columbia Business School even though my GMAT scores were way below the average for the school (I have always been a terrible standardized test taker);
► A student at Columbia happened to remember that another woman in our class happened to have interned at Families and Work Institute (one of the organizations highlighted in the special section of the *WSJ*) the previous summer and introduced me to her. This woman put me in contact with a researcher at FWI; and

► Right before I met with that FWI researcher, Families and Work Institute got a consulting job with a large New York bank. Even though I had no research experience, they thought my banking background would be helpful. I was hired. I was now working directly for two of the researchers I read about originally in that special section of *The Wall Street Journal*.

Now this might make it sound easy, but it wasn't. I hit *many* roadblocks along the way. Here are some examples:

► No one (except my husband and a few friends) believed achieving this new work+life fit was a good idea;
► Not one professor in the two years I was in business school told me they thought work/life strategy consulting was a valid field; and
► Even though the business school's recruiting department helped students find summer internships making $5,000 per week, I had to find my job at FWI on my own, a job that paid nothing. I went from a banker's salary to working for free. It was a bitter pill to swallow. Talk about having to redefine success.

As I said, it was my belief in something greater that helped me through the roadblocks of fear and resistance and helped me to see the possibilities for my life where before I only saw dead ends. As a result, I knew I was on the right path—wherever that might lead.

Fortunately, my belief paid off. Ultimately, FWI hired me as a full-time senior research associate a couple of months after graduation, but of course at a not-for-profit salary (read: low). Imagine how I felt as most of my friends graduated with two or more job offers making more than $100,000 per year. But I continued to redefine success and to persevere. Now as my work+life vision has evolved over time, I'm taking new leaps of faith daily.

When I first began typing the words of this book, I had no idea whether I'd ever see them in print. But I knew the new vision of my internal guidance was to provide people with the tools to create and implement a better way to fit work into their lives.

So in the beginning, whenever my daughter napped, I sat down and typed. Then I typed some more when my sitter arrived in the afternoon. During that period, long before I sold my book, I experienced the same coincidence and serendipity that confirmed that the universe supported my efforts. So I continued to trust. And two years later I finally signed a book contract. Two years.

Does that mean I didn't experience dark moments? No. In fact, on a trip to Florida during that period, I seriously questioned my sanity for putting so much time, energy, and money into this project. As part of my morning meditation, I walked on the beach alone early one day and argued with my higher power.

I asked for a sign, just one thing to tell me I wasn't crazy. Right then, out of the corner of my eye, I saw a huge shell in the surf. I walked over and picked up this enormous, almost perfect conch shell, completely intact.

I looked around and saw no other shells even remotely close in size. Two maintenance workers passed by me as I held the shell. "Where did you get that?" one asked, "I've never seen anything like it on this beach before." I knew then that my request had been answered.

In the peace of that morning, with the waves gently lapping, I heard my small still voice say, "This shell looks like the journey you're taking. The perfect spiral is like the order within which your work is taking place, and the small holes represent the bumps along the way. No experience is without challenge, but in the end it all makes sense and is beautiful whatever the outcome." I asked for and was reminded of the power of something greater. Now, I had to continue to trust it.

You might think, "Lucky coincidence." Yes, it could be. But the point is that it had meaning for me. Even though an experience or event—no matter how subtle—holds no meaning for anyone else, it could mean the difference between success or failure in achieving your work+life vision. So try not to dismiss the signs from the universe that tell you, "Keep going."

Notice the serendipities and coincidences that remind you something greater is supporting your efforts. Knowing this will give you the confidence and patience to identify and trust your internal guidance and to avoid succumbing to roadblocks, whether they're put up by you or by others.

"Finding the Time"

Over the years, I've shared the power of the mind, body, and spirit tools to resolve work/life conflict. And clients and workshop participants so often respond, "That sounds great, but when am I supposed to find the time to do all of that?"

When I reluctantly started down the path of seeking my internal guidance, I never believed I'd find the time to use one tool, never mind three. However, the more unhappy and unhealthy I felt, I knew that I simply needed to find the time. I looked at my life and found time by watching less TV and going to bed earlier so that I could wake up an hour earlier to meditate and write in my journal. I made sure I left work on time to make it to yoga class.

When I moved to the suburbs and commuted, I used the hour on the train for meditating and journal writing instead of reading the paper the whole time. Hey, it's the unwritten commuter code not to talk on the train in the morning anyway, so take advantage of the peace and quiet.

Now that I have children, it's even harder. I meditate and write when they nap, before they get up in the morning, after they go to bed. You may say, "That's when I do laundry and clean my house." Let me tell you my house is a little dirty and my wash waits until the weekend, but I'm happy.

Let's be honest . . . you can find the time if you want to. We certainly do waste a lot of it. I know I did, and often still do. View time as your most precious resource and apportion it only to things that enhance your life, not to things that keep you stuck where you are.

EXERCISES

1. How Connected Are You to Your Internal Guidance?

The goal of this exercise is to give you an idea of how much work you're going to have do with the mind, body, spirit tools in order to access your internal guidance.

Imagine you are lifting a pile of blankets in order to uncover a bright light. The blankets represent the "shoulds," "oughts," and "can'ts" that separate you from your internal guidance and your vision for a better work+life fit. Answer the following question in your Work+Life Fit Workbook:

How many blankets will you have to lift to get to your internal guidance? A lot/A few/Not many/None

You will find, as most of the people I work with have found, that your answer will change depending upon where you are in your life. Accessing your internal guidance isn't a linear process. It's more of a two-steps-forward, one-step-back process. So don't be surprised if at one time you answer "not many" and another time you answer "a lot." It only means that you may have to do a little extra work to reconnect to what your internal guidance has to tell you at this point in time.

2. Using the Mind, Body, Spirit Tools

While I always encourage clients to choose the tools that work best for them, I start them off by suggesting a combination of mind, body, spirit practices. I suggest that they follow this initial program and then adjust it over time to better suit their individual preferences.

217

The Mind:

- Identify the source of your particular work/life conflict: child care, caring for an aging relative, avocation, working retirement, further education, changing careers, changing lifestyles, etc.
- Conduct a web search and/or library search using keywords related to your work/life issues and identify relevant books, articles, websites, or chat rooms to provide you with facts about how to address your conflict.
- Network and try to find individuals who have faced similar challenges in order to learn from their experiences.

The Body:

- Move your body at least 20 minutes every day;
- Eat three healthy meals and drink six glasses of water every day; and
- Get at least eight hours of sleep per night.

The Spirit:

- Find time to meditate 20 minutes a day;
- Write at least three pages in a journal every day; and
- Identify a source that helps you feel connected to something greater than yourself, and then make it a daily part of your life.
  - Read one of the spirit-related books listed in the chapter;
  - Take a quiet walk through the woods;
  - Read a poem;
  - Spend an hour or two at a local museum;
  - Listen to some great musical works or other peaceful, soothing music;
  - If applicable, focus on your religious practice.

STOP: As I suggest to my clients, read no further in the book for at least a week. Take longer if you'd like. During that time, focus solely on getting familiar with and using the mind, body, spirit tools to begin accessing your internal guidance. Depending upon how unfamiliar you are with these kinds of things, one week may not be enough. But it does give you a start in getting familiar with what your internal guidance sounds like. And having at least some sense of what you want will help you in the next chapter as you to begin to create your work+life vision.

Putting It All Together

Ground Rules

Successful creation of your work+life vision depends upon following a few ground rules:

1. We're still leaving all limitations at the door. See only the possibilities and dream. In case you need to repeat the visualization from the beginning of chapter 14, I've made it part of the exercises here. Do it as many times as necessary in order to stay in the right frame of mind.
2. Continue with your daily mind, body, spirit practices, because visions emerge over time.
3. Be patient. You may have to complete the exercises over and over again before you have a sense of what you want.

Answers to Some Common Questions

"Does my vision have to be crystal clear before
completing the rest of the roadmap?"

Depending upon how disconnected you are from your internal guidance, it might take you quite some time to clarify your work+life vision. After using the mind, body, spirit tools for a while and completing the exercises in this chapter, you may still only have a vague idea of what your vision looks like. This is completely normal.

Keep using the tools, but don't wait to move on to the next part of the roadmap. In fact, working through the next part of the roadmap might help to clarify your vision more quickly, especially as you compare that vision to your work and personal realities. There may be incompatibilities between your vision and your current realities, and you may need to make compromises in order to resolve them.

And one of the best things you can do at this stage is talk to others in order to get feedback and information. As you share your developing vision, people will put you in touch with someone they know who can help you, or suggest a book or website. All of these resources, in conjunction with the mind, body, spirit tools, will further refine your vision.

Finally, there is nothing wrong with implementing a vision that's not yet completely formed, as long as you're open to the fact that your vision may change with experience—and lead you in a different direction.

"I don't have a job at the moment. How does that
affect my ability to create a work+life vision
and make it a reality?"

Actually, people who aren't currently employed—whether you've lost your job or you are someone transitioning back into the workforce after an absence—are some of my favorite people to work with.

Job seekers have a unique opportunity. They can sit back and ask themselves, unencumbered by the tasks and responsibilities of a current job, "What is my vision for my job and how do I want it to fit into the rest of my life?" It's as if they have a blank slate to work with.

The difference between someone with a job versus someone without emerges when you find an incompatibility between the work reality of a potential job and your vision. It's more difficult to change an incompatible reality connected to a potential job than it is to change an incompatibility related to a job you already have.

But don't let the lack of a job keep you from considering all of the limitless possibilities for your work+life vision. You'll have plenty of time for reality later.

"What if my vision is to not work at all?"

A work+life vision can be not to work at all. When completing the exercises at the end of this chapter, reword the questions to create a work-free vision. It's still important to complete the rest of the process because the realities in your personal life need to be compatible with that vision if it's going to succeed—particularly personal finances, career and personal expectations, and your partner's reality.

EILEEN AND JAMES

Eileen, a financial planner, and James, a computer engineer, recently completed this process when deciding whether or not James would be able to quit his job and stay home with their children full-time. As both of them began traveling more and working longer hours, it became clear that something had to change, especially as their older son's schedule was becoming more complicated with activities and homework.

Finally, the route they would take became clear when James's company restructured his division and, along with it, his job. No longer doing the type of work he really liked, James began to think about what he wanted. He decided that he wanted to give 100% of his time and energy to home and the kids for a while. He wasn't sure that they could swing it financially, but after a few rounds of budgeting and expense cutting, it seemed feasible.

Then he had to look at his expectations for his life. A stay-at-home dad is not the norm, and he had to consider how he was going to respond when people found out that Eileen was the sole breadwinner. This turned out to be a tough one, and James had to work really hard at redefining success. In fact, it actually took him a year longer than planned to begin his new work+life fit simply because it took him that long to get around the success roadblock. But now he felt really good about being able to get his kids to school, take them to their activities, and help them with their homework without the crazy rushing around that was the norm when he worked.

And, finally, what were Eileen's expectations for her life? Eileen loved her job and was doing very well professionally. She wanted to continue to advance and to make money. Plus, she was lucky that her hours still allowed her enough time with the kids every day. And James really relished more time with the kids since his hours hadn't been as family-friendly over the years. Eileen admitted that she found herself jealous of all of the time James was spending with the boys. But when she really thought about changing places with him, it just didn't feel right at this point in time. Would she change her mind someday? Maybe. But for now, she couldn't think of a better arrangement for the whole family. "Besides choosing to get married and having the kids, this is the best decision our family has ever made."

James wasn't sure how long this work+life fit would last, but for now he agreed with Eileen: "We're all winning, especially me."

Creating Your Work+Life Vision

Go to the front of your Work+Life Fit Workbook and review the entire Work+Life Fit Roadmap. Remind yourself of the critical role that creating your work+life vision plays in the entire process. When you start creating your vision, you're going to start hitting roadblocks. Make sure you're prepared with the strategies to bypass them and proceed toward your goal. Make sure you're comfortably maintaining the mind-set outlined in Step 1, challenging your misconceptions about work and life and embracing a new reality of what is possible.

Start Articulating Your Vision

The following exercises will help to start developing your vision.

Pick a day and a time when you'll have at least 30 minutes undisturbed. Find a quiet place with a space that allows you to write easily and comfortably. Grab your favorite pen and open your workbook to a blank page. Close your eyes and relax. Breathe deeply a few times. Without thinking, censoring yourself, or stopping to correct what you're writing, answer the following question. And remember, there are *no* wrong answers.

Describe in detail your perfect workday from beginning to end—what would I do from the moment I woke up until the time I went to bed? What would my surroundings look like? Who am I with? What activities do I engage in? How long do I do each one of them? What do I eat? What do I wear? How do I feel?

Debrief: Here are some questions to help you focus the vision that emerges from your answer to the question above:

Who are you working with?
- Are they similar to or different from the type of people with whom you currently work?

- If they're different, list the specific qualities that make them different.

What type of work are you doing?

- What are the tasks and responsibilities?
- How is it different and how is it similar to what you do now?

Why are you doing the work?

- How are you feeling about the work you're doing?
- How are you doing the work?
- How are you feeling when you're doing the work?
- Are you working differently than you are now?
- What are you wearing?

Where are you working?

- What is the environment like—are you in an office or at home?
  - Colors/Noise
  - Number of people present

When are you working?

- What days are you working?
- What are your hours?

How does your personal life fit into this picture of a perfect workday?

- What are you doing in your personal life?
- When are you doing it?

The goal of the previous exercise is to help you tap into your inner guidance and its vision for how work should fit into your life, without the limitations of your conscious mind.

Now that you have, I hope, at least the foundation of your vision, use the following questions to begin honing in on specifics. Record the answers in your workbook so that you can refer back to them.

▶ How hard was it to complete the exercise without judging or censoring your answer?

► Write down some of the "messages" that you heard as you tried to record your most honest, heartfelt vision of your work+life fit.

If you found it difficult to describe how you want work to fit into your life, you have a lot in common with most people, especially when they try the exercise for the first time. ROADBLOCK ALERT: As they try to articulate their perfect day, people typically report encountering the following resistance roadblocks: "That isn't realistic," "You can't do that," or the classic, "Are you crazy?" It may take many tries before the description of your workday truly reflects your nonjudgmental, uncensored vision. Have patience. Revisit the chapter on the resistance roadblock if you find yourself stuck.

Clarifying Your Vision

► Can you see the beginnings of your vision in the description of your perfect workday? If so, what might it look like?

► When you were a child, what did you love? What could you voluntarily do for hours and feel like only a few minutes had gone by? What activities gave you pure joy? When given a choice, how did you choose to spend your time? What were your dreams for your future?

Creating a vision full of possibilities and free of limitations often requires going back to your childhood, revisiting your interests and passions from that time before you bought into "reality" to find clues to your work+life vision.

How could you incorporate some of those childhood interests into a work+life fit now that you are an adult?

► Close your eyes. Imagine you're in a soundproof room where no one else can hear what you say and, therefore, can't judge it or hold you to it. With the freedom to say anything you want without ramifications, answer the following question as fast as you can without thinking: "Okay, what I really want to do is _____."

Finalizing Your Work+Life Vision

Hopefully, using the mind, body, spirit tools and completing the previous exercises have brought you to this point where you will finalize the vision that you'll use to complete the rest of the roadmap.

● ● ●

Let's take a moment to clear your mind:

- ► Get comfortable in your chair.
- ► Close your eyes and take three deep, slow breaths in and out.
- ► Now, imagine standing up and walking to the nearest door. Visualize yourself physically throwing all limitations and "realities" out that door.
- ► Now, visualize shutting the door and walking back to your seat.
- ► Next, look around and imagine that the walls of the room are gone and that light and air, which are symbols of all things that are possible, surround you.
- ► Open your eyes. It's time to finalize your vision.
- ► Remember your work+life vision is *an imaginative insight into how you want work to fit into the rest of your life.*
- ► In your Work+Life Fit Workbook, title a page "My Work+Life Vision."
- ► On that page, answer the following question, being as detailed as possible:

What is your vision for a better work+life fit, or how do you want work to fit into your life at this point in time?

HINT: You can proceed in one of two ways, either create one vision, or if it's less overwhelming, break your vision into smaller increments of short term, medium term, and long term. Choose whichever feels more comfortable to you.

Time and Energy Check: Is your vision realistic in terms of how much combined time and energy you are devoting to your work and personal life, recognizing that you only have 100% to give every day?

▶ If yes, you think it is realistic, then move on to the next part of the Work+Life Fit Roadmap;

▶ If no, you think it would require more than you have to give, try making some simple compromises to your vision to make it more realistic. But if that doesn't work, and if you haven't done this already, try dividing your vision into short term, medium term, and long term. Make sure to adjust your short-term vision so that it's realistic in terms of the time and energy you have to give today. You can do this by placing the work+life aspects that take up more than you have to give into the medium- and long-term versions. That way you don't have to give up any part of your original vision permanently. Instead, you may just be postponing some of it until the future.

Keeping Track of Coincidences and Serendipitous Moments

Now that you've articulated your work+life vision, start keeping track in your workbook of all of the coincidences and serendipitous moments—no matter how big or small—which occur while you complete the rest of the process. These are the moments that seem to confirm you are on the right track. And, remember, they don't have to be meaning-ful to anyone but you.

Review the list from time to time. It will help confirm the existence of and your connection to something greater sup-porting the implementation of your desired work+life fit.

With your work+life vision in hand, it's time to move on to mak-ing your vision a reality.

Making Your Vision a Reality

16

You've created your work+life vision—a vision full of imagination and possibility, and free of limitation. Now it's time to change direction and make that vision a reality. This is where the dreaming ends and the steps to actualize your vision begin.

Your vision must be compatible with the current realities of your work and personal life if your final work+life fit is going to succeed. This involves a "compare for compatibility" process whereby you compare your vision to each specific aspect of your work and personal life in order to identify any potential mismatches. The goal is to rectify any incompatibility *before* implementing your work+life fit, thus reducing the chance of being derailed later.

Resolving an incompatibility involves changing the reality if at all possible or, if that's not an option, adjusting your original vision. Depending on how far apart your vision and your realities are, all of the comparing and adjusting can transform your vision into a very different final work+life fit at the end of the roadmap. This may seem a bit disconcerting. You may wonder why you should exert the effort to create that vision in the first place if it's only going to change. There are two very good reasons.

First, if you have to adjust your vision to resolve an incompatibility, clearly you're going to choose to make the compromise that departs the least from your original vision. If you keep each compromise as small as possible, your final work+life fit will resemble your vision as closely as it can and still be aligned with the realities that currently prevail in your work and personal life.

And don't underestimate the power of conscious choice. There's a big difference between, "Okay, I'm unable to change this reality, so I'm choosing to make this compromise," and unconsciously moving forward with a work+life fit that is not only incompatible with critical aspects of your life, but will most likely fail.

Second, even though you may make compromises in the short term, it doesn't mean you can't pursue your original vision in the long term. Let your efforts to achieve your original goal influence future choices and decisions. It may take longer than you anticipated, but when you get there, all of the work and personal realities in your life will align and support your success.

With this in mind, instead of being discouraged when you have to make adjustments to your vision, view it as insurance that the work+life fit you implement today will succeed. And it only needs to be a detour in the journey, not your final destination.

Six Most Common Changes Your Vision Will Involve

Making your work+life vision a reality will most likely involve changes in one or more of the following:

▶ Why you are working
▶ What type of work you do
▶ Whom you work for/with

► How you work
► When you work
► Where you work

Changing "Why" You Work

Believe it or not, finding a better work+life fit can be as simple as re-framing why you're working. For some, the source of conflict is "Why am I doing this type of work or this particular job?" The good news is that you don't necessarily need to leave your current situation to dis-cover an enhanced sense of purpose.

JIM'S STORY

When I met Jim, he was in his late 40s and a general manager for a large manufacturing company. He introduced himself by saying, "You're looking at the embodiment of the midlife crisis. Also known as, 'Why the heck am I doin' this job?' It isn't really helping anyone if you think about it. I need to do something to make the world a bet-ter place."

We talked for a while and I learned that he liked his job, and en-joyed the fact that it afforded his family a comfortable lifestyle, but he wasn't convinced that was enough reason to stay.

He admitted that he did enjoy managing people and thought he might actually be good at it—or "at least that's what my people say in the reviews." Most of the people who worked for him were relatively young and inexperienced, and Jim truly enjoyed helping them master the various aspects of their jobs. So, his work+life vision was to leave the business world altogether and become a teacher.

At this point, Jim's primary goal was to find a job teaching young people in order to make a difference in their lives. I threw this ques-tion out to him, "Did you ever think that maybe you're already doing what you want to do?" He looked puzzled.

I continued, "Did you ever think that creating a supportive work environment within which the young people in your group can learn their jobs at the hand of a truly dedicated manager is a great service to them? You *are* their teacher. Maybe not in a school, but in a place that develops their careers and allows them to support their families."

After some silence, he responded hesitantly, "You know, I never thought about it that way before."

Maybe Jim could extend his responsibilities for the education of new employees beyond his group. Perhaps he could take over the company's training program. There were many ways he could accomplish his vision without leaving the company. He just needed to change "why" he did his job. Instead of viewing his job solely as that of manager, he could shift his perspective and think of himself more as a teacher. It seemed to work for him at this point and allowed him to achieve his vision in the context of his current career.

. . .

Maybe your vision is to find a job that allows you to have enough time, money, and energy to pursue an avocation or interest. While I believe that for every interest there is a job related to it somewhere, sometimes you aren't able to find a job doing what you love the most. And you can experience work/life conflict when you feel forced to choose a job unrelated to your true passion in order to finance that unpaid pursuit. You feel trapped in a job that "keeps you" from what you'd prefer to do.

In these cases, resolving the conflict involves embracing a vision that acknowledges two things. First, you can acknowledge that, at this point in time, you either can't or won't change the realities that keep you from having a job related to the activity you love. Second, you can change the "why" of working. You can acknowledge that your paid work is simply the means to devote time and energy to a non-paying avocation. By consciously acknowledging these two points, the conflict between the work you do out of necessity and the personal interest about which you are passionate can be replaced by a vision that embraces both.

Changing "What" You Do

Perhaps your vision for a better work+life fit includes a different job or career altogether. This was my experience when I resolved my work/life conflict by transitioning from banking to work/life consulting. It is also the experience of many of my clients. You can devote the same amount of time and energy to a job that you enjoy and a job you don't. One will make you feel great, while the other will result in work/life conflict.

If changing your job or career is part of your vision, making it happen involves many of the standard head-based, logical job-search techniques. These include resume writing, networking, and other ideas about which many great books have been written and with which career counselors or coaches can help (see resource section). Use all of these traditional job search tools, but don't allow them to constrain you.

Always remember that your internal guidance dreams bigger things than your logical mind can imagine. Keep in mind these "big dream" strategies:

- ▶ Make sure you're using the mind, body, spirit tools to provide that optimal context within which to analyze your job-search efforts.
- ▶ Contrary to much well-intentioned job-search advice, you *can* change careers. It may not be easy, but it can be done with a little patience, elbow grease, and internal guidance.
- ▶ Your passion will take you far. If you're passionate about a particular field, your interest will absolutely set you apart from the crowd and will impress those currently doing the work you want to do.

  The fact that you love what they do will make them willing to sit down and talk to you and give you not only helpful information, but good contacts. Ask yourself: What could I talk about endlessly without getting bored? What activity do I engage in that seems to make time stand still? The very thing that doesn't seem like work at all could be your ideal job.

▶ Do what you love and the money will follow. This is a title of a great book by Marsha Sinetar, and it couldn't be more true. Why? Because if you love what you do, again that natural passion will set you apart; it will guide you. You'll be willing to invest time and energy in order to be successful. Do I guarantee you will make a million dollars? No, but I believe you can make your vision into a paying venture, although you may have to take a reduction in earnings for a period of time in order to learn a new skill or to train in a different area of expertise. (ROADBLOCK ALERT: Unwillingness to compromise on the amount of money you make for a period of time could keep you from potential longer-term rewards).

Time and again, I've seen examples of this. Someone who started catering on weekends because she had kids and loved to cook, and went on to have her own show on the Food Network. A design assistant who loved handbags is now Kate Spade.

There are countless low-profile examples of the same experience: having a work+life vision that is achieved by changing what you do for work, and making it happen no matter how impossible it seems.

If changing what you do is one of your paths to a better work+life fit, take your vision and write down three concrete steps that you can take over the next two weeks toward achieving your goal. Once you've accomplished those three tasks, write down three more, and so on. Before you know it, you're on your way to a new career.

Changing "Whom" You Work For/With

One of the key components of work/life satisfaction is a supportive work environment.[1] To find it, you may have to work for a new company. Later on, we'll discuss the importance of a corporate culture that is compatible with your vision, and how to find it.

The other two key components of your work environment are a supportive manager and coworkers. By supportive, I mean overall and not just in the area of work/life. That said, it follows that either an unsupportive manager or an unsupportive coworker is enough to cause conflict. If this is your reality, your vision for a better work+life fit could involve changing whom you work with in order to resolve the conflict.

Like changing what you do, changing whom you work for or with involves many of the traditional job-search techniques discussed in the previous section.

DENISE'S STORY

Denise worked in the marketing department of a large pharmaceutical company. She pulled me aside after a focus group I'd conducted in her company to ask me to clarify something for her. "In your experience," she asked, "have you ever heard of anyone experiencing work/life conflict because of their manager, and not because they work too many hours, or have a long commute?"

I said, "Yes, I have heard of that, but tell me more."

She elaborated, "I don't actually have a problem with my hours per se, what I have a problem with is the stressful, uncomfortable environment that my manager creates every single day. The funny thing is he thinks he's great—but he's insane. For example, he'll say one thing in private, and then in meetings says another that makes you look foolish. You never know where you stand. The sad thing is the president of the company also thinks he's great, so nothing is going to change. I go home every night just wiped out from the day. I have enough *time* for my personal life, but my energy level is zero, so I just zone in front of the T.V. or go to bed. And then, I get up and start the whole nutty cycle over again the next day. Clearly, I'm going to have to find another job either within this company or elsewhere."

I regretfully agreed, "I'm afraid you're right."

Changing "How, When, and/or Where" You Work

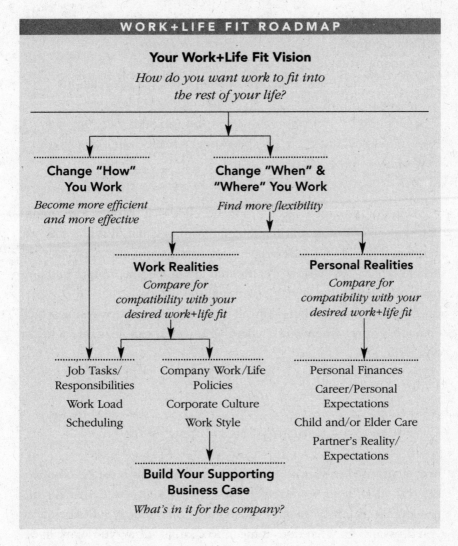

WORK+LIFE FIT ROADMAP

Your Work+Life Fit Vision
How do you want work to fit into the rest of your life?

Change "How" You Work
Become more efficient and more effective

Change "When" & "Where" You Work
Find more flexibility

Work Realities
Compare for compatibility with your desired work+life fit

Personal Realities
Compare for compatibility with your desired work+life fit

Job Tasks/ Responsibilities
Work Load
Scheduling

Company Work/Life Policies
Corporate Culture
Work Style

Personal Finances
Career/Personal Expectations
Child and/or Elder Care
Partner's Reality/ Expectations

Build Your Supporting Business Case
What's in it for the company?

Time to hit the Work+Life Fit Roadmap to begin making your vision a reality.

When you change how, when, and/or where you work, you are trying to reallocate time and energy away from work and devote it to your personal life. But there are certain realities in both your work life and personal life that influence whether or not these changes can be made. Addressing those realities is the focus for the next part of the roadmap. These critical realities are:

Work Realities	*Personal Realities*
Company work/life policies	Personal finances
Job tasks and responsibilities	Career/personal expectations
Workload	Child- and/or elder-care
Scheduling	responsibilities and supports
Corporate culture	Partner's reality and expectations
Work style	

Think of the process as a production line that manufactures the final work+life fit you will implement. Your original vision is the raw material that goes into the process, while the work and personal realities to which your vision is compared along the line mold it into a final work+life fit that is viable and realistic.

Before we begin, here's a quick overview of the ways in which changing how, when, and where you work can lead to a better work+life fit.

Changing "How" You Work

Any changes you want to make in how you work must be compatible with all of your work realities in order to succeed. Personal realities are not as critical here because they don't directly influence how you do your job. What does it mean to change "how" you work in order to find a better work+life fit?

First, let's admit that there's a lot of time and energy wasted every day on the job. Whether it's redundant or unnecessary job tasks and responsibilities (e.g., meetings, reports, etc.), or simply time-draining "face-time" behaviors (e.g., staying until the boss's office light goes off), you change how you work by first looking at how you do your job. Then you determine whether you could work more efficiently and effectively in order to find more time and energy to reallocate to your personal life.

In 1996, the Ford Foundation published the results of a groundbreaking six-year study.[2] The Foundation funded three teams of researchers, one from Families and Work Institute, to go into three Fortune 500 companies and look at how a change in how people worked helped resolve work/life conflict. The three companies were Corning, Inc., Xerox, and Tandem Company.

Not surprisingly, the study found that changing work practices to make them more efficient and more effective not only gives employees more time and energy to devote to their personal lives, but the resulting increase in employee satisfaction unleashes "individual energy and creativity" that increases productivity, which improves business results. In other words, it's a win-win for the employee and the company.

The FWI team's participation in this project shifted our consulting practice toward identifying and changing work practices that were counterproductive not only to employees' work+life fit but also to the business. Time and again, we discovered work inefficiencies and redundancies that unnecessarily drained time and energy away from employees' personal lives. And we saw how improving these work practices, even slightly, offered some relief from work/life conflict.

Comparing your vision to your work realities will help you take a similar look at how you do *your* job. The goal is to identify inefficient and redundant work practices that can be changed in order to make your vision a reality. The trick is to focus on the high-impact, high-value tasks and responsibilities and eliminate those that are not.

As a first step, everyone should try to change how they work, especially people who want to make minor changes in their work+life fit. You can free up an hour here and there, or you can reduce the amount of frantic energy you exert during work hours so that you aren't as wiped out at the end of every day. Everyone can benefit from making changes in this area.

Changing "When" You Work

Any changes in when you work must be compatible with all of your work *and* personal realities in order to succeed. Personal realities are relevant here because changes in either the time or in the amount of hours you work affect other aspects of your life.

There are two ways to change when you work. You can change the designated time that you work. For example, shifting your hours to 7:30 A.M. to 3:30 P.M. instead of 9:00 A.M. to 5 P.M. Or you can change the number of hours that you work, working 30 hours per week rather than 45 hours. Historically, changes like these fell under the standardized arrangements of flextime and part-time, respectively.

Another change you can make in when you work is to consciously choose when you perform certain tasks of your job. You can recoup lost time and energy by dedicating certain periods of the day or workweek to attend meetings, respond to emails, return phone calls, participate in training sessions, travel, entertain customers, and so on.

Again, the trick is to choose which activities have the highest impact at a particular time and exert influence over when you execute them, rather than having these tasks control you and your most precious resource—time.

Changing "Where" You Work

Any changes you want to make in where you work must also be compatible with all of your work *and* personal realities in order to succeed. Personal realities are relevant here because a change in where you work can affect other aspects of your life outside of work.

Historically, changing the location of where you work fell under the standard flexible work arrangement of telecommuting, which means working from a location other than your work site.

The beauty of telecommuting is that there's a lot of flexibility within that term. Telecommuting can be anything from taking care of answering your email at night after you've gone to an evening class, to working one day a week from home, to working full-time from a completely different state.

THE COMPARE-FOR-COMPATIBILITY EXERCISE

By now you understand that if achieving your vision requires making one or more changes in how, when, and/or where you work, these changes must be compatible with work and personal realities if your final work+life fit is going to succeed.

Let's begin the compare-for-compatibility exercise and transform your vision into the most viable work+life fit possible—one you'll have no problem building a business case to support, and one you'll feel more than comfortable proposing to your manager. And you will be able to do this because you will know beyond a shadow of a doubt that you've considered all of the possible contingencies.

NOTE TO JOB SEEKERS: If your vision involves finding a new job, complete the compare-for-compatibility exercise in the context of evaluating a potential job opportunity versus a job that you already hold.

Company Work/Life Policies

Chapter Goal: *To ensure that your work+life vision is compatible with the formal work/life policies and procedures of your current or prospective employer.*

Starting the
Compare-for-Compatibility Exercise

We begin by focusing on the work realities that are most critical to the success of your final work+life fit (see roadmap on p. 243). The first work reality you will examine for compatibility is the work/life policies of your current or prospective employer.

Specifically, what are the limitations and requirements for working part-time and for telecommuting? Are there any limitations that would prevent you from working a four-day week or from working at home? Would your proposed arrangement of combining these two types of flexibility meet all your company's requirements for each? In other words, are the policies compatible with your vision? If not, how can you make them fit?

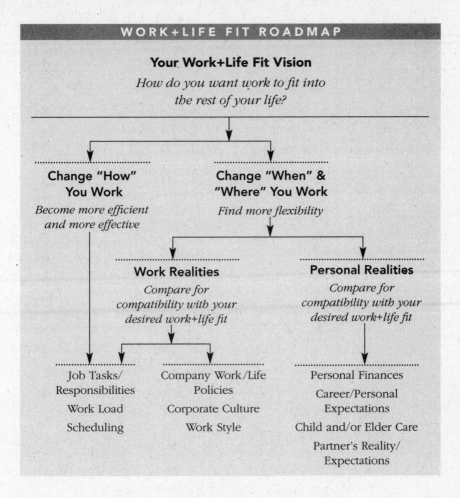

WORK+LIFE FIT ROADMAP

Your Work+Life Fit Vision
*How do you want work to fit into
the rest of your life?*

**Change "How"
You Work**
*Become more efficient
and more effective*

**Change "When" &
"Where" You Work**
Find more flexibility

Work Realities
*Compare for
compatibility with your
desired work+life fit*

Personal Realities
*Compare for
compatibility with your
desired work+life fit*

Job Tasks/
Responsibilities

Work Load

Scheduling

Company Work/Life
Policies

Corporate Culture

Work Style

Personal Finances

Career/Personal
Expectations

Child and/or Elder Care

Partner's Reality/
Expectations

Does the Company Have Formal
Work/Life Policies?

First, you need to determine whether or not your company has formal
work/life policies and procedures.

- ▶ Ask to see the company's human resource manual. Some
  companies, particularly smaller ones without an onsite HR
  department, may not have any formalized policies.
- ▶ If you can't find a record of any policies, call whoever is in
  charge of HR matters in your organization to confirm.

▶ If indeed none exist, then skip ahead to chapter 18, because you don't have to worry about whether the company's existing policies are compatible with your vision.

▶ If the company does have formal work/life-related policies, you specifically want to look at those that pertain to flexible work arrangements. These are the policies that will most directly effect your ability to change how, when, and where you work. Standard corporate policies typically define flexible work arrangements as follows:

Part-time: working less than full-time, or less than a 40- or 35-hour workweek

Flextime: working hours that differ from the 9-to-5 workday

Compressed workweek: working 80 hours (two full work-weeks) in a nine-day period instead of ten days, or 40 hours in a four-day period

Telecommuting: working remotely away from the workplace

Job-sharing: two people share a full-time 40-hour per week job, with each working three days per week allowing for one day of overlap.

Are the Details of Each Policy Compatible with Your Vision?

After you establish what formal policies do exist, you need to explore the details. Beyond the policy's definition of a flexible work arrangement, you need to understand the specific allowances and limitations. Why? Remember, most successful arrangements *do not* fit neatly into one of these five categories. In fact, a successful work+life fit is often a creative combination of two or more types of flexibility.

For example, if your vision involves working four eight-hour days per week with one of those days working at home, this is a combination of part-time and telecommuting. Therefore, it's important that you understand the detailed rules and regulations associated with both your company's part-time and telecommuting policies.

The following stories illustrate how, once you identify an incompatibility between the details of certain work/life policies and the changes you want to make in order to achieve your vision, you can either negotiate a change in the policy or change your vision in order to make them fit.

SUSAN'S STORY

Susan is a manager in a mid-sized company, and she has two junior officers and two administrative assistants reporting to her. Recently, she decided that she needed a different work+life fit so she could spend time with her mother who was in the final stages of cancer.

Her work+life vision was to work four 8-hour days per week in the office (instead of the typical five 12-hour days) and work about 4 hours from home on the fifth day, primarily returning calls and completing paperwork.

When she began the compare-for-compatibility process, she realized her vision and the company's part-time and telecommuting policies weren't compatible. According to the policy, if you worked less than the standard 40-hour workweek, you would not be able to retain managerial responsibilities and would have to take a reduction in title.

Susan's vision didn't include giving up the management of her team. She felt that her team would continue to have the same level of access to her, especially since she was willing to be available by cell phone and beeper even during the business hours she wasn't working.

During her negotiation, her senior manager agreed that the team wouldn't notice a big difference since she'd be available at all times if needed. And he agreed to waive the policy requiring her to give up managerial responsibilities. This worked because Susan identified these incompatibilities with her vision *before* the negotiation and addressed them up front. She changed the reality of the company's work/life policies to fit her vision.

ALEX'S STORY

Alex is a customer service representative for a large bank whose work+life vision is to work three 8-hour days (24 hours in total) in order to go back to college and take classes during his days off.

As he conducts the compare-for-compatibility exercise, Alex realizes that his vision and the company's work/life policies are not compatible. Specifically, the policy says that if you work less than 25 hours per week you lose your benefits. Because he's not married and doesn't qualify for the college's health care, he had planned on retaining his insurance, vacation, and 401(k) benefits.

Could he change the policy to match his vision, or would he have to change his vision to accommodate the policy? He realized that it would be easier to work 25.5 hours per week than to push to have the policy changed for such a minor gain. Plus he could use the extra income. So he proposed the following to his manager: He would work three 8.5-hour days and would make up that half hour by only taking a half-hour lunch the three days he was in. Also, he would prorate his vacation time and his 401(k) benefit contribution.

By recognizing in advance how the company's work/life policy and his original vision conflicted, Alex was able to adjust his vision, the "when" he worked, in order to accommodate this work reality that couldn't be changed.

ELIZABETH'S STORY

Elizabeth, a public relations manager for a large corporation, wants a work+life fit that allows her to work from home two days a week. She recently moved in order to be closer to her husband's new job, but the move extended her already lengthy commute of three hours round-trip by another hour. By working from home two days a week,

Elizabeth believes she will recoup an additional eight hours of productive work (two days without a four-hour commute), not to mention reduce her level of exhaustion.

When she sat down to compare her vision with the company's work/life policy for telecommuting, she realized that the company reimbursed only employees who telecommuted full-time for equipment they needed, such as a computer, online access, and a fax machine. While she hadn't envisioned the company paying for all of the equipment, she had hoped that they would pay for half.

She didn't want to change her vision. She felt that she needed to be in the office at least three days a week in order to do her job effectively. But she wouldn't realize the time savings from less commuting and reduced stress if she worked only one day from home. So she decided to negotiate with her manager for the company to cover half of the cost of the computer and the installation of a second dedicated phone line, as well as the monthly cost of her calls to the office. She would then pay for the fax machine and the monthly maintenance cost of the second phone line. To support her case, she calculated the benefit of eight more hours of productive time working versus sitting on the train, and her boss approved the plan.

COMPARE-FOR-COMPATIBILITY EXERCISE

1. Does your company have formal work/life policies? If no, then move on to chapter 18.

2. If yes, then specifically review the policies related to the following flexible work arrangements. Write down how they are defined, and write down any of their limitations:

   - Part-time:
   - Flextime:
   - Compressed workweek:
   - Telecommuting:
   - Job-sharing:

3. Go to the page in your workbook titled My Work+Life Vision. Does your vision involve working some form of part-time, flextime, compressed workweek, telecommuting, and/or job sharing? If yes, which ones?

4. Having determined which policies are relevant, compare this vision to each policy. Are they compatible? If yes, go to chapter 18.

5. If no, how would you negotiate with your manager to change the policy to make it compatible? Remember, everything is negotiable. I've seen many situations in which a term or condition of the "policy" is negotiated away as part of the final work+life fit. The key is to be aware of it in advance and build a strong enough case to change it.

   And if the policy can't be changed, you need to consider how you might change your vision to accommodate it.

6. If you've chosen to change your vision in order to resolve an incompatibility with the work/life policies of your current or prospective employer, record the revised version of your vision directly under the original version in your workbook. You will use this revised version of your vision in the compare-for-compatibility exercise in chapter 18.

Job Tasks, Workload, and Scheduling

Chapter Goal: *To ensure that your work+life vision is compatible with the tasks and responsibilities of your job, your workload, and scheduling.*

Changing how, when, and/or where you work will require changing the tasks and responsibilities of your job, your workload, and/or your scheduling of work. It can't be avoided. Together, all three of these realities represent what you typically think of as "work":

- ▶ **Job tasks:** the tasks and responsibilities that define the work that you do
- ▶ **Workload:** the volume of job tasks
- ▶ **Scheduling of work:** the scheduling of when you complete those tasks

Your objective, of course, is first to identify what your tasks, responsibilities, workload, and scheduling issues are, and then you can adapt these aspects of work to accommodate your vision. However, it's important to recognize before you begin that there are limits to what you may be able to change. At some point, the tasks of a job may simply not match the type of work+life fit you want. Or maybe your workload can be altered only so much. Or perhaps your schedule can't be adjusted beyond a certain point to accommodate your vision. In these cases, you will either need to adapt your vision to conform to the unchangeable realities of the job or look for another position with tasks, a workload, and a schedule that complement your vision.

A SPECIAL NOTE TO JOB SEEKERS: When considering the appropriateness of a potential job, it's important to determine whether the aspects of that job are in line with your vision. However, recognize that your ability to change the tasks, workload, and scheduling of a position prior to having the job may be limited. That doesn't mean that you can't consciously choose to take a job that isn't an optimal fit with the goal of adjusting the aspects of that job to match your original vision over time. Just make sure that there isn't too drastic a difference between the tasks, workload, and scheduling and your ultimate goal. Otherwise, you may be setting yourself up for work/life conflict.

How Can You Change "Work" in Order to Make Your Vision a Reality?

At this point, we've looked at two of the top three excuses for not seeking a better work+life fit: "I'm afraid" and "I can't afford it." Now it's time to address the third: "I have too much work."

If you think you have too much work, you probably do. People are indeed working longer hours and working harder during those hours than they did 20 years ago. And they're still unable to get their work done.[1] You can see that, if you want a better work+life fit, it's incumbent upon you to change either your job tasks, workload, and/or schedule in order to reallocate some of that time and energy back to your personal life.

Read Natalie's story of how she reevaluated her work and found great success with a new work+life fit.

NATALIE'S STORY

After finding out about my book, Natalie, a friend of mine from college, sent me an email about her experience with making work compatible with the work+life fit that she needed at this point in her life:

"You know, Cali, if I could tell people anything it would be this—it's amazing how, when you want more time for your personal life, it forces you to really focus on the parts of your job that have the highest impact. You are so much more efficient and effective.

"After I had my second child, I was ready to leave my job, but then my boss said, 'Here's the deal, you do what you need to do to get your job done and have the time you want. And I'll let you know if anyone has a problem with it.' So, here I am, three years later, lucky to get into work by 10 A.M. and out the door by 4 P.M., but getting as much if not more done than I did before. Not to mention the fact that no one has ever had a problem with the way I am working, *and* I've been promoted twice."

. . .

Let Natalie's story be an inspiration. Obviously, she had a vision of how she wanted work to fit into her life. When she compared that vision with her job tasks, workload, and schedule, and found aspects of them weren't compatible with her vision, she made changes.

She reprioritized the tasks of her job focusing on those that made the highest impact in the least amount of time. She addressed her workload by eliminating or delegating work that she couldn't accomplish in the allotted time. And, she more efficiently organized *when* she executed those tasks to accommodate her schedule. Simply put, she changed her work to make it compatible with her vision of a better work+life fit.

How Can You Influence Your Tasks, Workload, and Scheduling?

Let's revisit the concept of *level of influence* that we first discussed in the introduction to the roadblocks in Step 2. Influence is the power that you, as one person, have to make your work more compatible with your vision.

You have direct control over only your own tasks, workload, and schedule. Therefore, this is where you should exert most of your energy. But, the reality is, none of us works in a vacuum. The magnitude of the changes you can realistically make in your own work will be influenced by two other groups over which you have less influence: 1) your team and the people with whom you work directly, and 2) the larger organization that interacts with your team.

That said, on many occasions, managers have told me that when someone tries to become more efficient in the way that they work in order to find a better work+life fit, it forces everyone to step back and ask, "Should we be doing things this way? Is this task necessary? Do we need to have this meeting at that time? Could we do it better, more efficiently?" As a result, the whole team becomes more productive and efficient.

But remember, change takes time. Therefore, some of your suggestions that affect other people either on your team or outside the team could take longer to implement.

What Are Your Tasks, Responsibilities, Workload, and Scheduling?

Again, while these aspects of work are interrelated, each one has unique qualities that determine compatibility with your vision.

Tasks and Responsibilities

These are the activities in which you engage to do your job. For example:

> Writing reports
> Selling products and services
> Typing
> Filing
> Assembling parts
> Taking patient vital signs
> Answering customer questions
> Attending meetings
> Managing people

As you can see just from this short list, the list of tasks and responsibilities includes any and every detail of your workday.

ROADBLOCK ALERT: If you need to give up a certain task or responsibility in order to have the work+life fit that you want, you could hit a success-related roadblock, especially if that task or responsibility affects your level of prestige or advancement. For example, giving up a certain amount of seniority, no longer attending certain meetings that can't be rescheduled, or no longer traveling. As we discussed in the success roadblock chapter, there are trade-offs when you want a new work+life fit, and giving up certain tasks is a trade-off that often needs to be made to accommodate your vision.

Workload

Workload is the volume of tasks that you are expected to accomplish. If you are working longer hours, working harder during those longer hours, and still aren't able to get your work done, your workload must be increasing. In other words, the volume of tasks that you are expected to complete has increased.

If workload is standing between you and your goal, chances are there are plenty of inefficient and redundant tasks and responsibilities that you can change and maybe even eliminate. Why? Because with everyone working so long and hard, no one has a moment to step back and say, "Why are we doing this? Do we want to do it this way or is there some other, perhaps better, way to do it?" Betsy, one of my clients, recently had this experience.

BETSY'S STORY

Betsy, an insurance analyst, needed help formulating a work+life fit proposal to present to her boss. Her vision was to work from home one day a week. While this doesn't sound like a particularly drastic change, it would be the first time someone at Betsy's level proposed such an arrangement so she wanted to be prepared.

As part of the process, we spent a great deal of time making sure that her vision was compatible with her job. At one point, she said, "You know there's something we do that is so unnecessary from the client's perspective, but increases our workload and takes up a lot of time and energy."

She continued, "We have this unwritten rule that we complete every client project in one week, even though the client only needs a portion of the information we provide within a week and would be happy to receive the rest within two or three weeks. Not to mention the fact that a whole section of each final report that we produce is essentially a review of previous work we've done for the client. It takes a great deal of time to compile, and the information is irrelevant to the client's current deal. This artificially tight turnaround for every project makes my work+life fit somewhat incompatible with my work because it sometimes requires my presence on short notice."

We talked further and I told her that managers I've worked with have often found that having one person on their team change the way they do their work in order to have more flexibility forces *everyone* to do things more efficiently. Betsy agreed, "You know I just don't think anyone has ever said 'Why do we do this when the clients don't need it?'" So, instead of changing her work+life fit, Betsy decided to discuss changing the project management timeline and process with her boss, as well as eliminating the unnecessary client work review from the final report. In doing so, she was sure that she could arrange her workload to allow her to work from home at least one day a week.

. . .

ROADBLOCK ALERT: For some overworked people, their overwhelming workload is evidence of how indispensable they are to the company. This attitude is perpetuated in cultures where "face time" is prevalent. It's almost as if they think "I have an overwhelming workload, there-fore, I'm critical to the success of the company, and they can't get rid of me." Kind of like a security blanket.

What happens when this person decides that they want a different work+life fit, and achieving it requires them to reduce their workload? There is the fear that without the heavy workload, they may have to ask themselves, "What am I?" and "How am I doing?"

You may also encounter resistance, from within yourself and from others. As you try to change your workload, you may find yourself re-sisting the effort for all of the reasons we just discussed related to suc-cess and fear. You don't want to give up that particular task or responsibility, or you're afraid of what will happen if you do.

But also, as others see you give work away or question the ne-cessity of certain aspects of your work, they may resist—especially if they think it means more work for them. This is why it's imperative that you involve your work group in the implementation of your work+life fit, particularly if changes in your workload increases theirs. Moreover, if a coworker is going to take on more work, make sure he is recognized for his efforts.

Scheduling

Scheduling involves when and where you complete the tasks of your job. If you remember from the beginning of the book, when asked what would reduce their work/life conflict, people said, "time." Changing the way you schedule your work can free up a great deal of time. Time that you can then reallocate to your personal life.

In Betsy's case, the unnecessarily short turnaround time for client reports added to her workload, but changing that standard would also require a change in scheduling.

Whether it's meetings that start late and run long, constant interruptions from phone calls and e-mails, breakfast or dinner meetings that could be conducted during regular work hours, or unnecessary scheduling of shifts that has nothing to do with needs of the business, they all take up precious time.

By making certain changes in when you execute the tasks and responsibilities of your job, you can recoup lost time and divert it back to your personal life.

Are your job tasks, responsibilities, workload, and schedule compatible with your vision?

Again, because all three aspects of work are distinct yet so closely related, don't be surprised if you find that changing a job task to make it more compatible with your vision in turn alters your workload and changes your schedule. And vice versa.

It's easiest to begin with your job tasks and responsibilities. As you determine whether each one is compatible with the way you want work to fit into your life, also consider how a change in that particular task affects your workload and/or scheduling.

COMPARE-FOR-COMPATIBILITY EXERCISE

1. Review the most recent version of your Work+Life Vision in your workbook (the version from the end of chapter 17).

2. List all of the tasks and responsibilities related to your job, being as detailed as possible. Clearly, everyone will have a unique list since there is infinite number of different jobs. Here's a typical list:

   - Completing reports
   - Getting projects approved
   - Gathering data for a project
   - Turning raw material into a finished product

- Responding to customers' requests
- Managing people
- Attending meetings
- Writing and responding to e-mail
- Making and returning phone calls
- Traveling and entertaining

3. Is each task or responsibility compatible with the changes you want to make in order to achieve your vision? And how does that change influence your workload and/or scheduling? For example, ask yourself:

- Is this task or responsibility necessary? Can it be done more efficiently or differently? Can it be eliminated to reduce my workload?
- Can I retain this existing task or responsibility with my new work+life fit and still do it well? Do I want to do it? Do I need to give all or part of it to someone else? Does anyone else have the skills or the time and energy to take it on?
- What portion of each one of these tasks and/or responsibilities am I responsible for? How will my work+life fit affect those responsible for the rest?
- Can this task be done at a different time?
- Can I set a certain period of time aside and dedicate it solely to completing this one particular task or responsibility instead of doing it throughout the day?
- If I change when I execute this task, whom does that change affect?
- Can this task or responsibility be done in a location outside of the office? Would I have access to the information necessary to do that task? If not, can I get it and how?
- If I change where I do this task, whom does that affect?

4. If yes, each one of the tasks, as well as all workload and scheduling issues, are compatible with the most recent version of your vision, move on to chapter 19.

5. If no, then you need to try to change the task or adjust your workload or schedule in order to make it compatible with your vision.

6. If you're unable to adjust a task, workload, or scheduling reality, then you need to adjust your vision and record this new version in your Workbook directly under the prior version. You will use this new version in chapter 19.

ALICIA'S STORY

Alicia is going to start with one of her job tasks: meetings. Specifically, she needs to determine whether the meetings she attends are compatible with the work+life fit she wants to implement. Alicia's Work+Life Vision is to work in the office four days a week from 9:30 A.M. to 5:00 P.M. and work from home on the fifth day, which she would like to be Monday. Currently, Alicia works five days in the office from 9:00 A.M. to 6:00 P.M.

Will she be able to have that work+life fit and still attend the meetings for which she is responsible? Is the number of meetings compatible, and are the times the meetings are scheduled compatible?

- ▶ Alicia attends approximately 10 meetings per week.
- ▶ Five of them are standing meetings with her peers, her team, and her boss to track different aspects of the marketing project process. On average, five other meetings are added to her schedule each week by various individuals to discuss various issues.
- ▶ Of the five standing meetings, two take place on Fridays. One is supposed to begin at 9:00 A.M. but never starts before 9:30 A.M. and the other usually begins promptly at 2:00 P.M. A third meeting is on Tuesday at 4:00 P.M. and tends to run late.
- ▶ The unplanned meetings occur whenever the person planning them wants to meet.

So, the answer to the second question is no, her work+life fit is not compatible with all of Alicia's meeting obligations. Therefore, she's going to propose the following changes in her meeting-related workload and scheduling to make them compatible:

Meeting Workload

▶ Of the five standing meetings, two are probably not necessary, or could be handled by someone else.

▶ Clarifying the agenda up front to determine whether her presence is critical or if someone else could participate in her stead could reduce the number of unplanned meetings.

▶ As a result of reducing the number of meetings, Alicia would free up time to complete her other work, which would allow her to arrive later in the morning and leave earlier in the evening.

Meeting Scheduling

▶ To allow her to arrive by 9:30 A.M. on Fridays, Alicia is going to propose officially changing the meeting's start time from 9:00 A.M. to 9:30 A.M. That is when everyone arrives anyway.

▶ To ensure that all of her meetings are more efficient, especially the meeting on Tuesday, she's going to encourage the group to set an agenda in advance and commit to a start and end time.

▶ To ensure that the rest of her workweek doesn't fill up with other meetings, she's going to block off certain times for meetings on her calendar. When someone calls to schedule, she will suggest an alternative time recognizing that she may have to be flexible.

This is just one example of what happens when you eliminate or change a job task. You become more efficient, lighten your workload, and free up your schedule in a way that allows you to achieve your goal. Here are examples of changes you can make to other tasks, workload, and scheduling:

- ▶ **Reports:** Like Betsy did, look at the reports you complete. Are they necessary? Are you using the most efficient means to gather the information for the report?
- ▶ **Answering the phone and/or returning phone calls:** As with meetings, try to set aside a certain period of time when you or make phone calls in order to focus uninterrupted on other work.

  Do you have to pick up the phone when it rings, or can you set aside a period of time at the beginning, middle, and end of the day to review, prioritize, and return your calls? This allows the rest of the day to be devoted to other work.
- ▶ **E-mail:** Do you have to respond to your e-mail immediately upon receipt or, as with the phone, can you set aside specific times at the beginning, middle, and end of the day where you review, prioritize, and respond to e-mails?
- ▶ **Travel:** What is the purpose of the trip? Is it strategically critical to the business? Could the goal be achieved another way (e.g., conference call, videoconference, etc.)?
- ▶ **Entertaining:** What is the purpose of the breakfast, lunch, or dinner? Could the goal be achieved by another means (e.g., lunch instead of breakfast or dinner, or a meeting in the office)? Do you have to be available to entertain every day, or could you limit it to certain days?
- ▶ **Redistributing work:** If you determine that someone else could take over some of your tasks and/or responsibilities, make sure that person is adequately rewarded, and that the extra work is not a burden but an opportunity. Perhaps that opportunity is more exposure, a chance to develop a skill, advance to another level, or earn more money. Whatever it is, you want to make sure with the help of your manager that you limit potential resentment from coworkers who them-

selves may feel overworked already. You do this by acknowledging their increased contribution in some way.

▶ **Changing scheduling procedures**: If you work in an environment of rigidly scheduled shifts—manufacturing, retail, restaurants, nursing—propose building more flexibility into the scheduling process to accommodate the work+life needs of employees.

Corporate Culture

Chapter Goal: *To ensure that your work+life vision is compatible with your company's corporate culture.*

What is corporate culture and why is it one of the critical work realities with which your work+life fit must be compatible? Corporate culture is all of the unwritten rules—norms and values—that influence behavior within an organization. The power of these unwritten rules is that everyone in the company has chosen unconsciously to buy into them and behave according to their dictates.

Frequently, those rules contradict written policy, business realities, or both. Betsy's story from the previous chapter is a good example. The unwritten rule in her company dictated that every client project be completed in a week, even though there wasn't a real client need. It was "just the way we do things." And until Betsy challenged it, everyone continued to buy into that unnecessarily tight time frame.

Another more common example is face time. Everyone is at their desk by 8:00 A.M. and no one dares to leave until 6 P.M., even if their work is done, because "you don't want to be the first car out of the parking lot." This cultural norm often supercedes a written policy that says the official hours are 9:00 A.M. to 5 P.M.

Because of its intangible quality, you'll address corporate culture differently than the other work realities in the roadmap. When there is a mismatch between your vision and other work realities, you first try to change the reality. And then, if that doesn't work, you adjust your vision.

But with corporate culture the strategy is different because the actions of one person usually won't have enough power to change a corporate culture. Therefore, if you recognize an incompatibility between your vision and your company's culture, you have three options:

- ► **Come up with a strategy to mitigate the potential effects of the incompatibility.** For example, let's say the norm is that "we go out to dinner with our clients" even though the business could be as easily handled over lunch. But since your work+life vision includes leaving the office by 5 P.M. two nights a week and working from home one other day, it limits your availability for dinners. To counteract this norm, you plan to communicate to your manager about how daytime business meetings, lunches, and occasional dinners are effectively sustaining your client relationships.
- ► **Recognize the incompatibilities with the corporate culture with the sole purpose of not being unexpectedly derailed by them as you move forward.** In other words, consciously choose which cultural norms you will no longer buy into and then move forward with your unaltered vision. But understand that you may have to address the consequences of your choice not to conform, or
- ► **Adjust your vision to accommodate aspects of the corporate culture that you feel unable to ignore.** Sometimes the difference between your vision and the cultural norms in your company is just too dramatic to ignore. Adjust your vision accordingly and consider whether this position with this particular company is appropriate for you given the way you want work to fit into your life.

ADAM'S STORY

Adam is an associate at a large professional services firm, and he would like to have a new work+life fit whereby he gets to work at 9:30 A.M. three days a week. Currently, he arrives by 8:00 A.M.

Arriving later would allow Adam to go to the gym three mornings a week and drop off his daughter at school before coming into the office. Having just been diagnosed with high blood pressure at a young age, it was important to him to try to improve his health. Plus, his daughter was usually getting ready for bed by the time he got home at night. Taking her to school was a nice chance to visit. And he had no trouble working until 6:30 P.M. on the days that he came in later, which is what he typically did anyway.

The interesting part of Adam's conflict was how troubled he was about asking for what seemed to be a very small change in his schedule. He felt that he was asking for something huge that would most likely not work.

At first, I didn't quite understand why it was such a big deal. So I asked him about it, "Adam, I don't want to minimize your obvious discomfort with the work+life fit that you want to propose. But I don't see why your manager should have such a hard time approving an arrangement that essentially lets you arrive a half hour later than the formal start time of 9:00 A.M. three mornings a week."

"You just don't understand the way things are done at my company," Adam told me. "Basically, our annual review system is a joke. In eight years, I've probably had three reviews. So, what managers do is use the amount of time you spend in the office as an indicator of how hard you're working. That's why everyone gets in by 8:00 even though officially we don't have to be in until 9:00 A.M. And no one leaves before 6:30 even though by that time half the people are making personal calls or surfing the net.

"I'd much rather get in, do my job, and get out. But I also want to do well. So, believe me, if I start coming in at 9:30 A.M. I could be getting twice as much work done and they would only see that I was working less. Can you blame me for being worried?"

. . .

No, I couldn't blame him. His vision was incompatible with the corporate cultural norm that says you're working hard only if you put in a lot of face time. But Adam did have some choices.

First, he could change his vision, but there wasn't much wiggle room within his proposal. He already wasn't asking for very much.

Second, he could acknowledge the incompatibility and recognize it for what it is and present his proposal anyway, letting the chips fall where they may.

Or he could propose his work+life fit as is but prepare a strategy to combat the potential conflict with the corporate culture. In Adam's case, he could give his boss periodic updates on the status of critical projects, making sure he demonstrates a consistent ability to make deadlines even with his new schedule. Hopefully, this would help his manager to stop using face time as a proxy for Adam's performance.

Here's something else to consider about corporate culture and work+life fit. Corporate culture may be intangible, but it's relatively easy to identify (see the exercises at the end of the chapter). I believe it should be part of everyone's job-search process to study the culture of a prospective employer and ask yourself some tough questions about what type of work+life fit you want.

Remember the story of my friend Steve from business school who went into investment banking? That's an example of a drastic incompatibility between the work+life vision Steve wanted (regular involvement in the day-to-day realities of his family) and corporate culture (the investment banking philosophy of "we pay you a lot of money, therefore we own you").

I'm not saying Steve made a mistake going into this field, but I am saying the reality of what the investment banking world expects from its employees is pretty common knowledge. If you can honestly say, "Yeah, I can do that," then go for it. But, if you look at a company and its culture and say, "Gosh, I don't know," you may want to think twice.

It can be hard to know when you take a job exactly what your life will look like, even six months from now. But it's always worthwhile to ask yourself whether a company's culture is open to some type of flexibility and whether you are the kind of person who is comfortable rejecting a corporate culture to which the majority of other employees are conforming. There are certainly people like that; are you really one of them?

Evaluating a Company's Culture

To determine compatibility of an employer's corporate culture—either current or prospective—you need to identify the subtle nuances that make up a corporate culture by answering the following questions in your workbook. Then you will use the information to create a description, or corporate culture snapshot, to compare to your vision at the end of the chapter. Some of the questions will be easier to answer if you are evaluating your current employer; however, even as an interviewee, careful observation and discrete questioning can unearth helpful insights.

• • •

Look at how the company addresses employee work/life issues:

▸ Does the company have formal work/life policies and/or offer work/life programs, such as child care and elder care? (Remember, the mere fact that policies and programs exist *does* affect the culture by giving you a platform for a discussion with your manager.)

▸ Is the idea of placing value on an employee's work *and* personal life part of the company's recruitment materials? Does it come up in any of your interviews?

▸ Is *any* portion of your manager's compensation tied to his or her ability to help employees address their work/life conflicts? (Believe it or not, there are a few companies that do this, and it is usually included in the description of the companies on the Working Mother Top 100 Companies list.)

When you talk to people about the corporate culture, listen for phrases that are repeated—both positive and negative:

- ► "You can't turn down a spontaneous dinner request from a senior executive." (Think about how that affects family commitments or an evening class you're taking.)
- ► "We pride ourselves on being available to our clients 24/7." (You can't get a clearer message that work is an all-consuming focus here.)
- ► "This is a family organization." (Can indicate openness to commitments outside of work.)
- ► "We like to grow our own." (Can indicate commitment to employee development.)
- ► "You don't want to be the last car in or the first car out of the parking lot." (Can indicate a focus on face time instead of work outcomes to determine performance.)

Look at how employees are valued and treated:

- ► Are employees considered important assets of the organization, or is there an "if you don't want the job, there are three more right behind you" attitude?
- ► How were you treated during the interview process, either currently or when you originally got your job? This is often a foreshadowing of how you will be treated in the company. Were the people with whom you met respectful and true to their word? When you arrived the first day on the job, were they organized and prepared for you?
- ► How formalized and objective is the annual performance review process? Is there an emphasis on your long-term professional development and growth? Ask to see a copy of the

format for an annual review. What are the measures against which you have been or will be judged?

Look for environmental clues:

- ▶ Do employees keep pictures of their families on their desks?
- ▶ Do employees at all levels talk freely about their lives outside of work as a natural part of a discussion? If you do ask about the ability to have a rewarding personal life with this job, what's the response?
- ▶ If it's a smaller company, how do the owners behave with regard to their own work and personal life? This is important because the owner will set the tone for the organization.

Do some research:

- ▶ Is the company ever cited as one of the Working Mother Top 100 Companies (This list is not only helpful for working mothers, but for any employee who wants to know which companies support work+life needs of employees.) or the Fortune magazine's 100 Best Companies to Work For? (See the resource section for the most recent listing of companies.) Look deeper into the reasons that the company was included to see if any had to do with commitment to work+life and to the development of employees.
- ▶ If the company is smaller and more local, is it ever cited in local publications for corporate citizenship?
- ▶ Are there any other aspects of the company's culture that you think are important to address?

THE COMPARE-FOR-COMPATIBILITY EXERCISE

1. Using the answers to the questions above, it's time to create your corporate culture snapshot.

- Look over the information that you've gathered in your workbook. What does it tell you?
- Create your snapshot by answering the following question: "This company's unwritten values and rules related to work and personal life are . . . ."

2. Compare your work+life vision with the snapshot. Can you see any incompatibilities? If no, and your vision and the culture are compatible, then move on to chapter 20.

3. If yes:

- Can you think of a strategy to mitigate the potential effects of the incompatibility? For example, Adam's plan to communicate the status of his work more proactively in order to mitigate the impact of face time at his company.
- If you're unable to develop a strategy to address the potential incompatibility, are you able to handle the potential resistance from yourself and others when you implement your work+life fit? For example, without his communication strategy in place, there is a chance people will think Adam is not working as hard because he comes in an hour and a half later than everyone else.
- Or do you want to change your work+life vision to accommodate the aspects of corporate culture that you can't develop a strategy to mitigate—and don't feel you can ignore? Go to your workbook and adjust your vision accordingly.
- Finally, if you're analyzing the culture of a *prospective* employer and you've identified a mismatch, you need to ask yourself, "Is this the type of culture I want to work in?" Or are you willing to wait to find a culture that supports your vision either right away or in the future after you've established yourself? If more people made job choices based upon the supportiveness of corporate cultures, more companies would be forced to make positive changes.

Work Style

Chapter Goal: *To ensure that your work+life fit vision is compatible with your work style.*

There are two aspects of your personal work style that affect the success of your work+life fit. First, there are characteristics that managers feel you must possess for them to support your proposed arrangement life fit. And second, there are work styles that are more compatible with certain types of flexibility than others are. This compatibility influences your happiness with your new arrangement.

Your Work Style and Manager Support

When managers talk about why they supported a work+life fit proposal, they consistently mention the following characteristics as critical to the employee's success: self-starter, trustworthy, motivated, and reliable. In other words, without these qualities, a manager is much less likely to feel comfortable supporting your arrangement. However, with them, they're often more than willing to give it a try.

When I was working as a corporate consultant with Corporate-Family Solutions, our team identified personal work style as a key contributor to the success of a flexible arrangement. The story of how we discovered this will help you understand how to address this work reality in your negotiation with your manager.

In many companies, the official human resource policy states that requests for flexible arrangements by anyone with a performance rating below a certain level won't be approved. At first glance, that may seem fair because you want to retain your best performers, and your best performers are more likely to manage an arrangement properly. Here's the problem. Very few companies have an objective, fair, and consistent annual review process. Some do, but most don't.

Often I'd meet employees who hadn't had a review in two years. And what happens if someone had a performance problem in the past but had since rectified the issue? There would be no record of the improvement. Or what if someone didn't get along with their previous manager and that affected her last official rating? But now that person has a new manager and her rating has come up—again, there is no record. Should that person not be allowed to propose a new work+life fit?

Once we identified this problem, we realized that the managers and human resource departments were simply using ratings to identify the work style characteristics that tended to determine the success of a flexible work arrangement. So, to move the companies away from this practice, we identified the critical work style characteristics associated with high ratings—self-starter, motivated, trustworthy, and reliable—and had managers determine qualification based on the existence of these characteristics as they observed them in an employee.

CARRIE'S STORY

Carrie had been with her employer for less than 16 months when her mother unexpectedly was diagnosed with cancer. Grateful to live close by, Carrie wanted to change her work+life fit for at least six months to help her mother through a series of operations and chemotherapy treatments. Given what she knew of the treatment course, she wanted to propose working four 10-hour days (8 A.M. to 6 P.M. Tuesday through Friday, with Monday off), and working from home on Fridays. However, as she completed the compare-for-compatibility exercise, she realized that there was an incompatibility between her work+life vision and the work/life policies of her company. According to the policy, employees who wanted to implement a change in their work schedule had to have a performance rating of 2 or higher. The problem was that in the 16 months Carrie worked for the company, she had never had a formal review. And on top of that, she had a new manager.

Even though she had only worked for Steve for five months, she knew that he would say she was a self-starter, motivated, trustworthy, and reliable. And she also knew that he would be willing to work with her to adjust her schedule in order to be with her mother, especially because her proposal was compatible with the tasks and responsibilities of her job. When she presented Steve with her proposal, she asked that he talk to HR and have them waive the rating requirement since she'd never had a review. He agreed and, after speaking with the VP of human resources, was able to approve Carrie's proposal with confidence.

．　．　．

So, ask yourself how your manager would describe your personal work style. Are you a self-starter—meaning that your manager doesn't have to follow up and monitor your work in order for it to get done? Are you motivated? Do you take the initiative? Are you trustworthy and reliable? Do you do what you say you're going to do when you say you're going to do it? If you answer yes to all of these questions, then your manager is more likely to approve your proposal.

SPECIAL NOTE TO JOB SEEKERS: Use examples from your previous jobs to illustrate these critical characteristics to a prospective employer.

But what if your answer is "no, my manager would probably not use those words to describe my work style"? Well, there are a couple of options. First, sit down with your manager and discuss the situation. Explain that you'd like to pursue a different work+life fit, but you are aware that she might have difficulty approving your request because you haven't proven that you are a self-starter, motivated, and trustworthy. Therefore, you'd like to take the next few months to prove that you can change, with the understanding that in the future she would be willing to consider your request. This way your manager fully understands your motivation for improving your performance and can view your desire for a better work+life fit as an incentive.

Another approach is to address your performance problems before ever mentioning your desire for a new work+life fit. That way your manager won't think you're asking for a quid pro quo, because really these behaviors should already be part of your performance. But only you know your manager, and only you can decide what approach would work best.

There is also the possibility that your unreliability or lack of motivation is caused by an unresolved work/life conflict. If this is your reality, make sure that you present your proposed work+life fit as a way to resolve this problem. It will make your manager much more likely to support your request.

KEN'S STORY

Since his son started school, Ken finds that he often arrives 30 minutes late for his 8:00 A.M. shift. Because his wife's hours are 7:00 A.M. to 3 P.M., Ken is in charge of getting Jerome off to school. He's tried dropping him off before going to work, but the school is twenty minutes in the opposite direction from work. So now he's been waiting for the bus, but by the time it arrives and he drives to work, he's late most days.

While Ken's boss, Doug, has tried to be flexible, the company policy requires Doug to penalize Ken for his late arrivals. Finally, after Doug warned Ken he was in danger of being put on probation, Ken decided he needed to formally request a change of hours. After looking at his tasks and responsibilities, he realized that the team was always short of coverage from 11:30 to 1:00 when people went to lunch. He offered to reduce his lunch break by 30 minutes and to take his lunch after 1:00 P.M. so that he could cover for others. He presented the proposal to Doug who approved it for six months on the condition that Ken would arrive and be ready to work no later than 8:30 A.M. One slip-up and he would be forced to put Ken on probation. Ken understood and felt confident this extra half-hour would make all of the difference.

• • •

As explained in Work+Life Fit Fundamental #5, supporting an employee's request can't just be "the right thing to do"; it needs to make good business sense. It needs to be a mutually beneficial arrangement between equal parties. Would you pursue a business deal with someone who is unmotivated or untrustworthy? No. Why should your manager okay an arrangement if he or she would use those words to describe you?

Make sure that you are the kind of partner with whom you would want to do business before you present your proposal. And if you aren't already, lay the groundwork to become one.

Work Style and Your Happiness with Your Work+Life Fit

Not only does your work style influence whether your manager will be happy with your work+life fit, but it also influences whether you will be happy. Your work+life fit must be compatible with the way you like to work, and the way you work best, if it is going to succeed.

What does this mean exactly? Well, let's assume that your vision includes telecommuting three days a week, but you're the type of extrovert who likes having people around. You might find it difficult to sit in a home office alone all day. Instead, maybe consider telecommuting two days a week so that you conduct a majority of your work in an environment with other people. Or, if you really want or need to telecommute, make sure that your work+life fit includes a conscious effort to take a "people" break during the day.

Other examples are "early birds" and "night owls." Some people are better in the morning, while others are in their prime at night. If you know you are primarily an early bird, consider the wisdom of implementing a work+life fit whereby you work four 10-hour days by extending your workdays to 7 P.M. You're likely to be exhausted by that time of day, and not able to give 100%. Vice versa for night owls. Be aware of how you work best and consider your personal style when formulating your work+life fit.

COMPARE-FOR-COMPATIBILITY EXERCISE

1. Go to your workbook and review the most recent version of your work+life vision.

2. Take a sheet of paper and at the top write "How would my boss describe me as a worker?" Hopefully, your description includes some of the characteristics that managers consider necessary for a work+life fit to succeed: self-starter, reliable, trustworthy, and motivated.

3. Take your vision and then compare it to your list. Is your vision compatible with your work style, as your manager would describe it? If yes, move on to question #5.

4. If no, ask yourself the following:

   - What specific characteristics are incompatible with your vision?
   - How can you improve your performance over the next six months in order to change your manager's perspective?
   - How can you change your work+life fit to offset this incompatibility?

5. Take another sheet of paper and label two columns "How I like to work" and "How I don't like to work." Then make a list under each heading. For example:

How I like to work: with interaction and input from team members, but with direct control over and responsibility for my workflow.
How I don't like to work: I prefer not to work alone for long periods.

Compare your vision as it stands now to the work-style characteristics in each column making sure it's compatible with how you like to work and incompatible with how you don't like to work. Adjust accordingly. For example, if you like input from your team and like to work with others, your work style would be compatible with a work+life fit involving job-sharing. However, when you add the fact that you like to be in control of your work flow, job-sharing could pose a problem since you are relying on someone else to help complete your tasks. Therefore, you would have to adjust your vision to accommodate this incompatibility.

6. Having completed the compare-for-compatibility exercise for work style, record the newest version of your work+life fit vision in your workbook and go to chapter 21.

Personal Finances

Chapter Goal: *To ensure that your work+life vision is compatible with your personal financial reality.*

The focus now shifts to personal realities and their compatibility with your vision, beginning with what to many is the most challenging reality: money.

We've already discussed how money can be one of the success roadblocks standing between you and the work+life fit that you want. Remember, "I can't afford it" is one of the top three reasons cited for not pursuing a new work+life fit. But the truth is that you have much more power over your personal finances than you think. By this point in the book, you're well aware of how many issues related to work+life fit are about power—power over your time, your job tasks, your workload, and your schedule. And now power over your money.

Here's an example of the type of person for whom money and a new work+life fit are incompatible:

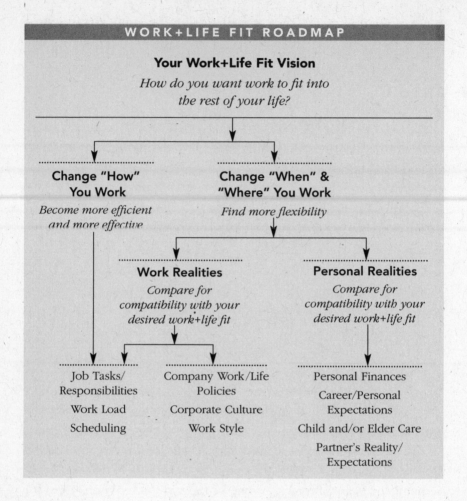

WORK+LIFE FIT ROADMAP

Your Work+Life Fit Vision
*How do you want work to fit into
the rest of your life?*

**Change "How"
You Work**
*Become more efficient
and more effective*

**Change "When" &
"Where" You Work**
Find more flexibility

Work Realities
*Compare for
compatibility with your
desired work+life fit*

Personal Realities
*Compare for
compatibility with your
desired work+life fit*

Job Tasks/
Responsibilities

Work Load

Scheduling

Company Work/Life
Policies

Corporate Culture

Work Style

Personal Finances

Career/Personal
Expectations

Child and/or Elder Care

Partner's Reality/
Expectations

JANE'S STORY

Jane is a successful professional who is married and has three children. In her job, she manages a team of people, travels on a fairly regular basis, and is often called to participate in the company's most high-profile projects and meetings. And Jane is at her wit's end. When she speaks, it's fast. When she walks, it's fast. When she eats, it's fast.

She wanted to meet with me because her children are starting to have difficulty in their private school, and she's finding that much of her evening—assuming she's not traveling—is spent helping with homework and dealing with the various crises of the school day. The evening used to be the only time she had to take care of her personal responsibilities. Now, without those hours at night, things are starting to fall apart in the five-bedroom house she bought two years ago.

We talked about how she could change her work realities to have more time and energy for home. But she felt that any material change in the number of hours she worked or in the tasks and responsibilities that she handled would reduce her compensation and "you know we just can't afford it."

. . .

Can't afford it, or won't afford it? These are two very different concepts that are easily confused. Clearly, there are people who truly *can't* afford to make less money; there aren't any expenses to cut, and budgeting wouldn't make a difference. That's one end of the spectrum.

On the other end are those who *won't* afford a change in lifestyle because "I like my lifestyle the way it is and I'm willing to work the hours and exert the energy required to maintain it." There is nothing wrong with feeling this way as long as you not only admit it, but also accept the work+life fit reality that goes along with that choice.

Conflict arises when you can't do that. You want more time and energy for your personal life but aren't willing to make the financial choices necessary to make that vision a reality. Then "can't" becomes "won't." Finding a better work+life fit involves trade-offs. One of those trade-offs may have to be the amount of money that you make. This is a hard pill for people to swallow. Sure, it would be great to achieve your vision and still make the same amount of money. But depending upon the details of your vision, that may not be possible.

It's important to differentiate which reality it is. If you decide that you "won't" afford a particular work+life fit, then you'll need to adjust your vision accordingly to accommodate the financial reality that you're choosing not to change.

But assume that you really, sincerely believe that you can't afford to make a change. That's a different story. Keep reading because there are strategies that can help you alter your personal financial reality in order to have the work+life fit that you want.

Sadly, Jane's belief that she can't afford to change her work+life fit in order to have more time and energy for her personal life isn't unusual. Yes, she may be more affluent than most people, but her predicament is the same: She feels overwhelmed and trapped by her lifestyle in a work+life fit that is no longer working. And she feels completely unempowered to alter it.

It doesn't have to be this way. What can you do if you find yourself in a similar situation? You can budget and make choices that can be tough, especially if you're grappling with money-related definitions of success, or fear. But you *can* make a change.

Budgeting

There are entire books written on the subject of budgeting and personal finances. But let's just highlight a couple of important points about budgeting as a way to make your personal finances compatible with the work+life fit that you want.

First, what is budgeting? Basically, it's being responsible with and thoughtful about the money that you have and spend. From both my personal and professional experience, people waste a lot of money. And if you don't have a budget, chances are you're one of those people and don't even know it. That's the bad news. The good news is that if you respect it and handle it wisely, you will have more money than you imagined. Enough money, ultimately, to at least pave the way for your work+life vision. I know it's true. I've witnessed too many examples to believe otherwise.

As with job tasks, workload, and scheduling, envisioning your work+life fit can be a great excuse to deal with your finances, perhaps for the first time. In fact, work/life conflict may be the reason you mishandle your money. It's a vicious cycle. When there isn't enough time for your personal life, then there isn't enough time or energy to set up a budget, monitor it, or consciously choose between what you need and want. As a result, you make bad, often spur-of-the-moment, spending choices, which then keep you from having the money you need to change your work+life fit and resolve your conflict.

Does this crazy money cycle sound familiar? What can you do to break it? Get started by planning a "financial sanity retreat," which can be anything from a Saturday to a weekend to a week, depending upon how disconnected you are from your personal financial reality. This retreat would involve the following:

1. Getting a couple of great money-related books.
   - ► As I said earlier, I believe the books by Suze Orman, including *The 9 Steps to Financial Freedom* and *The Courage to be Rich*, are the most helpful in changing your relationship to money. Her approach is unique because she mixes standard financial advice with insights into your feelings about, and respect for, money, which are helpful when dealing with redefining money-related success.
2. Following the instructions in the books, organizing a budget.
   - ► Use your old check registries, monthly bills, and credit card statements from the past 12 months to figure out how much you've actually been spending,
   - ► If you have a computer, use a program such as Money or Quicken to set up and monitor your budget throughout the year, and create a new budget for the following year. Or just designate a notebook that's devoted exclusively to keeping track of your finances.
3. Reviewing other parts of your financial picture.
   - ► Insurance coverage—make sure you've negotiated the best rates for the coverage that you need.
   - ► Wills—make sure that you have one.
   - ► Clutter—get rid of it in order to know exactly what you have, which helps you to know exactly what you need, so that you only spend what you must.
   - ► Financial updates—decide to set aside two days a month to input financial transactions into your budget so that you stay on track.

► Professional financial planning—if you need professional help above and beyond the books, contact a financial planner. Ask friends whom they use, or go to the website of The Financial Planning Association (www.fpanet.org) to find a planner in your area.

Making Choices about Money

Finding a better work+life fit means making trade-offs, and sometimes those trade-offs are not easy. Money-related trade-offs can be particularly difficult because, again, they can be tied up in how we define our success and ourselves.

I often listen to people who want a different work+life fit, but then run through a financial list of why they can't have it:

► Big mortgage/rent payment
► Two car payments
► Private school tuition
► Credit card bills

As we've discussed, in most cases, it's not that they can't afford it. It's that they won't. They *could* make different choices about how they spend their money. Even though they don't see it, they could:

► Reduce their mortgage by selling their house and buying a cheaper one, or rent a cheaper apartment;
► Sell their cars, and buy ones that they can afford;
► Move to a town with good public schools and save the private school tuition; or
► Stop spending money on things they don't need: the newest electronics, eating out all the time, vacations, expensive cable, cell phones, etc. Instead read a book, cook at home, visit

family and friends that live within driving distance, and limit your calls.

These steps may sound drastic at first, but if you really want to change the way work fits into your life, you *do* have the power. There is no law that says, "Once you buy a certain size house or rent a certain apartment, you must always buy or rent a dwelling of greater value the next time." Believe it or not, you can actually downsize.

Again, you may not *want* to but you can. And, if you don't want to, just admitting that can be very freeing. I've worked with a couple of people who stopped beating themselves up for not spending more time in their personal lives simply by admitting, "You know, I really like my lifestyle and I'm willing to do what it takes to have it."

However, if you still think you want a work+life fit that would involve your making less money, but find yourself resisting a budget or making some of those tough choices, what's going on? ROADBLOCK ALERT: Perhaps you've hit either the money-related success roadblock or the fear roadblock.

We covered the money-related success roadblock in detail in chapter 9. Refer back to the exercises in that chapter in order to bypass the roadblock that is keeping you from making difficult financial choices.

The fear roadblock is also pervasive when it comes to money and work+life fit. People use the excuse "I can't afford it," to avoid taking the sometimes scary steps to change the way work fits into their lives. As we discussed in the fear roadblock chapter, you need courage to create a financial reality that supports the work+life fit you want and then to take the other steps necessary to achieve your goal. Refer back to chapter 10 and review the exercises to bypass a fear roadblock should you encounter one related to finances.

You may also be worried that you can't afford your desired work life fit right now. But remember that you can always achieve your vision in small stages over a longer period of time. Maybe you can't afford to work three days a week right now. So start small. Shift your full-time hours in order to have more time to volunteer in the evening. In the meantime, implement a financial plan with an eye to working three days a week within two years.

"Can I reduce my hours and keep the same salary?"

Believe it or not, people ask this question all of the time. Feeling that they're underpaid, they want to resolve this perceived inequity by requesting to work fewer hours for the same pay. In the spirit of full disclosure, I have met a few people who reduced their hours but kept the same salary. While I'm not sure how their arrangements ultimately worked, I never had much hope for their success and here's why: Money equals expectations.

Your boss pays you $40,000 to work 40 hours per week. Then you ask to work 30 hours or "40 minus 10 hours" but still want to be paid $40,000. In theory, your boss may agree. But he still knows that he's paying you $40,000 and on some level probably expects you to do the same amount of work that you used to.

In other words, by keeping your salary, you've lost the leverage to say "I'm only being paid to work 30 hours a week," to combat the inevitable "work creep" that sets in after you've implemented your arrangement. It won't be as easy to push back and keep your workload and schedule within a range that is reasonable for a 30-hour workweek if you're still being paid for 40 hours.

Here's my advice: If you're unhappy with your compensation, deal with it *before* you reduce your hours, then negotiate your arrangement. Otherwise, reduce your compensation commensurate to the number of hours that you want to work. It aligns the money with the change in expectations—you are working "40 minus 10 hours," so you are being paid "40 minus 10 hours" worth of salary. Everyone is clear.

If you still think you're underpaid and really want to use your new work+life fit as a way to right this wrong, consider proposing a reduction in your salary that is smaller than the percentage reduction in hours. But do give something back. In chapter 27, we'll discuss how it's important in a negotiation to give something up in exchange for getting something.

COMPARE-FOR-COMPATIBILITY EXERCISE

1. What is your personal financial reality? Make a list in your Workbook:

   - How much do you earn annually?
   - What are your current expenses (you will probably underestimate unless you sit down with your checkbook and specifically catego-rize expenses)?
   - What are your long-term obligations?
       Retirement savings
       College savings
       Mortgage repayment
       Car payments
       Credit card debt repayment
   - What are your assets?
       Equity in home
       Savings (excluding retirement savings)

2. Look at the most recent version of your work+life vision in your Work-book. Is it compatible with your personal financial reality as it is to-day? In other words, can you afford it? If yes, go to chapter 22.

3. If no, then:
   Are you willing to make the changes necessary to make your personal financial reality compatible with your vision? This is important because there's a difference between "can't" afford and "won't" afford. There is no right or wrong answer; it's just important to know where you stand. If no, then adjust your vision to accommodate your financial reality as it stands today. For example, instead of reducing the number of hours you work, try to change when and/or where you work (e.g., telecom-mute or work longer hours in fewer days). If yes, then continue to the next question.

4. How can you change your personal financial reality to make it compatible?
   - Do you have a budget?
   - Do you keep track of all of the little things that you spend money on every day? A lot of money is wasted on little things.
   - Are there expenses that you could reduce or eliminate?
   - Do you have assets that you could sell (e.g., house, cars, etc.)?
   - Are there liabilities that you could refinance at a lower rate (e.g., mortgage, car loans, credit cards, etc.)?

5. If you still feel you can't afford your goal, then make sure you haven't hit a money-related success roadblock or a fear roadblock.

6. Change your work+life vision to make it compatible with your adjusted personal financial reality and record it in your Work+Life Fit Workbook.

Career and Personal Expectations

Chapter Goal: *To ensure that your work+life vision is compatible with your career and personal expectations.*

What are your expectations for your career and for your personal life? How do these expectations compare with the way you want work to fit into your life? For your work+life fit to succeed, you need to make sure it's compatible with the following career and personal expectations:

- **Advancement**—the consideration for and the timing of
- **Prestige**—status conferred by the company you work for and the projects you are assigned
- **Power**—access to others with power and others' perception of your power
- **Compensation**—what you will make, and how you will make more, in terms of salary and benefits
- **Personal responsibility**—what role you expect to play in the tasks and activities of your personal life

Advancement Expectations

Having thought about advancement in relation to how you define success as you read chapter 9, what are your expectations?

Maybe you're like Catherine, someone who wants to work four days a week and be available by cell phone on the fifth day, but still wants to be considered for all advancement opportunities. And remember my friend Natalie who was promoted twice after reducing her workday to 10:00 A.M. to 4 P.M.? Or maybe you're more like Jill, who likes working from home three days a week and is content to stay at her current level for a while in order to keep this arrangement.

Whatever your goals, defining your expectations around advancement will help you avoid being derailed the first time you aren't promoted and had expected to be.

Prestige Expectations

In chapter 9, you reflected on prestige and how it relates to your definition of success. Do you expect to work for a prestigious company? And if you didn't but had more flexibility, how would that feel? Do you have to be assigned to the more high-profile accounts or attend the most high-profile meetings? What if you didn't and therefore could work 25 hours per week? Are your expectations compatible with your vision?

Remember, typically, smaller, and perhaps less prestigious, companies tend to offer their employees more flexibility. And, while it's not always the case, the most prestigious projects often have the tightest turnaround times or require the most time and energy to complete. Some companies require you to take a step down in seniority or title if you work less than a full 40-hour week. But remember, everything is negotiable.

How would it feel to change your title in order to have the

work+life fit that you want? What are your expectations? If you want to keep your title and retain your seniority, make sure that you include that as part of your negotiation (which we'll cover in more detail in chapter 27).

Power Expectations

A conversation I had with a friend from business school illustrates this point perfectly. She told me about how she'd made the decision not to take on any additional work responsibilities. She had two kids and a long commute, and she felt that her current schedule and workload were enough for now. I was thrilled that she'd found what seemed to be the right work+life fit, but then she said, "I'm not sure it's going to work out." And after some discussion she admitted, "I just don't get called anymore by people wanting me to guide them or give them advice. I miss being the 'go-to' girl."

Even though her arrangement worked on one level, her expectations of personal power weren't in line with her vision. She had stepped back from work and wasn't visibly working on the highest-profile projects. As a result, she was being perceived differently by her peers, and it bothered her. It was a problem.

What are your power expectations? What are your expectations about access to powerful people in the organization, inclusion in critical meetings, etc., as well as your own power in your company?

Compensation Expectations

We've discussed money as it relates to your definition of success, and the compatibility of your personal finances with your vision. But what are your expectations regarding compensation under your new work+life fit? And are these expectations compatible with your vision? You need to consider:

- ▶ Salary
- ▶ Bonus
- ▶ Stock and stock options
- ▶ 401(k) retirement savings
- ▶ Health and life insurance
- ▶ Access to other benefits

Again, everything is negotiable. But be realistic, and remember that money equals expectations of the amount of work you will do—and this expectation will vary by company and industry. If your company is compensating you at a certain level, then be prepared to address the associated expectations as part of your proposal and negotiation.

ROADBLOCK ALERT: One common cause of resistance from others is any kind of perceived unfairness: "Gee, *I'd* love to work 30 hours a week and make 75% of my salary. I work 50 hours a week for my 100%." When calculated that way, it isn't fair, especially in today's corporate world where fewer people actually work the standard 40-hour workweek upon which their salaries, and bonuses, are based. This reality needs to be accounted for in your expectations for compensation as it relates to the level of work that you will be expected to complete.

How do you do this? To help you consider your expectations related to money and work, use something I call the "proportional work" rule of thumb. The more money you make, and the more average hours per week you are expected to work in your company above and beyond the standard 40-hour workweek, the more you need to use this gauge.

Consider the following example. Judith and other colleagues at her level make $100,000 per year working 60 hours per week, on average, as corporate consultants. The standard workweek in her company is 40 hours; therefore, Judith works approximately 150% of the standard workweek in order to make $100,000.

With her new arrangement, Judith wants to cut back to 30 hours per week. At first it seems clear enough: She expects to be compensated at 75% of her salary (30 hours is 75% of 40 hours) or $75,000. But, I point out to her, it's important to look at the norms in her company and industry to determine how much "above and beyond" those

30 hours she'll be expected to work in order to make that $75,000 and maintain equity with her coworkers. Applying the "proportional work" rule of thumb, she would have to work, on average, 150% of the 30 hours—or 45 hours per week—in order to retain that sense of fairness to others in the company. And, this would be the expectation of her manager and coworkers if she were making $75,000.

Judith thought about this and realized she really didn't want to work more than 30 hours per week, and she wanted the leverage to confidently push back when the work started to creep past that point. She realized that to do this, she would have to take 50% of *the average number of hours she would be expected to work for her full-time salary* (30 hours is 50% of the 60 hours she worked, on average, full-time) and make $50,000 per year.

You can see how maintaining this proportional sense of fairness becomes more critical when you work far beyond the standard 40-hour workweek you are expected to work in your particular company. But regardless, it's important to clarify your expectations related to compensation and the associated expected level of work. This is where the "proportional work" rule of thumb comes in handy. Again, it involves the following steps:

- ▶ Calculate the number of hours per week, on average, you are expected to work—in your company or industry—above and beyond the standard 40-hour, full-time workweek. Then determine the percentage above 40 hours those extra hours represent. For example, if you work, on average, 45 hours per week making $40,000 per year, you are working 113% of the standard 40-hour workweek.
- ▶ Then apply that same proportion to the schedule you want to have with your new work+life fit. Ask yourself if the number of hours that you would be *expected* to work are compatible with the number you *want* to work with your new arrangement. If you want to work 20 hours per week, would you really be expected to work 113% of 20 hours, or 22.6 hours per week?

▶ If you're fine going above and beyond by 2.6 extra hours per week, then calculate the proportional reduction in your compensation off of the *standard* workweek, whether it's 40 or 35 hours in your company. For example, 20 hours is 50% of the standard 40-hour workweek; therefore, you will make $20,000 for an average of 22.6 hours per week of work.

▶ If it's *not* okay for you to work one minute more than 20 hours per week, then you need to calculate your expected compensation proportionally from the *average number of full-time hours you would typically work for your full-time salary.* Say you want to work 20 hours per week, which is 44% of the typical 45-hour full-time workweek that you put in at your company to make your full-time salary of $40,000. Then you should make 44% of your $40,000 salary, or $17,780, if you want to work no more than 20 hours per week.

Apply the same parameters to the other aspects of compensation that need to be compatible with your work+life vision. In chapter 28, you will use this proportional work gauge once you've implemented your new work+life fit to avoid work creep. It will help you to monitor how many hours you should expect to work above and beyond what you are paid before you ask to revisit your agreement. But it's important for you to make sure that your compensation and the associated work expectations of others are compatible with your vision *before* you implement a final work+life fit. You don't want to be unpleasantly surprised by either working more hours than you wanted to or having your manager perceive that you're proportionally being paid more than others given the hours you are now working.

Personal Responsibility Expectations

At this point in the roadmap, your work+life vision is compatible with your *work* realities and expectations. But what about the other piece of the time and energy pie—your *personal* responsibilities? What are your expectations about what you want to accomplish personally with your new arrangement? Are your expectations compatible with your vision, or are they unrealistic given the vision as it stands now? It's easy to overestimate.

For example, a stay-at-home mother wants to devote more time and energy to work. This means that she no longer has as much to give to some of the personal tasks that she used to be responsible for. If her routine was to attend all of her children's after-school athletic events, perhaps her new work+life vision only includes enough time to attend half. Does she still expect to cook a three-course meal every night, clean the entire house, and do all of the laundry all by herself? If she does, she could find herself working the "second shift" at home that causes so many working mothers to burn out. She needs to lower her personal expectations and either give up or share some of her responsibilities with others if she wants to avoid this fate.

Those who are working but are reallocating more time to their personal life often expect to accomplish more than is realistic with their new work+life fit.

KEVIN'S STORY

When Kevin's wife relocated with her job, he saw an opportunity to propose the work+life fit he had wanted for some time. As a computer software engineer, he felt he could telecommute. And now that his wife made more money, he also wanted to cut back to four days a week.

Without having to commute and with one day off a week, Kevin looked forward to pursuing his hobby of playing the saxophone more seriously. People always said he had talent, but he never felt that he had given it his all. He planned to practice at least two hours every day, using the time during which he would have otherwise commuted. And, to save some money, he told his wife he would take over all of the responsibilities that their cleaning person used to handle, including the laundry. On top of this, he was committed to sticking with a daily exercise routine in order to lose the 30 pounds that had crept on over the past five years.

How did it work out? Well, six months into his new arrangement Kevin had lost five pounds. But the extra time he thought he'd have fell short of his expectations. He found that the cleaning and laundry took up a large portion of his day off. Plus, because his wife now worked longer hours, she didn't want to deal with errands and food shopping on the weekends, so he took over responsibility for these tasks as well.

The good news is that he did manage to find time to practice the saxophone for at least one hour a day. And he was feeling so good about his playing that he recently tried out for a local swing band. Now two evenings a week are devoted to practicing with the band, and almost every weekend they have a performance locally.

Kevin has had to lower his expectations about how much he would practice, how much he would exercise, and how much he could handle domestically. "By the way," he said, "I've just finished interviewing cleaning people. I just can't do it anymore now that I have evening and weekend commitments. But I am going to keep doing the shopping on my day off because it really does lower our stress level on the weekends."

· · ·

Review the following list of personal responsibilities (skip those that don't apply, and add those that aren't included). Estimate not only the number of hours per week you'd like to devote to each one, but try to gauge the percentage of your fixed amount of energy per week each one would require. Keep in mind that some things—exercise, meditation, journaling, sleeping, eating well—won't use much energy and can actually give you access to more of that fixed energy. And remember, allocating time and energy is not an exact science, but a process of estimating.

1. Caring for your body
   ▶ Exercise
   ▶ Eating well
   ▶ Sleeping

2. Caring for your spirit
   ▶ Journaling
   ▶ Meditating
   ▶ Connecting to something greater

3. Hobbies

4. Cleaning your house

5. Caring for your yard

6. Spouse/Partner-related activities

7. Child-related activities
   ▶ Participation in activities
   ▶ Homework
   ▶ Playtime

8. Friend-related activities

9. Elder care–related activities
   ▶ Doctors appointments
   ▶ Errands
   ▶ Visiting

10. Retirement-related activities
    ▶ Travel
    ▶ Time with Family

11. Volunteering

12. Education

Total the amount of hours per week for each responsibility and activity, and then total the estimated percentage of your energy you would like to allocate to each. Look at your work+life vision. How many hours do you hope to work (include commuting time)? What percentage of your fixed time and energy do you think work will require (remember some jobs require a faster pace, have a larger workload, etc., than others)? You have a total of 168 hours in a week, and 100% of your energy to give:

▶ Total the number of hours you will work and the number of hours you want to devote to personal responsibilities and activities. Does the total exceed 168 hours?

If no, then your vision and your personal responsibilities are compatible in terms of the number of hours you want to devote to them.

If the total *does* exceed 168 hours, then start to consider where you may need to adjust your expectations, whether by changing your vision to reduce the number of hours devoted to work or those devoted to personal responsibilities.

▶ Total the estimated amount of energy you will devote to work and your personal life under your new arrangement. Is it greater than 100%? Now this is not an exact science, so don't panic if it is greater than 100%. But do look at what the number tells you.

If the total is more than 100%, it's simply a red flag that you may still be overextended if you don't change your personal expectations. See where you might be able to ask for help with a responsibility that is particularly energy draining (e.g., cleaning your house, shopping, caring for the yard, doing homework with an older child, caring for an aging relative, etc.). If you either are unable or unwilling to change your personal expectations, then you need to consider changing the work aspect of your work+life vision.

When Your Expectations Change

Once you implement a work+life fit based on a certain set of work and personal expectations, you may find that these expectations change. For the first time, other areas of your life have equal or greater importance.

For example, today you may expect to be considered for all advancement opportunities, but six months into your new work+life fit, you change your mind. Or, a year from now, you no longer need time and energy to go back to school, and you want more responsibility at work.

So keep in mind that you may complete the Work+Life Fit Roadmap this time around using one set of expectations and then revisit it at some point with a whole different set of expectations.

COMPARE-FOR-COMPATIBILITY EXERCISE

1. List your current expectations related to all the categories we've discussed. Please also include any others that you may think of.
   Your list may look something like this:

   - Advancement—I would like to be considered for potential advancement opportunities with the understanding that I may have to change my work+life fit to accommodate the needs of a position;
   - Prestige—I expect to be assigned interesting work; however, I understand that certain tasks may be assigned to others with more accommodating schedules;
   - Power—I expect to have my perceived power in the group change in accordance with my reduced daily presence in the office;
   - Compensation—I expect my salary, bonus, and long-term compensation to be prorated based on the standard 40-hour workweek; and
   - Personal responsibilities (use the list of responsibilities to help you)—I've reviewed the personal tasks and responsibilities that I expect to accomplish with my new work+life fit. These include_____(be as specific as you want). I feel that I will have an adequate amount of time and energy to complete them, and I am willing to adjust my expectations as necessary and find help when needed if I begin to become overloaded.

2. Review the most recent version of your work+life vision in your workbook. Is your work+life fit compatible with all of your career/personal expectations?

For example: I want to work 35 hours per week (versus 45 hours on average) with one of those days working from home.

Is this vision compatible with the career and personal expectations you listed above? If yes to all expectations, continue to chapter 23.

3. If no, then:

How can you make your expectations compatible with your new work+life fit? For example, assume your vision is not compatible with your expectations related to compensation and personal responsibilities. Therefore, you need to adjust them accordingly:

- Personal responsibilities: Although you had hoped to take your mother to the doctor every Friday and take over the responsibility for her financial affairs, you realize this will be too much. Therefore, you've asked your brother to handle her finances and insurance matters.
- Compensation: You think that your salary should be easy to reduce proportionally to the standard 40-hour workweek. You work 35 hours so you earn 88% of your salary. But you usually work 45 hours per week, as do most people in your company. Therefore, you have to calculate all aspects of your compensation as a proportion of the average full-time workweek you worked to earn your full-time salary, or 78% of your salary.

4. If you can't change your expectation(s), how can you change your work+life fit to make it compatible?

5. If you are changing your vision to accommodate an unchangeable expectation, please record this new version in your Work+Life Fit Workbook.

Child Care and Elder Care

Chapter Goal: *To ensure that you work+life vision is compatible with your child-care or elder-care arrangement*

Nothing wreaks havoc in your life like a problem with child care or elder care. Without reliable and affordable child care and/or elder care, your new work+life fit will not succeed.

In the other chapters, the first step was to determine if there was compatibility with your vision. With the reality of child care and elder care, we are going to assume right off the bat that they are *not* compatible. Given the shocking lack of reliable, affordable care in our country, more than likely, this is the case. Therefore, this chapter will focus on strategies to resolve that. There are creative ways to find good child care and elder care, even when they aren't abundantly available or affordable.

Like personal finances, there are hundreds of books, numerous websites, and government organizations that provide in-depth information on the subjects of child care and elder care. I can only highlight key points, but please refer to the resource section at the end of the book for additional resources.

Care Strategies

If, like most people, you don't have access to either a company-subsidized or community-subsidized child-care center or elder-care facility, what are your other options? You can hire a baby-sitter to care for the child or a nurse to care for an elder. And depending upon your work+life fit, you could get creative. You could nanny-share or even trade caregiving with a friend. Either way, educate yourself! Here is a list of websites that are excellent sources of information about how to find all types of care and how to judge its quality:

- ▶ The National Association for the Education of Young Children (NAEYC), which is a national organization representing early childhood educators (www.naeyc.org).
- ▶ The National Child Care Information Center, which is the Child Care Bureau of the Department of Health and Human Services (www.nccic.org).
- ▶ The Administration on Aging, which is part of the Department of Health and Human Services (www.aoa.dhhs.gov and elder-care locator 800-677-1116).

You can't go forward with your new work+life fit until you resolve the incompatibility between child care and/or elder care and your vision. You may also be someone whose work/life conflict is the result of child-care or elder-care difficulties. Let's look at the details of these different strategies, both short term and long term. Tip: If you even *think* you are either going to have a baby or have to care for an elder in the near future, research and sign up for the local supports that you want as soon as possible. Waiting lists at the highest quality centers tend to be very long. And a good nanny or nurse can take awhile to find. Give yourself all the time you can.

· · ·

If you work for a large company:

▶ Does the company have a child-care center or subsidize employees who use other centers?

▶ Does the company offer a service called Dependent Care Resource and Referral (often it's coordinated through the company's Employee Assistance Program)? These services allow you to call an 800-number, tell them what type of support you need, and then they help you locate child-care and elder-care supports in your local area. Ask your HR representative.

If you work for a large company that doesn't have a center or a subsidy, for a smaller company, or you're independently employed, there are number of other options.

Full-time Child Care

▶ Community-based child-care centers: You can check with your local child-care resource agency (call directory assistance) and ask for the names of community-based centers. Many are affiliated with the YMCA or a religious organization. The websites previously listed and in the resource section offer information on how to choose a center.

▶ In-home care: A provider cares for children in their home. Look for a provider who is licensed by the state. Again, information on how to find and evaluate an in-home care provider in your area is available from the previously listed websites and in the resource section.

▶ Nannies: There are three routes to find a nanny. One option is a fee-based agency. This is the most expensive, albeit less labor-intensive approach. You could also run an ad in the newspaper. Get a book that walks you through the steps of how to advertise, screen prospective nannies, and hire and manage a nanny (see the resource section). Finally, there's word of mouth. If you can get a great referral from someone you know, it's always the best way to go. But, this method isn't always the fastest.

Part-time Child Care

If you need only part-time care, there are child-care centers and in-home caregivers offering part-time hours, but there are other options as well:

▶ Nanny-sharing: This strategy is great if you aren't working full-time hours. Sharing a nanny with someone else gives your nanny a full-time salary, but you don't have to cover it all. The trick is to find a partner who needs a sitter during hours that complement your needs.

▶ Swapping baby-sitting: I've seen this strategy work amazingly well in a number of instances, especially when your work+life fit requires that you only work a couple of days a week. Two parents swap child-care responsibilities. The real benefit with this option is that it's free.

ROADBLOCK ALERT: Often in an attempt to "save money," mothers and fathers working less than full-time will under-hire child care. They will piece together unreliable care that ultimately undermines the success of their new arrangement. The reality is that you need reliable care to make *any* work+life fit work; therefore, you may need to pay more money or adjust your schedule in ways you hadn't anticipated. Review the success roadblock related to making a certain amount of money. Perhaps you'll have to put more resources toward adequate child care—paying for more hours than you need, or paying a caregiver a premium for working part-time. Also, some people who telecommute mistakenly believe that they can watch their children while they work from home and save money. The simple answer is: No you can't. You need to find care for your child for all of the hours that you telecommute.

Elder Care

Child care is often easier to deal with their elder care because the type of care needed is more cut-and-dry and often more readily available in some form or another. But that doesn't mean there aren't community-based resources that can help you find the type of elder care you need. The goal is to make sure whatever that care looks like, it's compatible with the work+life fit that you want. Here are some steps you can take to identify proper elder care:

- ► National Alliance for Caregiving (www.caregiving.org) is a website dedicated to providing support and information to family caregivers and the professionals who help them.
- ► Contact a social worker specializing in geriatrics who practices in your community. Such a person can help identify and access most appropriate services.
- ► Another similar resource is the National Association of Professional Geriatric Care Managers (www.caremanager.org). This group locates fee-based certified professionals who can assess your needs and coordinate resources for seniors and their families including medical, legal, and financial.
- ► Contact your local Department of Aging's Senior Information and Assistance Unit, they may also be able to guide you. Either call directory assistance, or run an Internet search under "Department of Aging" and then find your state's listing.

COMPARE-FOR-COMPATIBILITY EXERCISE

1. Review the most recent version of your work+life vision in your workbook. Is your current child-care and/or elder-care reality compatible with this vision? If yes, go to chapter 24.

2. If no, then review all of the strategies listed above to help change that reality and make it compatible.

3. If you can't find the right child-care or elder-care arrangement, then you may need to adjust your work+life vision. Record this new version of your work+life vision in your workbook.

Your Partner's Reality and Expectations

Chapter Goal: *To ensure that your work+life vision is compatible with your partner's reality and expectations, both professional and personal.*

At this point in the process, you have a work+life fit that is compatible with all of the relevant work and personal realities in *your* life, but there's something still missing, or should we say, *someone* missing—your partner. As anyone who shares his or her life with another person knows, your ability to make changes in your own life is influenced by the reality of that other individual.

You may want to change how, when, or where you work, but do these changes complement how, when, or where your partner works? And what about his or her personal reality? Is your work+life fit compatible with their understanding of your financial reality, with their career and personal expectations, and with the role they want to play in caring for either your children or elderly relatives?

What happens when your *partner* hits a success, fear, resistance, or in-the-box-thinking roadblock? *Your* work+life fit can be derailed. That doesn't seem fair, but it's a fact. So, it's important, before you start the Three Steps that your spouse also learns to recognize the roadblocks that *they* might hit.

As you ponder these questions, it's easy to see why your work+life fit needs to work for your partner too. It's no wonder that traditional corporate work/life initiatives have had limited success, because they typically do not include the partner's role as a consideration. Who would feel comfortable telling a boss or HR about his wife's job, how much money she makes, and her career expectations? Not many people, which explains why these questions were ignored.

Make sure you don't make that same mistake. Use this chapter as an opportunity to sit down with your partner. Really discuss these issues—what are the realities of your joint work and personal life, as your spouse sees them, and how susceptible is your partner to hitting one of the roadblocks that could derail your efforts?

Are the work realities of your spouse/partner compatible with your work+life vision?

Company Work/Life Policies

What work/life policies and programs does your partner's employer offer? For example:

▶ Both of you might try to coordinate two complementary flexible schedules (e.g., one partner works two days a week; the other three days a week). Be sure to work through the process outlined in chapter 17 to make sure that your spouse's work+life fit conforms to his or her company's work/life policies.

▶ Does your spouse's company offer work/life supports that could help *you* change the way you work? Does the company have a child-care center or child-care subsidy? What about an elder-care resource and referral service that could help you find the type of care that you need?

Job Tasks, Workload, and Scheduling

You've developed a work+life fit whereby you will work a certain number of hours, at certain times, in particular locations. But how does that coordinate with your spouse's job tasks, workload, and scheduling? Consider:

▶ What are the tasks and responsibilities of his job?
▶ Does he have to travel or entertain clients at night and on weekends?
▶ Does she work rotating shifts?
▶ Is she on 24-hour call at certain periods?

Some couples work different shifts in order to provide care for either children or elders. This arrangement is fine unless one partner works in a rotating shift environment. But it can cause problems if there is overlap on a night shift when it's very difficult to find care.

Corporate Culture

What is the corporate culture at your spouse's company? How do these norms and values influence his or her ability to support the changes you want to make?

Let's imagine that the arrangement you want involves working four 10-hour days, 8 A.M. to 6 P.M., with every Wednesday off. In order for this to work, your husband needs to leave work by 5:30 P.M. so he can pick up your kids from child care. But, in his corporate culture, "no one leaves before the boss turns his office light off," which doesn't usually happen before 6:30 P.M. Clearly, his corporate culture and your work+life fit are not compatible, and you need to revisit the exercise in chapter 19 to decide how you're going to resolve it.

Are the personal realities of your spouse/partner compatible with your work+life vision?

Personal Finances—Perception and Expectation

If you are part of a couple, no matter who makes the money, two people spend it. Therefore, you need to know the following:

▶ What is your spouse's perception of your personal financial reality?

▶ If the changes you want require making some difficult financial choices, does your spouse support those choices?

▶ What are your spouse's expectations related to your personal finances? What do they want your joint financial reality to look like? Are you both on the same page?

▶ If your spouse is trying to simultaneously make a change in his or her work+life fit, what are the financial ramifications of his or her efforts?

For example, when I decided I wanted to work for myself and write this book, it was an adjustment for my husband. After I finished business school he never thought he'd be the sole source of income again. Our new financial reality was an adjustment for us both.

Your partner's lifestyle expectations are also a factor. My client Gerry wanted to reduce the number of hours he worked per week. After reviewing all of *his* work and personal realities, he had a strong, compatible work+life fit.

But when he considered his partner's reality, he realized, "This is never going to work. If I work fewer hours a week, I'm going to make less money. And, even though the extra time and energy would reduce my level of stress, my wife is not going to want to make the financial sacrifices this change would entail. Our lifestyle is too important to her. I'm going to have to find a way to work differently that has less impact on my income."

There's nothing wrong with his wife's reality, as long as they both acknowledge it and Gerry is okay with changing his vision to accommodate her expectations.

Career Expectations

Many professional couples find themselves in a situation where their individual career expectations aren't compatible with their joint personal responsibilities. Until they have children or an aging parent falls ill, both partners are ambitious and willing to log the long hours. Then a child arrives or Grandma breaks her hip, and caregiving requires a large amount of time and energy. The couple then realizes the extra effort has to come from somewhere. In the case of a child, if the dad maintains his career expectations, the mom often feels pressure to reduce hers. Again, your partner's reality directly affects the work+life fit you can achieve.

SHEILA'S STORY

After Caitlin was born, Sheila decided to cut back on the time and energy she devoted to work for at least a year. She worked four days a week, telecommuting two of those days. But she made it clear that she still wanted to be considered for future advancement opportunities. A promotion would most likely require her to reallocate some of her time and energy away from Caitlin and other personal responsibilities and give more time and energy back to work. Her expectation was that her husband, Rob, would pick up some of the slack when the time arrived. But when she sat down with him to discuss her plans, she realized that his goal to be the next CEO of his company was going to require him to focus primarily on work. This wouldn't leave enough time and energy for him to take on some of the responsibilities that she would have to give up if she increased her commitment to her job.

* * *

The expectation that a partner will *not* have any career also causes a problem for some couples. Even though most young women today work before they have children, there are still young men who ascribe to the "dad works and mom stays home with the kids" paradigm. So, when a stay-at-home mom decides that she wants to find a way to fit a few hours of work back into her life, it can conflict with the expectations of her partner.

Those considering working in retirement also face this dilemma as both husband and wife consider what their respective retirements will look like. I've seen a husband who has worked more than thirty years retire. He's married to a woman who may have gone back to the workforce after having raised children, and she either can't retire or doesn't want to. As the husband tries to create a new work+life fit, his wife has a full-time work schedule that may conflict with his vision.

Charles Handy, the former dean of the London School of Economics and a well-known business writer, caused a stir a few years ago when he announced his retirement in order to work only six months of the year. He would spend the other six months traveling with his wife, who is a photographer. His wife had spent her whole life putting her career second to his demanding schedule; now he was going to change his work+life fit to allow equal time and energy for her work.

Child Care and/or Care for an Aging Parent

How does your spouse or partner plan to be involved in the child-care and/or elder-care responsibilities you have? Do the changes you want to make in how, when, or where you work require a certain caregiving contribution from your partner? And what are his or her limitations? This is a mismatch of expectations many of my clients face.

As I shared in the introduction, my husband's work reality affected my work+life fit after we had our first child. His inflexible schedule and long hours made sharing drop-off and pick-up at a child-care center impossible. And unless we wanted a nanny, I would have to be available every day to coordinate child care. This meant I couldn't travel, which was a task critical to my consulting job.

Do you remember the story of the senior executive whose wife now works after years of caring for their children? Her attitude was "I stayed home with the kids, now it's your turn to take care of your mother." This wife did not intend to take on the same level of responsibility for the care of her mother-in-law as she did for her children. And that reality is going to affect the work+life fit of the senior executive as he faces coping with the needs of his aging mother.

· · · ·

ROADBLOCK ALERT: Finally, as you review the changes you want to make in how, when, or where you work with your spouse or partner, make it a point to identify any potential roadblocks:

- ► Success roadblock: What are your partner's definitions of success related to money, prestige, advancement, and caregiving? Are these definitions compatible with your work+life fit? If they aren't, then both of you should complete the success roadblock exercises at the end of chapter 9. Either your partner needs to adjust her definition of success or you need to alter your work+life vision to match the definitions she either can't or won't change.
- ► Fear roadblock: What are the fears that your partner expresses as you discuss your work+life fit? Go through the chapter 10 exercises together to challenge his fears.
- ► Resistance roadblock: Does your partner express resistance to your proposed work+life fit? Probe deeper and try to determine its source. Then review the exercises in chapter 11 to help your partner challenge the resistance in order to reach a point of support for what you are trying to accomplish.
- ► In-the-box-thinking roadblock: As you encounter incompatibilities between your spouse's work and personal realities

and your work+life fit, does he have difficulty seeing creative ways to change his realities to make them compatible? Take some time to review chapter 12, and have your partner complete the exercises to help him see possibilities instead of limitations.

In the future, I hope that couples will naturally look at their work and personal realities together and create a joint work+life vision that gives them adequate time and energy at work and at home. But until it becomes second nature for moms, dads, those caring for an elder, working retirees—all of us—we can start by making a conscious effort to go through this process as a team. I recently met two couples who are perfect examples of this symbiotic work+life fit partnership.

MARCIA AND BRUCE'S STORY

Marcia and Bruce both work full-time, and they have two children under the age of four, which would seem like a lot for any couple to juggle. But they have created a work+life reality, both individually and as a family, which seems to fulfill their combined vision of how they want work to fit into their lives.

Bruce is a professional scriptwriter whose hours tend to be 4:00 A.M. to 1:30 P.M. He is home by 3:00 P.M. to relieve the baby-sitter and spend time with the kids. He's responsible for dinner and bath. Marcia is a producer, and her hours are 10:00 A.M. to about 5:30 P.M. (even though she works 37.5 hours per week on average, Marcia considers her schedule part-time since most people at her company work more than 50 hours per week, often well past 8:00 P.M.). This means she doesn't have to catch the train until 9:00 A.M., giving her plenty of time to get the kids up, dressed, fed, and off to preschool. As Marcia points out, "We have arranged it so that the kids have one of us for a good part of the morning and for most of the afternoon before bed. Are we asleep by 8:30 P.M. most nights? Sure. But the kids are only little once, and this is a perfect match of our schedules that allows us to give them what we think is important right now."

JANICE AND AIDAN'S STORY

Janice came to me for help negotiating a reduction in her work schedule. After a long, successful career in the high-powered world of finance, Janice was pregnant with her third child and needed more time and energy for home. But, as she said to me, "I love working—it's an important part of who I am." Together we put together a proposal for her to work four days a week, with one of those days working from home. Somewhat to her surprise (but not to mine), the arrangement was approved as she proposed. Six months later Janice calls to tell me that she and her husband had agreed to implement the next step of their work+life transformation: Her husband was going to quit his high-stress albeit lucrative career in international marketing to become a high school teacher and coach. Today, Janice continues with the schedule that gives her the time and energy she wants for her family *and* the salary that allows her husband to pursue his dream and care for the kids in the afternoons before she gets home. "We both couldn't be happier," she said, "and two years ago I only thought this was a pie-in-the-sky dream."

COMPARE-FOR-COMPATIBILITY EXERCISE

1. Sit down with your spouse or partner to look at your vision and answer the following questions about *his or her* realities:

   How are the specifics of this vision either compatible or incompatible with the following realities of your work?
   - Your workload
   - Your schedule
   - Your company's culture
   - Your work style
   - Your career expectations regarding advancement, prestige, power, and compensation

How are the specifics of this vision either compatible or incompatible with your personal realities, and your expectations about things like finances, retirement, and family structure?

2. If all work and personal realities and expectations are compatible, then skip to chapter 25.

3. If not, then:
   - How can your partner make changes to work and/or personal realities and expectations in order to make them compatible with your vision?
   - If your partner cannot make changes, then how can you change your vision to accommodate any realities or expectations that can't be altered?

4. If you've adjusted your vision to accommodate a reality or expectation of your partner's that can't be changed, remember to record the most recent version of your vision in your workbook.

Building Your Business Case

Chapter Goal: *To develop the business case, or "What's in it for the business?" to support your final work+life fit.*

Take a moment to look back at the transformation of your original vision throughout the compare-for-compatibility exercises. Your final version is a work+life fit that's compatible with your current work and personal realities that are most critical to its success. Now it's time to answer the question: What's in it for the company?

From Work+Life Fit Fundamental #5, you know that your work+life fit should be approved because it's a solid business proposal and not just because it's the "right thing to do." So now we'll look at your work+life fit through a business lens to determine how it makes sense for your employer or prospective employer. In other words—what is the supporting business case?

There are five basic business cases to be made for a new work+life fit:

- ▶ Productivity
- ▶ Business needs
- ▶ Retention
- ▶ Recruitment
- ▶ Expense control

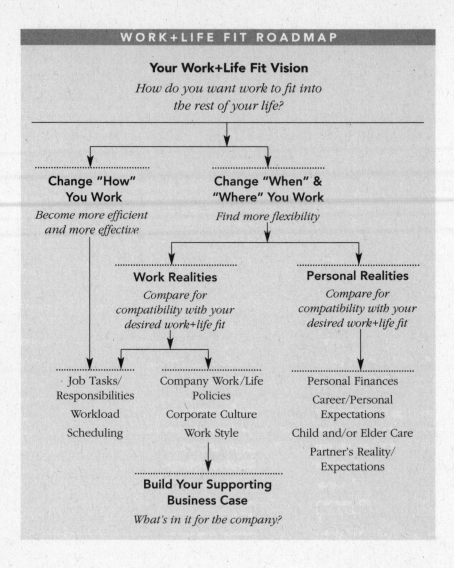

When developing your own business case, you can include one, some, or all five. But the most important thing is to approach your proposal as you would any other business negotiation, making sure the outcome is a "win-win" situation. When you build the business case, you're articulating what the "win" is for your company in supporting your arrangement.

It's important to develop your business case prior to the negotiation when you'll want to be able to confidently articulate how your work+life fit will benefit the business.

As we discussed at the beginning of the book, you already know that achieving a better work+life fit would make you more satisfied with your job, more loyal, less likely to quit, and feel a heck of a lot less burned out. In turn, you would work more efficiently, which makes your company more profitable. But now let's look at each aspect of the business case a little more closely to see which piece supports your particular arrangement most effectively.

Productivity

When you find a better way to fit work into your life, you are more productive because you are less stressed, less distracted, and therefore more focused. It's really that simple. As a manager said to an employee with a reduced work schedule, "This is great. I pay you 80%, but you give me 120%."

In fact, people with jobs that require uninterrupted time to concentrate often propose telecommuting arrangements because they get more work done at home without the distractions of meetings, ringing telephones, and so forth.

As you consider the productivity business case think back to some of the stories you've read. Remember Natalie and Betsy? Natalie is my college friend whose new work+life fit improved her productivity by forcing her to prioritize work and focus on what made the most impact. She's been promoted twice even though she works fewer hours.

Wanting to work from home one day a week, Betsy challenged the necessity of certain tasks she felt added little value but required a lot of time. Her critical review of her work will not only improve her efficiency and productivity, but that of her whole group.

Marie is another client who used the productivity business case. As a financial analyst, she's responsible for writing reports but often finds that difficult to do during regular work hours because of constant interruptions from the phone, meetings, and colleagues. As a result, she was forced to complete most of her concentrated writing after 5 P.M. which caused her to get home past 10 P.M. most nights. She knew this wasn't healthy in the long run, so she proposed a work+life fit that would allow her to work from home two days a week. She devoted those two days to the uninterrupted writing of her reports. After only two months into the new arrangement, not only was she more productive but she felt that the quality of her work had improved.

As you consider the productivity business case to support your work+life fit, ask yourself:

▶ What changes in your job tasks, responsibilities, workload, and scheduling did you identify in chapter 18? Do these changes improve your productivity, and how?

▶ Can these productivity improvements help the group as a whole work more efficiently? How?

▶ How will your job benefit from the resolution of your work+life conflict? Reduce stress and burnout? Allow you to focus? Will you work even harder out of gratitude and loyalty?

Business Needs

Could your work+life fit fulfill an unmet need of the business? Here are a couple of arrangements that did:

Eve, a mother of two children, works in a manufacturing plant as an engineer. Her manager couldn't find people willing to work the third shift from 12 A.M. to 8 A.M. Always the night owl, Eve offered to permanently work that shift in order to be home when her children get home from school in the afternoon, thus ending the manager's struggle to staff the third shift with an engineer.

Joe works for an international bank, and his group's clients are all in the Far East. He proposed a work+life fit that shifted his hours from 9:00 A.M. to 5 P.M., to 6:00 A.M. to 2 P.M. The group's customers love the arrangement because they have access to Joe during a part of their regular work-day, and now Joe is able to attend school in the afternoon.

Judy wanted to transition back to work after staying home full-time with her kids. With a background in finance, she wanted to find a position that would give her the flexi-bility to work primarily from home, during school hours, or in the evening after her husband got home. She met a local financial planner who was looking for someone to run an investment workshop for women one night every month and to create reports on stocks that he was thinking of including in his clients' portfolios. He had been responsible for these tasks but was trying to find a way to reduce the time and en-ergy he spent at work. With Judy on board, he could spend more time at home. They enjoyed a mutually supportive arrangement for a number of years, with Judy ultimately working her way up to portfolio manager of client accounts.

Charlie had been an engineer with the same aerospace company for more than 30 years. When he decided to retire last year, he approached his supervisor with a proposal to become essentially an engineer-for-hire. He knew the way the project flow worked and also that there were crunch times in the project cycle where they could use an extra body in order to get the work done. He proposed coming in approximately 10 days per month and being paid a per diem rate, based upon his salary at the time of his retire-ment. His boss thought it was a great suggestion, consider-ing that turnover in the team had left it staffed with relatively inexperienced engineers. Charlie would be a big help to them, and to his manager.

Retention

The retention business case: A flexible arrangement that resolves your work/life conflict makes you more loyal and committed and allows your employer to retain you, along with all of your talent and knowledge. As one client told me, "When I get headhunter calls now, I say that I'll think about it only if I can continue working from home three days a week. And they can't match it. So I stay."

Let's review Work+Life Fit Fundamental #4. You add value. We discussed the different ways you can add value to your employer's business. Review the list you compiled. Since you add value, it's worthwhile for your company to retain you. You are an important asset of the organization. And even in an economic downturn, there's still a competitive market for retaining quality employees.

As the research at the beginning of the book indicates, increasingly, work+life fit is an important retention tool for companies, especially as employees' values change and projected employee shortages emerge. Thirtysomethings want more time and energy for their families; fiftysomethings want to work in some capacity when they retire; fortysomethings are facing the responsibility of caring for an aging relative; and, finally, workers across all these demographics are reevaluating what is important in their lives. The new common reality among all of these groups is a willingness to make a decision about where and how they are employed based in some part on finding a work+life fit that allows them to have a personal life. If, because of your values and personal responsibilities, you're willing to change your employment in order to find more flexibility, then the retention business case applies to your work+life fit too.

People ask me, "If retention is part of my business case, when do I share that in the negotiation? It sounds a little bit threatening, although I *will* probably leave if I don't find a better work+life fit." We will discuss negotiation strategy in chapter 27; however, suffice it to say you don't want to begin the negotiation by saying that you're willing to walk if you don't get your way. That doesn't set the desired mutually supportive tone that you want. You probably won't have to mention the retention business case at all—your manager will most likely infer that turning down your request could result in your departure.

Why include retention as part of your business case if you aren't necessarily going to use it? Because *just knowing that you're willing to walk away is the strongest position from which to negotiate.* If you find the negotiation at an impasse, you can use the retention business case to jump-start the process. You can say, "I really hope we can work out some sort of an agreement because I would like to be able to stay and use my experience and customer relationships to help the group achieve this year's goals." Hopefully, a well-placed comment will make your manager realize what will happen if they don't support some version of your proposed work+life fit—you will quit. When faced with the reality—they will lose this employee who adds value to the organization—most managers are catalyzed to seek a mutually beneficial solution.

Recruitment

The recruitment business case is relevant if you're seeking a new job and want a particular work+life fit as part of that job. And, to accomplish this goal, you're more likely to seek a company that allows you to negotiate an arrangement that benefits you and the company.

Again, the market for attracting and retaining quality employees is competitive even in an economic downturn. Research confirms that more job seekers are basing their decision about what company they want to work for on work/life criteria. In fact, as more employees appropriately place greater value on work/life supports, more companies will have to create environments within which work+life fit negotiations can take place. I just love competitive market forces!

Recently, I participated in a women's business conference at Columbia Business School. In talking with students over lunch, several of them mentioned that their future employers were considered to be more work/life friendly than other companies in that industry. I was particularly struck by this, since none of those students were married or had children, but it definitely was a factor in their decision. And they had told their new employers it was one of the reasons that they were chosen over other organizations. These women would be considered top talent—ambitious students from an Ivy League MBA program—and they made work+life a factor in their decision-making. It was part of their business case.

Expense Control

In the profit-oriented world of corporate America, expense control is a very popular business case, so include it wherever you can. There are three categories of expense savings that could be relevant to a new work+life fit:

1. Recruiting and training expenses
2. Salary and benefit expenses
3. Real estate expenses

Recruiting and Training Expenses

This expense is directly related to retaining you. The bottom line is that it costs a lot of money to recruit and train a new employee to replace you if you leave. Depending upon your level of experience and the complexity of your job, researchers estimate it can take up to 12 months for a new employee to start generating profit.[1] That's a lot of profit opportunities lost. In other words, it's not only the direct costs of recruiting. It's also the loss of the individual's ability to contribute fully today and the missed business opportunities in the future that factor in to the calculation.

Even losing less-experienced employees with relatively unskilled jobs can cost a company a lot of money. It's amazing how much money companies could save if they included work+life fit as a strategic management tool. Listen to the story of Clueless Company.

CLUELESS COMPANY'S STORY

As part of a consulting project at one large company, our Corporate-Family Solutions team was asked to visit its 24-hour call center. Because many of the call representatives were young single mothers, senior management wanted to understand their work/life challenges, especially since they were experiencing 65% turnover annually. Paying to recruit and train 65% of the workforce every year was very expensive.

We learned that new recruits traditionally have to start working the night shift, 12 A.M. to 8 A.M., and work their way up to the day shift by increasing their seniority. But the night shift is the most difficult time to find quality, affordable child care. Therefore, these single, minimum-wage mothers were predestined to fail. When asked why they were thinking of leaving, they *all* said a lack of affordable, reliable care for their kids.

We also learned that some of the more senior representatives would be willing to work the night shift if they got paid more. This would free up slots in the day shifts for the new recruits. The solution seemed simple: Pay more per hour to entice senior reps to work the night shift, which would allow more new reps to work the day shift when they could find child care. The company would offset the increased salary expense with the reduction in recruiting and training of 65% of the workforce every year.

We presented our findings and recommendations to senior management who said, "We can't afford to pay any more than we already are per hour."

"How much do you spend each year to recruit and train this endless stream of new reps only to see a majority leave within the same year?" I asked. They weren't sure. "If you paid some people more to work at night, the accompanying decrease in recruiting and training expense would more than offset the increase in salary expense."

While the expense savings business case was very clear to me, they still weren't sure. Even in an environment with relatively unskilled employees, lower turnover still saves you money.

. . .

As with the retention business case, the associated expense savings will most likely not come up in the negotiation. However, if your manager is really resistant to approving your arrangement, you can point out that if you need to leave because you can't resolve your work/life conflict, it could be expensive to find a replacement. Go back to the list of ways you add value from chapter 4. Emphasize the benefit to the company from keeping you employed, and how much would be lost, both tangibly (e.g., direct training expenses) and intangibly (e.g., customer relationships, efficiency because you know how to do the job, etc.). Wouldn't it be more cost-effective to try to find a compromise that allows you to stay and continue contributing to the business? But again, even if you never discuss the details, use as a source of confidence the knowledge that replacing you would be costly.

Salary and Benefit Expense

I have a fantasy. In a depressed economy, before companies lay people off, they would first reduce the number of "employee hours worked," by asking the workforce who would be willing to reduce their hours. I think there would be a lot of takers. In many cases, the associated decrease in salary and benefit expense could be enough to avoid massive layoffs. Plus the company would retain the valuable employee talent it will need when the inevitable recovery begins. But a few barriers stand in the way—Wall Street's obsession with the "number of employees" laid off, and HR's obsession with "head count." Until these two concepts give way to "number of employee hours" or "fractional head count" as a measure of expense control, you will have to make your own individual argument for the expense-saving benefits of your arrangement.

A work+life fit that reduces the number of hours you work, and proportionally reduces your salary, has a strong business case supporting it. Your arrangement could save benefit expenses as well if you don't work enough hours to qualify for health and retirement benefits.

The direct salary and benefit savings are a powerful business case in any negotiation, especially if you link it with improving productivity. Saving money while helping you work more productively? Can't beat that. The company gets about the same amount of output for less money. Always good news in a bottom-line-oriented world.

Real Estate Expenses

This business case is reserved for telecommuting, and then really only applies to situations in which you don't need an office at the company at all. But if your work+life fit involves working from home most of the time, then you could present the real estate cost savings as part of the business case to support your arrangement. Contact a local commercial real estate broker to get the average per square foot cost of real estate in your area. For example, if you worked in office space that costs more than $150 per square foot, and you have a 20-square-foot cubicle, it costs your company $3,000 per year. Assuming your telephone expense is less than $3,000 per year, the company saves money on the deal. But when calculating the savings be sure to factor in your telecommuting expenses, such as monthly telephone bills, fax machines, FedEx deliveries, and so forth.

BUILD YOUR BUSINESS CASE

1. Review the final version of your work+life fit in your workbook.

2. Which business cases support this vision as a formal "win-win" business proposal? Note how they support it specifically, in terms of:

   - Productivity
   - Business needs

- Retention
- Recruitment
- Expense savings

3. Taking the individual arguments together, write out the underlying business case to support the final version of your work+life fit in your Workbook. This description is solely for *your* purposes so try to be as detailed as possible. Later, we will include parts of it in your formal proposal. For example:

> Approving my proposed work+life fit of working four nine-hour days per week will allow me to be more productive. I will be less distracted and will be forced to focus on the tasks with the greatest impact, and I will also manage my schedule more efficiently to accomplish the tasks that I retain. In addition, the accompanying 15% reduction in my salary will save the company money. Furthermore, I will be able to remain at the company and use my experience and knowledge to contribute to achieving the team's goal. And the company will save the direct expense of recruiting and training my replacement. I will continue to contribute to the business using my unique knowledge of our product and services, my network within the company, and my customer relationships that help me efficiently and profitably get my job done.

Proposing Your Work+Life Fit

Chapter Goal: *To create your formal work+life fit proposal.*

You now have a work+life fit that is not only compatible with all of the work and personal realities most critical to its success, but is supported by a business case that articulates the "win-win" for both parties. From that strong base, it's time to create the formal proposal that you will present to and negotiate with your manager or prospective employer.

One Last Internal Guidance Check

Before you begin, let's do one last check with your internal guidance that the final work+life fit you are proposing truly represents how you want work to fit into your life. Your arrangement will only succeed if it represents what, in your heart of hearts, you want.

Compare the final version of your work+life fit to your original vision, and ask yourself:

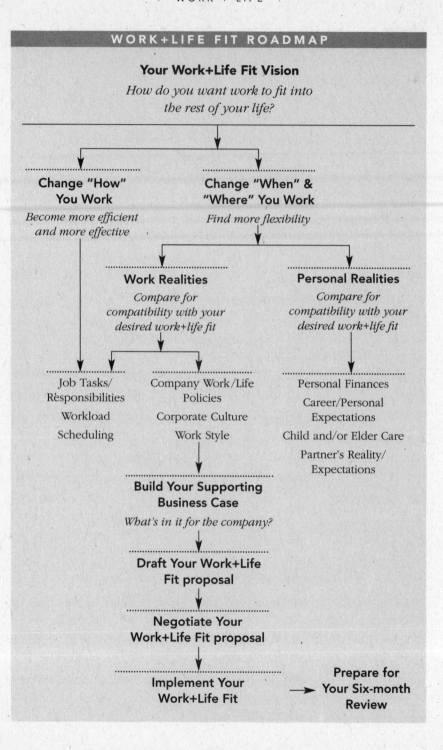

WORK+LIFE FIT ROADMAP

Your Work+Life Fit Vision

*How do you want work to fit into
the rest of your life?*

**Change "How"
You Work**

*Become more efficient
and more effective*

**Change "When" &
"Where" You Work**

Find more flexibility

Work Realities

*Compare for
compatibility with your
desired work+life fit*

Personal Realities

*Compare for
compatibility with your
desired work+life fit*

Job Tasks/
Responsibilities

Workload

Scheduling

Company Work/Life
Policies

Corporate Culture

Work Style

Personal Finances

Career/Personal
Expectations

Child and/or Elder Care

Partner's Reality/
Expectations

**Build Your Supporting
Business Case**

What's in it for the company?

**Draft Your Work+Life
Fit proposal**

**Negotiate Your
Work+Life Fit proposal**

**Implement Your
Work+Life Fit**

**Prepare for
Your Six-month
Review**

Given the work+life fit I originally envisioned, can I live with the final adjusted version, or have I compromised too much?

Take some time to reflect. You developed your original vision using the mind, body, spirit tools. Use these same tools to help you consider whether you're comfortable with your adjusted vision.

If you're still comfortable proposing this final version, then skip to Creating Your Formal Work+Life Fit Proposal on page 330.

What if the answer is "No, the adjusted version of my original vision is not how I want work to fit into my life?" You still have options.

First, redo the compare-for-compatibility exercises. Reexamine the work and personal realities that were incompatible with your vision and that you felt were unchangeable. Look carefully at those factors that caused you to adjust your vision. Challenge your determination that the reality can't be changed. Is there *any* possible way to change the reality instead of changing your vision? Use the mind, body, and spirit tools to help you. Make sure that a success, fear, resistance, or in-the-box-thinking roadblock isn't standing in the way of your making a change. You may need to refer back to Step 2 and use a bypass strategy to get beyond a particular roadblock.

For example, maybe you initially thought you couldn't change your personal financial reality. But upon reflection, you decided to downsize your house. Or you believed that you couldn't give up certain tasks to reduce your workload. After giving it a second thought, you decide to give them up even if it affects your status in the company. Or, maybe you couldn't change your career expectations regarding advancement. But you now realize that you'd be willing to plateau, at least for a while, if it meant more hours at home.

If you complete the compare-for-compatibility exercises again and *still* can't find a way to change your incompatible work and personal realities, you can still achieve your original vision, but in stages. You might want to revisit Work+Life Fit Fundamental #8: patience and perseverance. Then proceed as follows:

▶ First, propose and negotiate the adjusted version of your original vision, and implement it for six months.

▶ Over that six-month period, make the necessary changes to the work and personal realities that are incompatible with your original vision. The goal is to bring you closer to your original goal.

▶ As of the six-month review, if your work and personal realities are now in line with your original vision, propose a work+life fit that is closer to that vision and implement that for six months.

▶ Finally, if you still aren't quite there, take those next six months to make even more changes, until you're able to propose your original version.

This approach will obviously take more time, but it will help you ultimately reach your original goal. I've worked with a number of people who've taken this approach in smaller stages. One client wanted to either work part-time or job-share, but her personal financial reality was incompatible with that goal. Personal finance is the reality most often incompatible with an original work+life fit. So she started by working 35 hours a week for six months. Over that period, she focused on getting a handle on her finances. Then she went down to 30 hours for six months, and during that time searched for an appropriate job-share partner. And finally, one year later, she and her new partner proposed a job-share arrangement that allowed her to work two and a half days a week, which was her original vision.

Another client was struggling with her husband's expectation that she wasn't going to work at all while the kids were in school. But she wanted to work part-time as a speech therapist. Initially, she took on two clients for about 6 hours per week. As her husband and children became more comfortable, six months later she increased her client load to 15 hours, and six months later 25 hours. After a year, she had achieved her original goal and was able to reconcile her husband's expectations with her original vision.

Remember the example of the woman who was the first person

on her team to ever propose a different work+life fit. Her corporate culture was heavily focused on face time. Her original vision was to work four days a week, but as a team leader she was sure her boss wouldn't be comfortable with her working four days and handling her workload, even though she had carefully considered how she would do it. So she first proposed working from home one day a week. She felt this arrangement would help her manager develop a comfort level with her not being in the office. And then, in six months, when she had proven the work could still get done when she wasn't there, she proposed her four-day workweek.

What do you do if you really can't change the incompatible work and personal realities, and you don't think you can wait to achieve your original vision in stages? This is a tough and rare situation, however, there are still options:

▶ Maybe you need to revisit your original vision. I know you think it's how you want work to fit into your life, but is it *really* what you want? Go back to the mind, body, spirit tools. Talk to a counselor or coach. Spend more time reflecting and connecting to your inner guidance.

▶ If your impasse is work-related, maybe you need to consider the other paths to a better work+life fit: changing what you do, changing who you work for, or changing why you work. Maybe you don't need to change how, where, or when you work; maybe you need a new job or career, a new manager, or just a new sense of purpose.

▶ If your impasse is personal, you may have hit a success, fear, resistance, or in-the-box-thinking roadblock that's so big you either aren't able to see it, or haven't been able to get around it. Get some help redefining success, challenging your fears, overcoming resistance, and thinking creatively in order to reach your goal.

Bottom-line: *You must be happy and content with the work+life fit you propose for it to succeed.* If you feel like you're settling in any way, give the version that you want to propose a serious second thought before moving to the next step.

Creating Your Formal Work+Life Fit Proposal

There are a couple of important points to clarify before we begin creating the proposal that you will present to your manager: Review the rule of thumb from Work+Life Fit Fundamental #5. It's best to approach changing your work+life fit in the same way you would conduct any other important business transaction: formally negotiating and signing an agreement that lists the terms and conditions agreed to by both you and your manager. Why? Because it only benefits you. How? By doing the following:

- ► Lending credibility to your work+life fit
- ► Giving you credit for all of the work you do
- ► Clarifying expectations of all parties affected
- ► Supporting your manager's decision
- ► Surviving the peaks and valleys of corporate performance
- ► Allowing your work+life fit to continue despite management changes

And remember your formal proposal is a statement of understanding that clarifies mutual expectations, and it can be renegotiated at any time by either party if work and/or personal realities warrant. It's *not* a binding contract. There is boilerplate language in this chapter that you can include in your proposal document to clarify this.

* * *

I used to prescribe how the formal proposal should look, but then I realized that every organization has its own culture around business proposals; how detailed they should be, what they should and should not include, what format they should be in, and so on. Lawyers always seemed to need more detail, whereas an advertising agency wanted it simple and to the point.

Plus, I find that when you give people a form, even if it's only a suggested form, they're afraid to deviate from it. The important thing is that you present a formal proposal that you're comfortable with, that conforms to your industry and company norms of business agreements, and that can be easily understood by all parties. There is no right or wrong way to construct it. That said, I do have a few guidelines on what you should and should not include.

You should include:

- **Specifics of your work+life fit**: "Work three nine-hour days per week, Monday, Tuesday, Wednesday from 8:00 A.M. to 5:00 P.M."
- **Changes to aspects of work**: If you are making changes to your tasks, workload, or your schedule in order to achieve your work+life fit, then specifically list the changes you are going to make. Be sure to include how those changes may affect the rest of the team.
- **Business case**: Include any relevant productivity and salary benefit, and real estate expense savings–related arguments. Remember to reserve retention and its related expense arguments as discussion points during the negotiation in case you encounter resistance from your manager.
- **Potential concerns**: Think about any possible concerns that your manager might have about this arrangement and your ability to get the job done. Write down each concern and then underneath explain the steps you will take to mitigate it. For example, you think that your manager may question your ability to respond promptly to client inquiries. List the concern in your proposal and then next to it record the steps to address it. For example, "I will have my calls forwarded to my home office so that my absence from the office is seamless from the client." Also, leave space to list any other issues that are brought up during the negotiation.

Then record the steps that you and your manager agreed will be taken to mitigate them. This list is an excellent resource to support the success of the arrangement at the six-month review, especially if none of the concerns ever became a problem.

▶ **Specific expectations**: Specify your expectations related to the following areas (include any others that you may want to clarify during the negotiation):

    Responsibilities—those you will keep and those you won't

    Unexpected business needs—how you will handle problems that require you to work unscheduled days or hours

    Advancement—what you will and will not be considered for

    Compensation—salary, bonus, long-term compensation, etc.

    Benefits—retirement and health benefits

▶ **Disclaimer paragraph**: This attorney-prepared boilerplate language clarifies the nature of the agreement as a non-binding document of understanding, not a binding contract.

This is not a legally binding agreement or contract between the parties. The parties affix their signatures to this document indicating only that they have read and understand its contents. By signing this document, the parties understand that it does not constitute an employment contract and the terms of the document may be altered, modified, or rescinded by either party at any time.

▶ **Signatures and date of approval**

▶ **Date you reviewed the work+life fit with the group**: Include who was present at the meeting and list any concerns the group raises along with the strategies to mitigate those concerns.

▶ **Review date**: Six months is the standard.

▶ **Forms required by human resources**: Make sure that you include any of the forms related to your arrangement that need to be completed. The goal is to make sure that you are in compliance with company policy, *and* if you are negotiating changes to company policy (e.g., keeping health insurance even though you work less than 30 hours per week), making sure that it is formally documented. Many companies have "flexibility agreements" that you should complete.

You should *not* include:

▶ **The reason**: As much as you might like to include the reason for your request (e.g., to pursue an avocation in bird watching, take care of my sick mother, have more time to travel with my retired husband, have time to be with my kids) in your formal proposal, don't. This is a business proposal, and you want it to be approved based on its mutually beneficial merits—not because your manager is afraid to challenge your request to spend time with your aging mother.

As we discussed, managers want the ability to review your request objectively. They don't want to be put in the position of valuing one person's reason for a better work+life fit more than another's. The fact that you're asking is evidence that the arrangement is something you want and need. That's enough. Take the emotion out of it, and it's more likely to succeed on its business merits.

▶ **The retention and related expense business case**: Yes, being willing to walk away if you are unable to reach a mutually agreeable compromise is a position of strength as you enter any negotiation. However, you *do not* want to include that in your formal proposal. Use it only as a negotiating tactic of last resort, which we will discuss in the next chapter.

Scheduling Your Negotiation

Now that you have your formal proposal drafted, schedule a time to sit down with your manager to present and negotiate your arrangement. The question of when you should include human resources depends upon what role human resources plays in your company. If your HR representative is a strategic thinker who has a track record of facilitating creative solutions, then consider involving him at any point you would like. However, if he tends to be more administrative, then perhaps wait to involve him after the negotiation has taken place. Provide him with a copy of the formal proposal and the appropriate related documentation required by the HR department.

Negotiating Your Work+Life Fit

Chapter Goal: *To walk through the steps involved in the formal negotiation of your work+life fit arrangement.*

Why Is It Important to Negotiate?

You've drafted your formal proposal, now it's time to conduct the negotiation with your manager or prospective employer. What does it mean to negotiate? It's easy to get intimidated by the word and the process. To negotiate simply means *to reach an agreement by discussion.*

Approach your negotiation as you would any other business discussion. Doing so legitimizes your arrangement from the very beginning and sets the tone for how all parties—you, your manager, your team—will regard the arrangement once it's implemented.

Consider the alternative approach. You walk into your manager's office while he or she is on the phone, and you slip the proposal on the desk with a sticky note attached saying, "Let me know what you think☺."

What message does this send? It says you don't have enough confidence in the proposal to discuss it face-to-face. This won't give your manager much confidence, or reason to take the request seriously, especially if he or she is one of the resistant managers we've discussed.

Furthermore, if you don't sit down, discuss the proposal, and try to reach a consensus, you've undermined the legitimacy of your arrangement in other ways. You've surrendered all of your power to your manager. It's her decision now. In other words, even if she says "yes," it will not be an equal partnership. It will be a one-sided agreement.

You also need to make your manager feel invested in the arrangement. Otherwise at the first sign of trouble (and, as with anything in life, everything will not be perfect), it will be too easy for her to discontinue it. A negotiation during which you and your manager share your needs and concerns is critical to establishing this investment and commitment.

This all may sound very symbolic, and you still may be thinking, "Wouldn't it be fine to just slip the proposal into my manager's hand as we're walking out of a meeting?" But these symbolic steps of presenting your proposal, discussing it with your manager, coming to a consensus, and signing a formal agreement *are* important. They raise your work+life fit to the level of a business arrangement—an arrangement to be handled professionally and with respect, which is where you want it to begin. And only by negotiating will you both feel like you walked away with a win-win.

How to Negotiate

To prepare you for your negotiation, it's helpful to follow the same strategies you would use to negotiate any other type of business deal. The steps you need to follow include:[1]

Before the Negotiation

- ▶ Clarify your work+life fit and its objectives.
- ▶ Determine your Best Alternative to a Negotiated Agreement

(BATNA). In other words, what will you do if the answer is "no"?

▶ Determine which aspects of your work+life fit are "must haves" and which are "would likes."

▶ Understand your manager's goals, interests, values, objectives, fears, and predisposition to work/life issues.

▶ Give your manager your proposal in advance.

▶ Read a book on negotiation.

During the Negotiation

▶ Go in with the right attitude; avoid taking a position.

▶ Build trust.

▶ Build in time for brainstorming.

▶ Appreciate the power of silence.

▶ If you disagree, listen. Don't assume you and your manager want opposite results; avoid win-lose thinking.

▶ Don't agree to something "just to get it over with."

▶ Be flexible with your "must haves" and "would likes."

After the Negotiation

▶ Complete the formal work+life fit agreement

Before the Negotiation:
Prepare, Prepare, Prepare

Clarify your work+life fit

Check this off your to do list right away. You did this when you created your final work+life fit. You completed the compare-for-compatibility process to ensure your proposal was realistic given your work and personal realities. The work+life fit you are proposing is the optimal outcome.

Now, what do you want this negotiation to achieve; what is its objective? Essentially, it's laid out in your proposal. You want to reallocate "X" amount of time and energy to your personal life, which gives you "Y" amount of time and energy for work.

What is your BATNA?

The work+life fit you are proposing represents the best-case scenario for you. Now it's time to determine what you will do if you and your manager are *unable* to negotiate an agreement. In the world of negotiation, this is called your Best Alternative to a Negotiated Agreement, or BATNA.[2] In other words, what is the worst-case scenario? What if you aren't satisfied with the final arrangement your manager offers? Or what if your manager says "no" to the minimal compromise you will accept? What will you do?

Remember, *"no" is okay as long as you negotiated in good faith*. This is important. You must go into this negotiation hopeful and optimistic, but understanding that it is possible that you and your manager will not be able to agree.

Why is it important to consider this before the negotiation? Establishing your BATNA is the only way to know what your bottom-line, walk-away point is. What is the minimum portion of your proposal that you will agree to, before your alternatives look better, and you walk away from the negotiation? What are some possible alternatives to a negotiated work+life fit?

Your alternatives very much depend on your work and personal realities. Perhaps given your reality, if you can't reach an agreement, you'll have to continue with your current work/life conflict unresolved. This is the weakest BATNA. And depending upon your work and personal realities, you may have no other alternative. In this situation, you have the least amount of negotiating leverage. You would willingly accept any change no matter how small in your existing work+life fit, because any little change would improve your current situation.

The strongest BATNA, of course, is a willingness and ability to leave. That can mean finding a new job either with a new manager or a new company or even quitting without another job. This is the most powerful negotiating position. It means that you can determine the minimum change you will settle for, and for anything less, you will walk away. We've discussed numerous times, if you're willing to leave anyway, why not ask? You have nothing to lose.

Obviously, you don't want to start the negotiation threatening to leave if you don't get your work+life fit exactly as you propose it. Give the negotiation process a chance to create a mutually acceptable arrangement. But, when the time is right, you may need to present your limit.

Determine your "must haves" and "would likes"

Before you go into a negotiation, you need to know what concessions you are and are not willing to make. You do this by taking the best-case scenario, which is your work+life fit as you've proposed it, and your worst-case scenario, which is your BATNA, and then looking at all of the acceptable versions that lie between the two extremes.

Start by making a list of your "must haves" and your "would likes." The must haves are your walk-away, non-negotiable points. Your would likes are the aspects you would be willing to negotiate. If you enter the negotiation from a position of strength with a BATNA that allows you to leave, then your list of must haves will be longer than someone with a weaker BATNA. The weaker your negotiating position, the fewer must haves there can be.

Incorporate all of your must haves and would likes into an alternative version of your work+life fit. This will give you an idea of where you have room to negotiate. And then create the "walk away" version of your work+life fit that includes only the must haves, which will be your bottom line in the negotiation. For example:

▶ Proposed work+life fit: Work Monday, Tuesday, and Wednesday from home, and then Thursday in the office from 10 A.M. to 6 P.M., and Fridays off.

► Alternative with must haves and would likes: I must work Monday and Wednesdays from home, and I must be able to arrive on Thursdays by 10:00 A.M. However, I would like to work from home on Tuesdays, but would be willing to work in the office if I could arrive by 10:00 A.M. And, I don't need to take Friday off. I could take either Tuesday or Thursday off instead and come in on Friday arriving at 10:00 A.M. Whatever makes the most sense for my manager.

► Alternative with only must haves: I must work from home on Mondays and Wednesdays; on the days that I come into the office, I must be able to arrive at 10.00 A.M., and I must have at least one full day off every week.

In the example above, I focused solely on the changes in "when" and "where" you work. However, before you negotiate, you want to expand this exercise to include "how" you will work under the arrangement—the must-have and would-like tasks, responsibilities, and schedules. Also, consider the must-have and would-like expectations related to promotion, compensation, benefits, and so forth.

What if you feel that most of your proposed work+life fit is non-negotiable, and you are willing to walk away if you don't get almost exactly what you proposed? Still give the discussion with your manager a chance. He might bring up some valid concerns about your ability to do your job with this particular arrangement that you hadn't thought of. Concerns, that if ignored, could effect the success of your work+life fit. Together you could adjust the arrangement in a way that accounts for these realities of your job but also that gives you the time and energy you want for your personal life.

Work+Life Fit Fundamental #3 states that if you are a good employee then you should propose your work+life fit because nine times out of ten, your manager will approve it. While this is true, remember also that your manager may not be overly enthusiastic with his approval, especially if this is his first time. Therefore, you may encounter some initial resistance in the negotiation that can be diffused if you try to determine what type of negotiator your manager might be and consider your response before you begin. There are five general types of negotiator:[3]

Type: Bully, "You can't do this."

Response: Create a boundary of consequence; this is a perfect time to calmly and professionally articulate your willingness to leave, "Just so you know, I have carefully considered not only my needs but the needs of the business when crafting this arrangement. I would like an opportunity to discuss it with you; however, I must let you know that if we are unable to come to some sort of mutually agreeable solution, then I may have to consider other alternatives." Hopefully, facing this reality will force your manager to see the negative consequences of his behavior and that he can't impose his preference for how you will work simply by rejecting your request outright. In this situation, the ability to leave is critical. If you must stay, then merely emphasizing how your arrangement will increase productivity and job satisfaction may not be enough to stand down a bully boss. He knows that his intimidation will result in the outcome he prefers—no change in your work+life fit.

Type: Avoider, "I don't have time right now," or Withdrawer, "I don't know."

Response: Make this person feel safe enough not to avoid or withdraw from your negotiation. Try to understand what he is afraid of. Make sure you're not doing anything to make him uncomfortable: your tone of voice, approach, etc. Draw him into the negotiation by asking questions such as, "What can I help you understand better?" or "Is there something I can do to help you find some time because this is important to me or I wouldn't be asking?"

Type: High Roller, "You either work the hours you have, or you don't work at all."

Response: "Can you tell me the criteria for making that decision?" or "I understand what you're saying, but I was hoping we could have a mutually beneficial discussion that addresses my current work and personal realities, as well as the realities of our business." Again, in this situation, if you can't restart the negotiation, you may have to pull out the negotiating tactic of last resort, "If we can't come to an agreement, I may have to consider other alternatives." If you are a good employee, your manager doesn't want to lose you. Hopefully, she will be forced to see the negative affect of her behavior and proceed with the negotiation. And always remember to emphasize the six-month review. It gives the manager a sense of control.

Type: Wad Shooter, "That's my bottom line," or "Take it or leave it."
Response: Take a break in the conversation for a minute and then try to restart the negotiation by asking to continue but in a fairer manner, "I would prefer not to be pressured into an agreement. I believe there is still room to reach a compromise." Or you could ask for clarification: "Why is this version final when I've shown you that the job can be done with the arrangement as I've proposed? What are your real concerns?" Also, remind him that you will sit down and review the arrangement in six months. How you respond depends upon your BATNA. If your realities are such that you have little leverage, then you may have to accept his final version of the work+life fit even if it includes few of your "must haves" and "would likes." In this case, something may be better than nothing.

However, if his proposal doesn't meet your minimum threshold, and you are willing to walk away, then it's worthwhile to calmly and professionally state this reality in the hopes that he will understand that saying "no" means saying "good-bye." You may be surprised how quickly the tone of the negotiation changes.

Another tactic is to try silence and see what happens. This is hard because the natural tendency is to fill the silence. But see if your manager reads your silence as an indication of dissatisfaction and puts forth an alternative that then restarts the negotiation.

• • •

In addition to determining what type of negotiator your manager is, it's important to understand your manager's goals, interests, and values. This will help you anticipate his specific concerns, as well as his initial reaction to your proposal, and make you better prepared to negotiate. How do you do this?

- ► **Role-play.** Role-play the negotiation with someone, with you playing the role of manager. This will help you understand your manager's point of view and be better prepared to address it.

- ► **Ask third parties for insight.** Ask around to try to get the scoop on your manager. How does your manager perceive herself, more supportive or more dictatorial? How has she responded to similar requests in the past? To whom does she defer or compare herself? How does she handle her own work and personal life? What are her values? What is her relationship with her boss like?

- ► **What is your manager's BATNA?** Think about what your manager will have to do if the two of you can't reach an agreement. If he will have to find and train a replacement, it's going to be a pain in the neck for him. Assuming you are a good employee, most managers would be willing to try any work+life fit that keeps you around. I believe this is the reasoning that makes even the most resistant managers willing to approve at least a six-month trial period. If you're comfortable with "I'm willing to leave," but your manager's facing the less attractive "I have to go through the hassle of finding a new person," you have a lot of leverage.

- ► **Understand your manager's fears.** This is a big one. Almost every manager that I've ever worked with has the same two fears: the "floodgates" fear and the "I will never be able to say 'no' once I say 'yes'" fear.
    "Floodgates" fear: It goes something like this, "If I approve this for you, then everyone else is going to want it."

Know that this is going to be an issue, especially if your manager has never approved a flexible arrangement.

Your response: As always, acknowledge your manager's concern. However, let her know that you would hope she would consider everyone's request individually as she has with your proposal. And offer to reevaluate your arrangement should the number of arrangements in the group begin to negatively impact the business. Offer to sit down with the others who are requesting a change and address her concerns as a group so that the work doesn't suffer.

Finally, from all of my experience consulting to companies and working with managers, I can tell you (and you can tell your manager) that I've never once seen the floodgates fear materialize. Yes, perhaps one or two people proposed changing their work+life fit also. But rarely are any two requests the same; therefore, there is little overlapping impact on the business. And what little impact there might be is easily addressed by adjusting each individual's work+life fit. More important, I've observed an unexpected dividend when a manager approves a work+life fit for one person in a group. Even though no one else may want to change their schedule now, it's affirming to know that they could at least ask if they needed to.

The "I can never say 'no' once I say 'yes'" fear: The basis of the fear is discomfort with having to take something away that you may perceive you're entitled to.

Your response: First, assure your manager that you understand this is a nonbinding business agreement and that business needs may change. Therefore, at the six-month review date, both of you will sit down and reevaluate the arrangement based upon the prevailing realities of the business. If at that time the business realities dictate the discontinuation of the arrangement, you will respect that.

You are reminding your manager of the review date, which gives her a sense of having an "out." And you are defining the grounds for discontinuation as business-oriented rather than personal, which, again, lends a sense of legitimacy and professionalism to your agreement. You understand that this is not an entitlement but a mutually beneficial business decision.

▶ *Give your manager your proposal in advance.*

Allow him time to review it and consider his goals and objectives prior to the negotiation.

▶ *Read a book.*

Prepare by reading more about negotiation if you feel you need to consider other strategies and techniques.

During the Negotiation

Now it's time to sit down and discuss all of the aspects of your formal proposal with your manager.

Go in with the right attitude

Avoid taking any one position before the discussion begins. Be open to the possibilities that might evolve. And don't assume that your manager wants the opposite of what you want. Chances are what you want is more time and energy for your personal life, and your manager wants a productive employee to contribute. These are not mutually exclusive desires. You probably aren't as far apart as you think. That said, don't expect your manager to dance the "jig of joy" either. She will most likely approve some form of your work+life fit for six months, but she might not be particularly happy about it. Don't let her hesitation deter you.

Build trust

Listen. State your needs and try to understand your manager's needs. Actively listen to your manager's point of view without becoming defensive. The key is to make it easy for your manager to agree by emphasizing how carefully you thought through every aspect of your job when crafting your proposal. Acknowledge her fears, address them, and negotiate in good faith.

Build in time to brainstorm

Let go of your attachment to one particular outcome for a set period of time—say, 15 minutes—and just throw out ideas and concerns without any particular goal. Both you and your manager may think of alternatives or concerns that could make your arrangement even more successful.

Appreciate the power of silence

This negotiating strategy was developed especially for me. I'm someone who hates silence, and I'm not alone. If this is a problem for you, make a conscious decision to just sit in silence if it's appropriate during the negotiation. Silence gives both you and your manager time to process the conversation, to think of alternatives and compromises. It gives you time to hear and consider each other's concerns and ideas.

If you really can't stand it, try asking leading questions such as, "What are you thinking?" or "Can I clarify anything?" And remember, if your manager gives you an ultimatum—"take it or leave it"—silence is a great response. See how he reacts. It may jump-start the negotiation.

If you disagree, listen

Avoid win-lose thinking. Don't assume you and your manager want opposite results. There is usually a way to work things out if you stick with it.

Don't agree just to get it over with

Don't feel pressure to agree to something quickly "just to get it over with," or because "I was glad to get anything." Remember your manager's BATNA. Chances are that he or she feels as much pressure as you do to find a workable arrangement.

Be flexible with your "must haves" and "would likes"

It's important to have a clear idea of what you will and will not negotiate before you start the conversation, but be flexible.

Know which aspects of your work+life fit are most valuable but be willing to make trade-offs. But never give away something of value for nothing. Say, for example, that one of your "must haves" was working from home two days a week. You can give that up, but not without getting something of value, such as hours that allow you to get home in time for your painting class two days a week.

Your best approach, of course, is trading something that is cheap to you but valuable to your manager for something valuable to you but cheap for your manager. For example, if your manager values having access to you on your day off in case he has questions, perhaps carrying around your cell phone is cheap for you. Or maybe, you value being able to work a four-day week, but it's cheap for your manager because she isn't paying you for that fifth day.

After the Negotiation

What if the answer is "No"?

You asked and, after a good faith negotiation, the answer is "no." What do you do now? First, as long as both you and your manager had a chance to express your needs and concerns, and opportunities for compromise were explored, then "no" needs to be okay.

In fact, instead of considering "no" the end, think of it as the beginning of the next chapter of your life. As we discussed earlier in the book, "no" can be a gift. Depending upon your particular work and personal realities, you essentially have two choices:

1. Keep your current work+life fit as it is.
2. Start looking for a work environment and/or manager that is more compatible with or supportive of the kind of flexibility you need. Go back to chapter 19 for some questions to ask when analyzing a workplace.

What if the answer is "Yes"?

Using your formal proposal as the template, create the formal Work+ Life Fit Agreement. Record the negotiated version of your work+life fit, being as specific as possible. Be sure to update all sections of the proposal to reflect changes made in the negotiation. Get the appropriate signatures, and make copies of the document for the relevant parties.

Now you've done it! Congratulations, your work+life fit is approved (bells ring, whistle blows, confetti falls)! Let's go to chapter 28 and implement your new work+life fit arrangement.

Implementing Your Work+Life Fit

Chapter Goal: *To review the implementation steps that are critical to your work+life fit arrangement's success.*

First, you envisioned how you wanted work to fit into your life. Then you tested that vision to see if it was realistic, given realities in your work and personal life, and if it wasn't, you made it compatible. Finally, you sat down and hashed it all out with your manager. And, presto, you have a new work+life fit! Now, you need to take the steps to make that arrangement a successful reality.

Review Your Arrangement with Your Team

What's one of the fastest ways to ensure failure of your work+life fit? Don't inform your team of the details of your arrangement. Why do you need to inform your team?

- ▶ Whether they know the details or not, your team will know something is going on. Wouldn't it be better for them to hear the details from you as opposed to letting the gossip super-highway fill the void with misinformation?

▶ As was the case with your manager, it's critical that your team feels invested in your arrangement. And they will if they're given a chance to hear the details, ask questions, and have their concerns addressed. This is not to say that they have veto power. But they may raise valid concerns about how your new arrangement could affect them and their work. Hopefully, you've already addressed most of their concerns, and you will be able to be reassuring.

▶ None of us works in a vacuum. Our success depends upon the people with whom we work. Sharing your work+life fit arrangement gives your coworkers a roadmap that spells out how the work is going to get done and who's responsible for what. It gets everyone on the same page, with the same expectations. And as we've discussed, aligning expectations is critical.

▶ Sharing your arrangement with the group also diffuses any potential hint of favoritism. Anyone can ask, and if the proposal makes sense for the business then they too can have a new work+life fit. There are no secrets.

Review Your Arrangement with Internal and External Clients

▶ Explain the arrangement.
▶ Reiterate the client's value to you, the group, and the company.
▶ Ask for feedback about the arrangement and offer to address any concerns.
▶ Discuss how you plan to handle the relationship, how coverage will work, how you plan to communicate, etc.

▶ If someone will be backing you up, introduce him or her prior to starting the arrangement.

Be Flexible but Avoid "Work Creep"

One of the things you should have discussed with your manager is how you plan to respond to unexpected business needs that may require you to work on a day you were supposed to have off or work from home, or attend a meeting during hours that you weren't supposed to work. How are these situations supposed to be handled?

Managers I've worked with believe flexibility and willingness to step up to the plate if the business requires it are critical to the success of flexible arrangements. *But,* there is a point when stepping up to the plate becomes working and not getting paid for it.

As we discussed earlier many people in today's world work more hours than they're paid for. And when you have an arrangement that reduces your hours or days in the office, it's easy to let the extra work become so consistent that you're not getting paid adequately. This is called "work creep" because it can slowly and unexpectedly sneak up on you.

How do you discern between making the appropriate extra effort and doing work for which you are not being adequately paid? Go back to the "proportional work" rule of thumb in chapter 22. To review, let's say that as a full-time employee at your company, the standard workweek is 40 hours, but the norm is to work 45 hours. If under your new arrangement you work 30 hours a week, then, the appropriate level of "going above and beyond" would mean working up to 33 hours a week on average. But if you're working above this level on a consistent basis, you need to speak up. Ask your manager if you can sit down together and review the terms of your arrangement (see how that formal document comes in handy!). Discuss how you can get back to the original terms of the arrangement or see if you need to renegotiate it before the review date.

In my experience, most people know when they're going too far above and beyond given their compensation. Trust yourself and don't wait too long to sit down and review with your manager. You don't want your extra effort to become expected and abused. You want it to be appreciated and respected.

Communicate, Communicate, Communicate

If you have an arrangement that allows you to work hours that are not the same as the rest of the team, or work in a location outside of the office, then immediately the burden shifts to you to take the initiative to communicate. Communicate with your manager, your customers, and your coworkers.

If your hours or your location are different, people are going to be afraid to call you at first. They won't want to bother you. You're going to have to set the tone. Check in regularly, even if you don't have a particular reason. This gives your manager and your coworkers permission to do the same and not feel uneasy.

If you aren't being included in meetings, lunches, or dinners that you want to participate in, then ask. If you aren't being cc'd on emails or reports that you'd like to see, again, ask. Soon people will understand that you want to be included.

Communicate constantly with your manager and your teammates about your progress on tasks for which you are responsible. Of the 100 employees we interviewed, a majority said that their communication with their manager actually improved after they implemented their new work+life fit, because they had to be more conscious of communicating.

This is especially important if you're in a heavy face time culture where presence is a proxy for performance. If you aren't there, all anyone will see is that you aren't pulling your weight. It is your periodic updates that will take the place of those missed hours. Ideally, your updates should be in written form—email or memo—in order to create a record of progress.

Be certain that either you or someone on your team always responds to customers in a timely manner. Check your voice mail and email regularly, even on your days out of the office, to make sure nothing is inadvertently overlooked.

The bottom line: You can't communicate enough with all of the people who are affected by and supportive of your arrangement.

Don't Expect Perfection

While finding a better work+life fit should enhance your sense of job and personal satisfaction, it will not be perfect. Nothing is. In the beginning, you will have to work out the kinks as everyone becomes accustomed to the day-to-day reality of your arrangement. Don't be overwhelmed by needing to clarify the parameters, or address the questions and concerns of coworkers and customers.

To help you overcome any challenges you experience once you've implemented your new work+life fit, please turn to page 361 and you will find the work+life fit "Quick Fix" Checklist. Make a copy and keep it handy as a guide to help you quickly identify the source of any difficulty and get back on track.

For example, just because you bypassed roadblocks while creating your final work+life fit, doesn't mean you can forget about them. On the contrary, the success, fear, resistance, and in-the-box-thinking roadblocks still lurk out there, waiting to derail you after you've implemented your arrangement.

In fact, you may be going along smoothly, working from home three days a week, until you are one of the few people not given a raise this year because of budget cuts. All of a sudden you hit the success roadblock related to money and advancement. Or everything is fine until someone from another team makes a comment about your arrangement: "You work four days a week? I thought only mommies did that, Jim. I didn't know you were pregnant (ha,ha)." You've hit the resistance roadblock.

What happens when you feel that you are being asked to do more work than was agreed to in the proposal? Even though you can prove that you consistently go "the extra mile," you feel you need to sit down with your manager to review the terms of the agreement, but you are afraid. You've hit a fear roadblock. Now that your son plays in the band, he has practice four evenings a week. This means that someone needs to be home in time to take him to practice, but you and your wife can't figure out how to rearrange your schedules. You've hit an in-the-box-thinking roadblock.

These are just a few examples of roadblocks you may encounter even after you and your manager have signed on the dotted line. Being aware of this possibility, refer back to the roadblock chapters and implement the appropriate bypass strategy to get yourself back on track. Or you can use the "Quick Fix" checklist to identify the source of your challenge and to quickly implement a strategy to resolve it.

Keep Track of Issues That Arise

It doesn't matter how thoughtfully you considered all of the possible contingencies. Things will happen. That's life. But instead of viewing it as the end to your arrangement, look at any difficulties as learning opportunities. Address the issues that arise and then keep track of how you resolved them. Bring this list to the table at your six-month review and use it to show how effectively you handled the challenges, and reassure your manager that you will continue to be on top of things.

Use the Mind, Body, Spirit Tools

Use the tools to stay connected to your internal guidance and to help you around any roadblocks that emerge even after you've implemented your arrangement.

No experience in life is without some bumps in the road. And as you settle into your new arrangement, you need to get down to the business of living with this new reality. And that experience, especially in the beginning, can be difficult. How will it feel the first time you miss a prestigious meeting or you don't get a promotion? When the going gets tough, use the tools to help you refocus on why you went through all of this effort in the first place. Remember that your work+life fit is how you want work to fit into your life today—and that vision will inevitably change.

This brings us to the second reason the mind, body, spirit tools are useful even after implementing your work+life fit. They will help you recognize when you need to make a change. And next time around, you can take that information and make the necessary adjustments in your work+life fit *before* you endure a long period of conflict.

Prepare for Your Six-month Review

To prepare for your six-month review, complete the following steps:

- ▶ Reflect upon any difficulties that evolved over the past six months and how they were resolved. Did you learn anything that would cause you to adjust your work+life fit going forward?
- ▶ Use the mind, body, spirit tools to be certain that the work+life fit you have supports your vision six months later.

▶ Has your vision has changed? Go back and complete the visioning exercises in chapter 15. If you had a medium- and long-term version of your previous vision, refer back to them now. Have certain work and personal realities changed in your life to allow you to incorporate aspects of these versions this time? Complete the roadmap to make sure your revised work+life vision is compatible with the work and personal realities prevailing six months after you implemented your original arrangement.

▶ Schedule a meeting with your manager to either continue the existing arrangement or negotiate a revised work+life fit.

Enjoy your new work+life fit. My hope is that it resolves your work/life conflict in a way that leads to both personal and professional fulfillment and success, however you define it today, and in the years to come.

Author's Note

I'm going to take this opportunity to make a final request. If you are motivated and courageous enough to complete the Three Steps to a Better Work+Life Fit, please reach out and encourage others who want to improve their work+life satisfaction to do the same. Offer your story, including all of your triumphs and pitfalls, to inspire and support their efforts. Because it will.

I'm also very interested in hearing your story. Please write to me at www.worklifevisions.com. We will compile all of the stories we receive and make them available on our website to inspire an even broader audience.

Beyond that, if you are someone in a position of authority and influence in an organization, encourage your managerial peers and those who report to you to complete the Three Steps themselves. I have found that if you, as a manager, *consciously* embrace your work+life fit choice—even if that choice is to willingly devote a majority of your time and energy to work—you are more open to the choices of others that may be different. You aren't as likely to expect all valuable employees to choose the same path you have. Employees will be more likely to propose a work+life fit that will allow you to retain them and their skills.

Remember, it's not important that every request is approved. But it is important that the negotiation is allowed to take place, and that people are heard.

With that, I wish you continued work+life peace and prosperity.

Work+Life Fit "Quick Fix" Checklist

Once you've implemented your new work+life fit, make a copy of this checklist and keep it handy. Use it whenever you experience challenges to remind you of the Three Steps to a Better Work+Life Fit and help get you back on track quickly:

▶ **Have you embraced the Eight Work+Life Fit Fundamentals?**

1. I can take the initiative with all aspects of my work+life fit.
2. There are an infinite number of work+life fit possibilities between the extremes of all work and no work; even the smallest change can make a big difference.
3. I'm going to ask, because most likely the answer will be "yes" to at least a six-month trial period.
4. I add value to the business—60% of me is better than 0%.
5. My manager will approve my formal work+life fit proposal because it makes sense for me and the business.
6. I can seek a better work+life fit for *any* reason.
7. As my work and personal life change, my work+life fit will evolve.
8. I will be patient and persevere.

▶ **Have you hit a Work+Life Fit Roadblock?**

Success Roadblock: Do you need to review and redefine success—in terms of money, prestige, advancement, or caregiving—and make it compatible with your work+life fit?

Fear Roadblock: Do you need to challenge a fear?

Resistance Roadblock: Are you experiencing resistance from within yourself or from others that you need to overcome?

In-the-Box-Thinking Roadblock: Are you thinking creatively enough to overcome this challenge?

▶ **Are there any unforeseen incompatibilities between your work+life fit and your work and personal realities that need to be resolved either by changing the reality or changing your arrangement?**

Work Realities
Company Work/Life Policies
Job Tasks & Responsibilities
Workload
Scheduling
Corporate Culture
Work Style

Personal Realities
Personal Finances
Career and Personal Expectations
Child-Care and Elder-care Supports
Your Partner's Reality and Expectations

Resource Section

Please visit our website www.worklifevisions.com for up-to-date work+life fit information, including current links to relevant websites, research, and information. You can also join our work+life fit sharing communities, where you'll meet and learn from others pursuing similar work+life visions.

General Work/Life Information

Websites

FAMILIES AND WORK INSTITUTE (**www.familiesandwork.org**)
A nonprofit work/life research organization dedicated to studying a broad range of cutting edge work/life issues.

WORK & FAMILY CONNECTION, INC. (**www.workfamily.com**)
A clearinghouse of information related to a broad range of work/life issues affecting both companies and individuals. Although most of the services are fee based and company oriented, portions of the site can be accessed for free.

CATALYST (**www.catalystwomen.org**)
A research and advisory organization working to advance women in business. Part of their focus includes conducting research related to a variety of work/life topics and corporate effectiveness.

TELECOMMUTING WEBSITES
www.gilgordon.com: the website of telecommuting expert Gil Gordon offers information and support to help you telecommute successfully.
www.jala.com: another telecommuting expert, Jack Niles, offers tools to help you create a cost-benefit business case to support your telecommuting arrangement.

Working Mothers

Websites

NATIONAL ASSOCIATION OF MOTHERS' CENTERS (www.motherscenter.org)
Through its website and a network of community-based centers, NAMC offers resources and support to mothers—both working and nonworking—in all stages of life.

WORKING MOTHER MAGAZINE AND WEBSITE (www.workingmother.com)
Both the website and magazine provide timely information to mothers who work while raising children. Source of the annual Top 100 Companies for Working Mothers list.

WOMEN WORKING 2000 (www.womenworking2000.com)
A website dedicated to helping women successfully combine work and life.

Books

Linda Mason, *The Working Mother's Guide to Life: Strategies, Secrets, and Solutions* (New York: Three Rivers Press, 2002)

Fathers

Websites

NATIONAL FATHERHOOD INITIATIVE (www.fatherhood.org) and NATIONAL
   CENTER FOR FATHERING (www.fathers.com)
Both organizations are dedicated to providing men with information and support to be better fathers.

ABOUT.COM (www.about.com), SEARCH UNDER SUBGROUP
   "FATHERHOOD"
This site offers a wide range of information for fathers.

Stay-at-Home Fathers Transitioning
Back to Work

Websites

SLOWLANE (**www.slowlane.com**)
A website dedicated to fathers who have chosen to take time-out from the workforce to provide care for their children.

Elder Care

Websites and Organizations

All websites and organizations listed below help caregivers find care for their aging relatives as well as provide them with information and support in their role as caregiver.

National Association of Professional Geriatric Care Managers (**www.caremanager. org**), locates fee-based geriatic professionals to support your search for the appropriate care.

Administration on Aging, part of the U.S. Department of Health and Human Services (**www.aoa.dhhs.gov**), and eldercare locator 800-677-1116

AARP (**www.aarp.org**), search under subgroup "Life Answers," and then "Caregiving"

ThirdAge (**www.thirdage.com**), search under subgroup "Caregiving: ThirdAge Guide to Health"

About.com (**www.about.com**), search under subgroup "Senior Care"

National Alliance for Caregiving (**www.caregiving.org**)

Family Caregiver Alliance (**www.caregiver.org**)

National Family Caregivers Association (**www.nfcacares.org**)

Today's Caregiver Magazine and Website (**www.caregiver.com**)

Books

Lynn Lancaster and David Stillman, *When Generations Collide: Who They Are. Why They Clash. How to Solve the Generational Puzzle at Work* (New York: HarperBusiness, 2002)
Mary Pipher, *Another Country: Navigating the Emotional Terrain of Our Elders* (New York: Riverhead, 2000)

James A. Levine and Todd Pittinsky, *Working Fathers: New Strategies for Balancing Work and Family* (Reading, MA: Addison Wesley, 1997)

Stay-at-Home Mothers Transitioning Back to Work

Websites

NATIONAL ASSOCIATION OF MOTHERS' CENTERS (www.motherscenter.org)
Through its website and a network of community-based centers, NAMC offers resources and support to mothers—both working and nonworking—in all stages of life.

MOTHERS & MORE (www.mothersandmore.org)
A national and local organization dedicated to supporting formerly employed professional mothers who have chosen to take time-out to provide primary care for their children.

Working Retirees

Websites and Organizations

The websites and organizations listed below provide information on a wide range of retirement-related issues.

AARP (www.aarp.org), search under subgroup "Money and Work"

About.com (www.about.com), search under subgroup "Senior Living"

Child Care

Websites and Organizations

NATIONAL ASSOCIATION FOR THE EDUCATION OF YOUNG CHILDREN
   (www.naeyc.org)
Even though NAEYC is an organization for early childhood educators, it offers excellent information for parents on various child-care–related topics. Search under subgroup "Parents" for information on pamphlets and books about finding quality care.

NATION'S NETWORK OF CHILD CARE RESOURCE AND REFERRAL
(www.naccrra.org)
After entering the site, go to "Resource Exchange" for information on finding quality care.

NATIONAL CHILD CARE INFORMATION CENTER (www.nccic.org)
A government-sponsored website offering resources and information related to child care.

ABOUT.COM (www.about.com)
Search by city and then look under "child care" in that city.

Books

Ellen Galinsky and Judy David, Ask the Children: *The Breakthrough Study That Reveals How to Succeed at Work and Parenting* (New York: Quill, 2000)

Job Search

Books

Richard N. Bolles, *What Color Is Your Parachute?* (Ten Speed Press, 2003)

Herminia Ibarra, *Working Identity: Unconventional Strategies for Reinventing Your Career* (Boston: Harvard Business School Press, 2003)

Barbara Sher, *I Could Do Anything If I Only Knew What It Was: How to Discover What You Really Want and How to Get It* (DTP, 1995)

Body

Websites

FitDay (www.fitday.com)
An online food and fitness journal.

Books

Bob Greene, *Get with the Program!;* (New York: Simon & Schuster, 2002)

Dr. Caroline Myss, *Why People Don't Heal and How They Can* (New York: Three Rivers Press, 1998)

Dr. Andrew Weil, *8 Weeks to Optimum Health* (New York: Ballantine Books, 1998)

Spirit

Books

Richard N. Bolles, *How to Find Your Mission in Life* (Berkeley, CA: Ten Speed Press, 2001)

Joan Borysenko, Ph.D., *Inner Peace for Busy People* (Carlsbad, CA: Hay House, 2003)

Sarah Ban Breathnach, *Simple Abundance* (New York: Warner Books, 1995)

Julia Cameron, *The Artist's Way* (New York: J.P. Tarcher, 2002)

Julia Cameron, *The Vein of Gold* (New York: J.P. Tarcher, 1997)

Phil McGraw, Ph.D., *Self Matters: Creating Your Life from the Inside Out* (New York: Free Press, 2003)

Marsha Sinatar, *Do What You Love, the Money Will Follow* (DTP; April 1989)

Gary Zukav, *The Seat of the Soul* (Fireside, 1990)

Meditation

Books

Herbert Benson and Miriam Z. Klipper, *The Relaxation Response* (New York: HarperTorch, 2000)

Joan Borysenko, *Minding the Body, Mending the Mind* (New York: Doubleday, 1993)

Jack Kornfield, *A Path With Heart* (New York: Bantam Books, 1993)

Jack Kornfield, *The Inner Art of Meditation* (Boulder, CO: Sounds True, 2004)

Journaling

Books

Sarah Ban Breathnach, *Simple Abundance* (New York: Warner Books, 1995)

Julia Cameron, *The Artist's Way* (New York: J.P. Tarcher, 2002)

Financial Planning

Books

Suze Orman, *The 9 Steps to Financial Freedom* (New York: Three Rivers Press, 2000)

Suze Orman, *The Road to Wealth* (New York: Riverhead Books, 2001)

Suze Orman, *The Courage to Be Rich* (New York: Riverhead Books, 1999)

Elaine St. James, *Simplify Your Life* (New York, Hyperion, 1994)

Redefining Success

Books

John Drake, *Downshifting: How to Work Less and Enjoy Life More* (San Francisco: Berrett-Koehler Publishers, 2001)

Beth Sawi, *Coming Up For Air: How to Build a Balanced Life in a Workaholic World* (New York: Hyperion, 2000)

Challenging Fear

Books

Don Greene, Ph.D., *Fight Your Fear and Win* (New York: Broadway Books, 2002)

Working Mother Magazine's
Top 100 Companies
For Working Mothers 2004

(www.workingmother.com)

Abbott Laboratories
Accenture
AFLAC Incorporated
Allstate Insurance Company
American Electric Power
American Express
Ameritas Acacia Companies
Arnold & Porter LLP
AstraZeneca
Aventis Pharmaceuticals

Bank of America
Baptist Health South Florida
Bayer Corporation
Blue Cross Blue Shield of
    Massachusetts
Bon Secours Richmond Health
    System
Booz Allen Hamilton
BP America, Inc.
Bristol-Myers Squibb Company
Bronson Healthcare Group

Carlson Companies
Cinergy Corp.
Cisco Systems, Inc.

Citigroup
Colgate-Palmolive Co.
Corning Inc.
Credit Suisse First Boston LLC

DaimlerChrysler Corporation
Deloitte
Deutsche Bank
Discovery Communications Inc.
Dupont

Eli Lilly and Company
Ernst & Young

Fannie Mae
First Horizon National Corp.
First National Bank
Ford Motor Company
Freddie Mac

Genentech
General Electric Company
General Mills
General Motors
GlaxoSmithKline
The Goldman Sachs Group, Inc.

Harvard University
Hewlett-Packard Company

IBM
IKEA
Inova Health System
Intel Corporation

JFK Medical Center
Johnson & Johnson
JPMorgan Chase

King's Daughters Medical Center
KPMG LLP
Kraft Foods

LEGO Systems Inc.
Lincoln Financial Group
Lucent Technologies Inc.

Marriott International, Inc.
MasterCard International
MBNA America Bank, N.A.
Merck & Co., Inc.
MetLife, Inc.
Microsoft Corporation
MITRE Corporation
Morgan Stanley

New York Life Insurance Company
Northern Trust Corporation
Northwestern Memorial HealthCare
Novartis Pharmaceuticals Corp.

Pearson Education
Pfizer Inc.

Phoenix Companies, Inc.
Pitt County Memorial Hospital
PNC Financial Services Group
PricewaterhouseCoopers LLP
Procter & Gamble Company
Prudential Financial Inc.

Republic Bancorp Inc.

S. C. Johnson & Son, Inc.
Schering-Plough Corporation
Sears, Roebuck & Co.
St. Mary's Medical Center

Target Corporation
Texas Instruments, Inc.
Thomson West
Timberland Company
TriHealth
Turner Broadcasting System, Inc.

UBS
Union Pacific Railroad
USAA

Verizon Wireless
Virginia Commonwealth University
    Health System

Wachovia Corporation
Wells Fargo & Company
Wyeth

Yale New Haven Hospital

Zurich

Fortune Magazine's
100 Best Companies
To Work For 2004

(www.fortune.com)

A.G. Edwards

Adobe Systems

AFLAC

Alcon Laboratories

Alston & Bird

American Cast Iron Pipe

American Century Investments

American Express

American Fidelity Assurance

Amgen

Arbitron

Arnold & Porter

ARUP Laboratories

AstraZeneca

Baptist Health Care

Baptist Health South Florida

Barton Protective Svcs.

Bright Horizons

Bronson Healthcare

CDW

Cisco Systems

Container Store

Continental Airlines

Duncan Aviation

Edward Jones

Eli Lilly

Ernst & Young

Fannie Mae

FedEx

First Tennessee Natl. Corp.

Four Seasons Hotels

Genentech

General Mills

Goldman Sachs Group

Granite Construction

Griffin Hospital

Harley-Davidson

HomeBanc Mortgage

Hot Topic

Hyperion Solutions

Intel

International Data Group

Intl. Business Machines

Intuit

J.M. Smucker

JM Family Enterprises

Marriott International
Mayo Clinic
MBNA
Medtronic
Memorial Health
Men's Wearhouse
Merck
Microsoft
Milliken
Mitre
Monsanto

National Instruments
Network Appliance
Nordstrom
Northwestern Mutual
Nvidia

Paychex
Pella
Perkins Coie
Plante & Moran
Principal Financial
Procter & Gamble
Publix Super Markets

Qualcomm
Quicken Loans
QuikTrip

REI
Republic Bancorp
Robert W. Baird

S.C. Johnson & Son
SAS Institute
Scooter Store
SEI Investments
Simmons
SRA International
St. Luke's
Starbucks
Sterling Bank
Stew Leonard's
Synovus Financial Corp.

TDIndustries
Texas Instruments
Third Federal S&L
Timberland

Ukrop's Super Markets

Valassis
Valero Energy
VHA
Vision Service Plan

W.L. Gore
Washington Mutual
Wegmans
Whole Foods Market

Xilinx

AARP's
Best Employers for
Workers Over 50 for 2004

(www.aarp.org.)

Adecco Employment Services

Beaumont Hospitals
Bon Secours Richmond Health System
Brethren Village

Centegra Health System.
The Charles Stark Draper Laboratory, Inc.

Deere & Company
Delaware North Companies Inc.
DentaQuest Ventures, Inc.

First Horizon National Corporation

Gemini, Incorporated

Hoffmann-La Roche Inc.

Lee County Electric Cooperative
Lincoln Financial Group
Loudoun Healthcare, Inc.

The Methodist Hospital
Minnesota Life
Mitretek Systems.

New York University Medical Center
North Memorial Health Care

Pitney Bowes, Inc.
Principal Financial Group

Scottsdale Healthcare
Scripps Health
Smurfit-Stone Container Corporation
Sonoco
SSM Health Care
St. Mary's Medical Center
Stanley Consultants, Inc.

The Vanguard Group
Volkswagen of America, Inc.

WELBRO Building Corporation
West Virginia University Hospitals
Westgate Resorts

Zurich North America

Notes

INTRODUCTION

1. "Survey: Labor Shortage Coming," *CFO* magazine (6/27/03).
2. Employment Policy Foundation, *American Workplace Report, Challenges Facing the American Workforce* (www.epf.com) September 2002.

WHAT IS WORK+LIFE FIT?

1. James T. Bond, Ellen Galinsky, and Jennifer Swanberg, *The 1997 National Study of the Changing Workforce (NSCW)*, (Families and Work Institute), p. 28.
2. Ibid., p. 152.
3. Ibid., p. 35.
4. Ibid., p. 30.
5. James T. Bond, Cyntha Thompson, and David Prottas, *Highlights of the National Study of the Changing Workforce,* vol.3, (Families and Work Institute, 2003), p. 1.
6. NSCW, p. 152.
7. Ibid., p. 73.
8. Ibid., p. 75.
9. Ibid., pp. 76–77.
10. Ibid., p. 63.
11. Ibid., p. 76.
12. Ibid., p. 65.
13. Ibid.
14. Ibid.

15. Ibid., p. 117.
16. Ibid., p. 58.
17. Ibid., p. 59.
18. Ibid.
19. Ibid., p. 73.
20. Ibid., p. 6.
21. "Randstad North American and Roper Starch Worldwide 2000 study," Business Wire (3/16/00).
22. Work and Family Connection "2001 MetLife study" (www.workfamily.com).
23. Employment Policy Foundation, "2001 Building America's Workforce for the 21st Century Study" as reported on the Work and Family Connection website, 100 Most Important Studies of the Past Decade (www.workfamily.com).
24. Work and Family Connection website (www.workfamily.com).
25. Work and Family Connection website, 100 Most Important Studies of the Past Decade.
26. Ibid.
27. Ibid.
28. Ibid.
29. Ibid.
30. Ibid.
31. Ibid.
32. Ibid.
33. Ibid.
34. Ibid.
35. Adapted from Joan Kofodimos, *Balancing Act* (San Francisco: Jossey-Bass, 1993).

CHAPTER 1

1. "National Report on Work and Family" (5/5/98), as reported in the *Work & Family Newsbrief* (July 1998).
2. "2001 Building America's Workforce for the 21st Century Study."
3. *NSCW*, p. 2.
4. Ibid., pp. 83, 84 and 113.
5. Ibid., p. 114.

CHAPTER 2

1. "World WIT survey," *Work and Family Newsbrief* (July 2003).
2. *American Demographics* (February 2002).
3. Whirlpool, and Families and Work Institute, "New Providers Study" (May 1995).
4. *American Demographics* (January 2002).

CHAPTER 3

1. *NSCW*, p.11.

CHAPTER 4

1. "2001 MetLife study."

CHAPTER 5

1. "Brigham Young study," Work and Family Connection website, 100 Most Important Studies of the Past Decade (www.workfamily.com).

CHAPTER 6

1. "2001 Building America's Workforce for the 21st Century Study."
2. *NSCW,* p. 144.
3. Ibid., p. 145.
4. *American Demographics* (May 2002).
5. "Make Room for Daddy," *Working Mother* magazine (October 2002).
6. *American Demographics* (January 2002).
7. "Make Room for Daddy."
8. *NSCW,* p. 146.
9. James E. Levine and Todd Pittinsky, *Working Fathers* (Reading, MA: Addison-Wesley, 1997).
10. *NSCW,* p. 73.
11. Ibid., p. 66.
12. "Make Room for Daddy."
13. *Highlights of the National Studty of the Changing Workforce,* vol. 3, 2002. p. 29, Bureau of Labor Statistics.
14. *Work and Family Newsbrief* (July 2003).
15. *Work and Family Trend Report* (May 2002).
16. Robert Samuelson, "Managing a Mature Workforce," *Washington Post* (12/11/02).
17. *Work and Family Trend Report* (May 2002).

CHAPTER 9

1. *NSCW* (Families and Work Institute), p. 106.
2. "New Providers study," p. 30.
3. Families and Work Institute, "1998 Business Work-Life Study."
4. Whirlpool, and Families and Work Institute "New Providers Study" (May 1995), p. 49.

CHAPTER 14

1. *NSCW,* p. 58.
2. John Dunne, *Reading the Gospel* (South Bend, IN: University of Notre Dame Press, 2000).

CHAPTER 16

1. *NSCW,* p. 103.
2. Rhona Rapoport and Lotte Bailyn, *Relinking Life and Work* (Ford Foundation: 1997).

CHAPTER 18

1. *NSCW,* p. 73.

CHAPTER 25

1. Jacqui Abbott, Helen De Cieri, and Roderick D. Iverson "Cost of Turnover: Implications of Work/Family Conflict at Management Level" *Asia Pacific Journal of Human Resources* 36 (1).

CHAPTER 27

1. *Negotiation.* Edited by Roy J. Lewicki, Joseph A. Litterer, David M. Sauders, and John W. Minton. Articles: "Resolving Conflict through 'Win-Win' Negotiation" by Phillip I. Morgan, p. 125; "Interests: the Measure of Negotiation" by David A. Lax and James K. Sebenius, p. 130; "Ten Guidelines for Effective Negotiations" by Joseph F. Brynes, p. 25.
2. Robert Fisher and William Ury, *Getting to Yes: Negotiating Agreement without Giving In* (New York: Penguin USA, 1991).
3. Len Lervitz, *Negotiation, "Taking the Bull Out of Bully."* (Burr Ridge, IL: Irwin, 1993).

Cali Williams Yost is the president and founder of Work+Life, Inc., a company dedicated to providing individuals and organizations with the products, services, and support they need to effectively and strategically implement work+life flexibility in a way that meets the needs of both the individual and employer. Her clients include General Electric/NBC, JPMorgan Chase, Lehman Brothers, GlaxoSmithKline, Claremont EAP, Ernst & Young, Kellogg Business School, University of Chicago Business School, La Salle/ABN Amro Bank, Seattle Bar Association, the Corporate Real Estate Executive Women's Association, and the Healthcare Businesswomen's Association. Cali earned her MBA at Columbia University prior to becoming a work/life strategy consultant to Fortune 500 companies with the Families and Work Institute, and then with Bright Horizons Family Solutions. Before that, she worked as a commercial banker in New York City.